MAZDA

MX-5

Renovation Manual

First published as *Do it up! Mazda MX-5* in January 2007
This edition published in December 2010
Reprinted February 2013

A catalogue record for this book is available from the British Library

ISBN 978 0 85733 006 2

Library of Congress catalog card no. 2010927390

Published by Haynes Publishing,
Sparkford, Yeovil, Somerset BA22 7JJ, UK

Tel: 01963 442030 Fax: 01963 440001
Int. tel: +44 1963 442030 Int. fax: +44 1963 440001
E-mail: sales@haynes.co.uk
Website: www.haynes.co.uk

Haynes North America, Inc.,
861 Lawrence Drive, Newbury Park,
California 91320, USA

Jurisdictions which have strict emission control laws may consider any modifications to a vehicle to be an infringement of those laws. You are advised to check with the appropriate body or authority whether your proposed modification complies fully with the law. The author and publishers accept no liability in this regard.

While every effort is taken to ensure the accuracy of the information given in this book, no liability can be accepted by the author or publishers for any loss, damage or injury caused by errors in, or omissions from the information given.

Printed in the USA

PHOTOGRAPH CREDITS
All photographs appearing in this book are courtesy of the author, except for the following:

BMITA
P27

Draper Tools
P38–42, P43 left

James Mann
Front cover, P7, P8, P10–11, P15 upper pair, P17 upper, P34 upper, P45, P46–48, P69 lower, P114

LAT
P14, P15 lower, P16, P17 lower, P21, P26

Manheim Auctions
P29

Mark Brewster at Dandycars.com
P54 lower pair

Mazda
P5 lower, P6/7 main, P12–13, P18–20, P28, P34 lower. P35, P168–170

Peter Wu
P91 top left and right, P92, P94, P95

MAZDA

MX-5

1989-2005

Includes
Miata & Eunos

Renovation Manual

Paul Hardiman

CONTENTS

KI55 PKO

INTRODUCTION

Since the original Mazda MX-5 was launched at the Chicago Motor Show in 1989 it has gone on to win hearts and influence people all over the world. This simple, attractive, well-built and nimble-handling car reintroduced a concept – driving fun – that had been sadly lacking from mainstream motoring for too long.

On first publication of this book the earliest MX-5s were approaching their 18th birthdays, and had proved they could stand high mileages. Various observers – the author included – had been watching closely and asking themselves 'does anything really go wrong?' The answer seems to be, not very much.

Because of their fundamental quality design and build – and because they are so well served by performance and aftermarket suppliers – MX-5s lend themselves well to home care and modification, from mild to wild.

This book is aimed primarily at owners wishing to deal with Mk1, or NA, cars in both 1.6-litre and 1.8-litre forms, built from 1989–1997; though most of the procedures still apply to the Mk2, or NB, which is mechanically almost identical. The Mk3, which appeared in 2005, is a different animal: though still offering the same unparalleled driving experience, it runs RX-8 and Ford technology under the skin, and is beyond the scope of this book. Look out for a new edition in a couple of years, though.

Above all, this book is about getting to know and enjoying your MX-5/Miata/Eunos. Don't be scared to have a go at maintaining or fettling it – the knowledge is here, and freely disseminated through club and specialist websites. MX-5ers are a friendly bunch and, whatever you plan, somebody will almost certainly have been there before you. You need look no further than the incomparable www.miatanet.com – although a list of useful contacts and specialists is given at the back of this book.

ACKNOWLEDGEMENTS

Many people have offered their advice and knowledge in the writing of this book, but the author would particularly like to thank the following for putting up with him while he slowed them down taking photographs: Sam Goodwin and Steve Butler at Sam Goodwin MX-5 Specialists; Val and Jackie Walker and Michael Loader at mx5parts.co.uk (Scimitar International); and Steve Gladden of Soft Top Windows (UK) Ltd.

For help with photography, thanks to Peter Wu, who kindly supplied the clutch renewal photographs used in Chapter 6, and to Mark Brewster at Dandycars.com who kindly supplied the automatic transmission photographs appearing on page 54

Thanks also to John Cookson for his handy, no-nonsense guide to interrogating your MX-5/Miata's 'brain' via the diagnostic connector, mentioned in Chapter 5, and available from mx5parts.co.uk.

Thanks to Paul Guiness for his invaluable reasearch and advice on the MX-5's evolution and on buying and running a car.

And thanks to Keith Tanner of Flyin' Miata for sharing with us his favoured suspension settings.

CHAPTER 1

EVOLUTION OF THE SPECIES

When the wraps came off the all-new Mazda MX-5 at the Chicago Motor Show on 9 February 1989 it created an amazing reaction, not just in the USA but throughout the world. This wasn't just because the two-seater sports car market had been through such difficult times during the 1980s; it was also because the MX-5 marked such a massive change of direction for Mazda.

Here was a company better known for its dull but worthy family saloons and hatchbacks than for out-and-out enthusiasts' cars, with only the RX-7 and all-wheel drive 323 Turbo providing welcome relief from such tedium throughout the '80s. Just as that decade of conspicuous wealth was about to draw to a close, Mazda shocked the world by virtually reinventing the affordable two-seater sportster.

In truth, the exciting new MX-5 (known in Japan as the Eunos and in most other markets as the Miata) had been an open secret for some time, with heavily disguised prototypes being spotted by eagle-eyed photographers throughout the late '80s. Even so, once the official production version was unveiled in 1989, onlookers couldn't help being pleasantly surprised by just how 'right' the new MX-5 was.

DESIGN MASTERPIECE

This long-awaited little two-seater was curvaceous, cute and full of character, with styling that almost everybody fell in love with. From its simple pop-up headlamps to its rounded tail, the MX-5's proportions were so damn perfect they made every other rag-top sports car of the time look awkward by comparison.

The 1980s hadn't been a great time for traditional open-top sports cars, especially in the UK. The demise of the MGB and Triumph Spitfire had been particular low points, as had the failure of the promising but flawed Reliant Scimitar SS1. Britain desperately needed a brand new two-seater convertible to bring traditional fun back to motoring. That such a vehicle arrived with Mazda badges rather than those of MG – and happened to be built in Japan rather than Britain – was seen as sad by some enthusiasts and inevitable by others.

In essence, Mazda took the concept of a conventional two-seater sports car, improved it massively without robbing it of its fun appeal, and launched it on to an eager market with the promise of driver enjoyment, low maintenance and running costs and, of course, reliability. It was the latter point that especially marked the MX-5 out as something very different from Britain's sports car efforts.

The decision to make the MX-5 front-engined and rear-wheel drive was a vital one for the car's long-term appeal. Mazda certainly considered the logical option of front-wheel drive during the early days of the MX-5's development, a course pursued by Fiat for its Punto-based Barchetta, launched later. But Mazda's engineers were adamant that if the MX-5 was to have the traditional feel of a 1960s British sports car combined with the ease of ownership of a more modern machine, then rear-wheel drive was the only way forward.

It was one of the best decisions ever made by Mazda, and it's a philosophy that still stands. What perhaps surprised some onlookers the most, though, was that the MX-5 came with nothing more powerful than a 114bhp 1.6-litre engine upon its launch. Admittedly it was an excellent engine, a 16-valve twin-cam four-cylinder design with a free-revving nature and an enthusiastic feel. But compared with some of the best performance cars to have already come from Japan, an output of 114bhp wasn't exactly spectacular.

MX-5 TIMELINE

1989 – Miata/Eunos/MX-5 range unveiled in the USA in February.
1989 – New MX-5 shown to British public at Earl's Court Motor Show.
1989 – *Car Australia* magazine awards MX-5 its 'Car Of The Year'.
1990 – MX-5 goes on sale in the UK.
1991 – Limited Edition launched to celebrate MX-5's first year in the UK.
1991 – Special edition 'Le Mans' announced in UK; just 22 produced.
1991 – American-spec 'Special Edition' introduced (4,000 units built).
1992 – 250,000th MX-5 is produced.
1992 – Rear subframe braced, to reduce vibration at speed.
1992 – 130bhp MX-5 M2-1001 launches in Japan in December; 300 produced.
1993 – Catalytic converters now fitted to UK-spec cars.
1993 – Limited edition (150 units) 1.8i SE introduced.
1994 – Minor MX-5 facelift includes launch of 1.8 version to replace 1.6.
1994 – Front and rear subframes stiffened and braced for extra rigidity.
1995 – MX-5 1.6 reintroduced, albeit with just 88bhp.
1995 – 133bhp Japanese-spec 1.8 version introduced.
1995 – Limited edition 'Gleneagles' and 'California' launched in the UK.
1996 – Limited edition 'Merlot' and 'Monaco' launched in the UK.
1997 – Limited edition 'Dakar', 'Monza', 'Harvard' and 'Classic' models announced.
1997 – New Mk2 MX-5 launches at Tokyo Motor Show in October.
1998 – Limited edition 'Berkeley' launched to mark end of Mk1 production.
1998 – Latest MX-5 range (below) goes on sale in the UK.
1998 – Limited edition 1.8i Sport launched, with body kit and red paintwork.
1999 – Limited edition 1.8i Sport launched in Racing Blue.
1999 – MX-5 '10th Anniversary' announced to celebrate the first decade.
2000 – Revised MX-5 launched with restyled front end and six-speed gearbox.
2000 – 'Jasper Conran' special edition (500 units) introduced in British-spec.
2000 – 'California Mk2', 'Isola', 'Icon' and 'Divine' limited editions launched in UK.
2002 – 201bhp MX-5 SP developed and launched in Australia.
2002 – Limited edition 'Phoenix' and 'Arizona' launch in Europe.
2005 – Preview shots of disguised new MX-5 released by Mazda in January.
2005 – Mk3 MX-5 unveiled at Geneva Motor Show in March.
2005 – New MX-5 range on sale in most export countries by early autumn.

THE FUN FACTOR

Such criticisms faded as soon as you took the wheel of one of those early MX-5s. They were all about fun rather than spectacular on-paper performance figures – and the MX-5 was soon acclaimed as one of the most fun-to-drive machines the Japanese had ever invented. Not the fastest, having a top speed of 121mph and 0–60mph in 8.7 seconds; but one of the most enjoyable. And, as a result of the MX-5's low-slung driving position, the eagerness of its engine and the slickness of its five-speed gearchange, it felt a whole lot faster than its official figures suggested.

The world's motoring press was amazed by the MX-5's fun factor, something previously rarely associated with Mazda. And they were equally full of praise for its handling and roadholding, two areas in which the MX-5 truly excelled. With independent double-wishbone coil-sprung suspension all round, tuned to offer just the right compromise between day-to-day ride quality and impressively flat handling, the MX-5 was tremendous fun when pushed to the limit, any rear-end breakaway being commendably easy to bring back under control with a touch of opposite-lock steering and an unfaltering right foot. Whether pottering through cities or tackling winding B-roads, the MX-5 was one of those rare machines that made modern motoring so much fun. No wonder MX-5 drivers were soon renowned for the size of their grins every time they took to the wheel.

And no wonder the MX-5 generated such positive headlines throughout the world, with Britain's motoring press being particularly enthusiastic. *What Car?* magazine awarded the MX-5 its 'Best Sports Car of 1991' award in October of that year, citing Mazda's finest as '... everything a sports car needs to be – fun to drive, good to look at and affordable'. It went on to say the MX-5 was '... huge fun to drive, with lovely handling and good ride', a view echoed by just about every other British magazine of the time.

Such praise wasn't confined to the British press: American journalists were just as vocal in their enthusiasm for the MX-5. Dennis Simanaitis, writing in *Road & Track* in March 1989, commented: 'Its combination of communication, responsiveness, predictability and forgiveness make it the best-handling two-seater I've driven in recent memory – and my memory for such things is good.'

Journalist Peter Egan, again writing for *Road & Track*, this time in November 1990, really enthused about the MX-5: 'Its quick steering, willing engine, short-throw gearbox, taut suspension and fits-like-a-glove driving position give it an instantaneous response that conjures up memories of the old Elan, only this time the headlamps work and the water pump lasts a bit longer.'

That last comment summed up perfectly the all-round appeal of the MX-5, for here was a hilarious-to-drive sports car that was also totally practical and reliable. That was a combination that evidently suited whole swathes of buyers, for Mazda's inspirational creation soon found itself experiencing huge demand worldwide.

DID YOU KNOW?

According to Mazda UK in October 2005, there were more than 200 MX-5 and Miata enthusiasts' clubs worldwide at the last count. In the USA alone there are 132 clubs (according to the website www.miata.net), with a further 15 in Canada. The UK's MX-5 Owners' Club boasts around 4,500 members, while the German website www.mx-5.de lists no fewer than 28 clubs.

Using those figures as a base, Mazda reckons there are at least 10,000 fans of the classic sportster who are members of an MX-5 club – an astonishing achievement for any vehicle introduced as relatively recently as 1989.

FURTHER DEVELOPMENT

Demand for the MX-5 almost caught Mazda off guard, for the company only ever intended its tiny sportster to be a niche vehicle. It was a way of bringing attention back to the Mazda marque while boosting company sales by a few thousand a year. But for an enthusiastic public, niche-market appeal just wasn't enough. That's why by 1992, less than three years after the MX-5 first went into production, the 250,000th example rolled down the line. It was a phenomenal achievement, the kind of success story that even the most optimistic of Mazda insiders never thought possible during the MX-5's gestation.

Despite the sheer competence of the MX-5, though, no car is immune to changing demands and the need for updates. By 1992 Mazda was fitting the MX-5 with a stiffer rear subframe to reduce motorway-speed vibrations, while the following year catalytic converters were installed on all UK-spec cars. The biggest change came in 1994 when the new 1.8-litre version was introduced to replace the 1.6 – along with more chassis cross-bracing under the floor. Offering 128bhp, the newcomer was usefully more powerful than its predecessor, though in reality its performance was broadly the same because of the extra weight of the increasingly well-equipped MX-5.

The 1.8 was more expensive too, which meant a possible gap at the bottom of the MX-5 range that arguably needed filling. This occurred in 1995 when the 1.6-litre model was reintroduced, this time with a mere 88bhp to make it significantly different from the 1.8. Performance obviously suffered, but the new entry-level MX-5 still offered the same kind of fun appeal and countless smiles-per-mile, therefore proving a useful new addition to the range. It also offered terrific value for money in a market where fun cars seemed to be getting increasingly sophisticated and complex in design.

LIMITED EDITIONS

To keep interest in the MX-5 at heady heights throughout the life of the Mk1, or NA, Mazda made sure there was a steady supply of special editions from which to choose. In the UK it all started as early as 1991, with the unimaginatively but logically titled MX-5 Limited Edition going on sale to celebrate the first year of British-spec models. Finished in British Racing Green with leather trim and a wood-rim steering wheel, it was exactly what so many UK buyers of open-top sports cars were looking for, and all 250 examples sold out remarkably quickly.

This spurred Mazda on to launch numerous other special editions throughout the life of the Mk1 range, comprising such diverse names as Gleneagles, Monaco, California, Merlot, Dakar, Monza, Harvard, Classic and Berkeley.

This trend continued with the subsequent launch of the Mk2 MX-5, or NB, with one of the most desirable examples being the 10th Anniversary, introduced – logically enough – to mark the first decade of MX-5 production. This was also the first MX-5 'special' to be sold worldwide, with 7,000 produced in total – although just 600 of those were destined for the UK. Based on the 1.8i S, the 10th Anniversary featured Innocent Blue mica paint, highly polished five-spoke alloys, Bilstein dampers and – for the first time outside the Japanese market – a six-speed close-ratio gearbox.

The way in which Mk1 MX-5 special editions destined for the UK market came about was fairly straightforward. They were, in fact, modified for their new status in Britain, thanks to the efforts of the UK importer of the time, MCL. Between 1990 and 2001 (when the Mazda import franchise was lost), MCL would take fairly base-model MX-5s and transform them into special editions at its distribution centre in Sheerness. It was cost-effective and gave MCL a useful marketing tool over the years.

One of the first limited editions created that way was the Le Mans of 1991, produced to celebrate Mazda's victory with the quad-rotor 787B in the Le Mans 24-Hour Race. The highly praised Brodie Brittain Racing (BBR) turbo conversion under the bonnet was worth having, but the model's bizarre green and orange paint scheme (designed to match the Le Mans racer) was controversial, to say the least. A total of just 24 Le Mans MX-5s were due to be built, but sales proved so slow that the final tally came to a mere 22. Survivors now are sought after, but when new the MX-5 Le Mans tended to remain in the showroom for quite some time.

The best feature of the Le Mans was, of course, that BBR turbocharger. Buyers of early MX-5 1.6s could order their cars in BBR Turbo guise if required, thanks to the BBR conversion kit being supplied to and fitted by Mazda dealers in the UK. It proved pretty popular among enthusiasts for whom a standard MX-5 just wasn't fast enough, and in all around 200 BBR Turbos were created. Excellent survivors are, once again, extremely sought after these days – a tribute to what was one of the most interesting and most effective modifications available at the time.

DID YOU KNOW?

The Mazda MX-5 has a serious motorsport following. In Switzerland, the UK, Portugal and Belgium there are manufacturer's one-make racing series dedicated to the MX-5. In the car's home country of Japan, MX-5s race competitively against each other, too. But it's in the USA where Mazda MX-5 racing series are most popular – and always have been.

The Mazdaspeed Miata Cup is one of the fastest growing racing series in all of American motor sports. According to estimates by the Sports Car Club of America, there are more than 1,000 identically-tuned first- and second-generation Mazda Miatas actively involved in racing.

There is good reason for this. Using for the most part standard technology, these racing series offer drivers an extremely affordable way of entering professional sports car racing. And, thanks to identical racing standards throughout North America, it provides drivers with an opportunity to demonstrate their talents nationwide in front of a large audience. What could be better than that?

THE JAPANESE EUNOS

UK-spec MX-5s weren't the only members of the family to be treated to a line-up of limited editions over the years. The Japanese-market Eunos model also came in for such treatment, with special editions such as V-Special, V-Special Type II, J Limited, S Limited, Tokyo Limited, G Limited, R Limited, VR Limited, B2 Limited, R2 Limited and SR Limited all appearing between 1989 and 1997.

Mazda created the Eunos moniker as a brand rather than a model name, in much the same way that Toyota created the Lexus marque. It was hoped that Japanese enthusiasts would see Eunos as the sporting side of Mazda, which might then lead to other models being launched in the future. It seems odd now, given the more sporting image of Mazda in the 21st century; but back at the end of the '80s, it did make some sort of sense.

Many Eunos models have been brought to the UK as 'grey' imports over the years, sometimes direct from Japan, sometimes via Ireland. And apart from different badging, a different back panel (to accommodate a square Japanese number plate) and other minor changes, it's very much the same breed as any MX-5 or Miata. Owning a Eunos is no hardship, and many owners still refer to them as MX-5s. But you need to be aware of the origins of your particular Mazda/Eunos before taking the plunge; if it's specifically a UK-spec MX-5 you're seeking, you'll need proof of this before handing over any cash (though this will be discussed in greater depth in the next chapter).

During its long life, the original-style MX-5 evolved into a genuinely timeless classic, a legend in its own lifetime. The day would eventually come, though, when it would need replacing completely – and that was a real dilemma for Mazda's management and stylists alike. How do you replace something so loved, so uniquely styled and so utterly desirable? Very carefully.

NEW GENERATION

The new Mk2 MX-5 took a bow at the 1997 Tokyo Motor Show, going on sale in the UK the following year. At first glance, photographs of the newcomer showed a car apparently little changed from its predecessor. In the metal though, the differences were immediately obvious, for the latest MX-5 was usefully larger than the old-style model and, most noticeably of all, did away with the original pop-up headlamps.

What the stylists did with the Mk2 was very clever, for some of the changes – such as the new-style headlamps – were dramatically different, and yet the car was still instantly recognisable as an MX-5, even with its telltale badges removed. Putting a Mk1 car alongside a Mk2 really emphasised this.

Under the bonnet of the Mk2, there was still a choice of 1.6-litre or 1.8-litre power, this time offering outputs of 108bhp and 140bhp respectively. The latter meant a top speed of 126mph, with 0–60mph in a healthy 7.8 seconds. And if that doesn't sound like much of an improvement over the Mk1, bear this in mind: the newcomer was bigger, heavier and better equipped than its predecessor, so to maintain the same lively performance figures was a success in itself. In any case, this MX-5 was – as ever – about more than mere figures.

The latest version was more than ever about the driving experience, and some genuinely useful improvements had been made here. Although the previous MX-5 had offered terrific handling capabilities thanks to its superb chassis design and excellent weight distribution, the Mk2 was even more of a step forward. Where the old MX-5 had an occasional tendency to understeer when pushed to the limit, for example, the latest model was better balanced and even more predictable. And yet, very cleverly, it was still just as much fun to drive.

Yasushi Ishiwatari, writing in *Top Gear* in 1998, claimed the MX-5 '… understeers less and … it's easier and more controllable to drift,' for example. While David Vivian, no stranger to driving some of the world's greatest supercars during his journalistic career, wrote of the new MX-5 in *Autocar* the same year: 'There's nothing small or dainty about the driving experience any more. It's fast, focused and fun.'

Mazda's engineers had achieved the near impossible. They had come up with a replacement for a nine-year-old design classic – and it was still great to look at, even better to drive and just as much fun as any other four-wheeled device of the time. The old-style MX-5 was dead, but the mourning was generally short-lived; its successor was just as much of a design masterpiece.

Part of the reason for the new MX-5's superlative handling and roadholding was Mazda's latest development of its double-wishbone independent suspension set-up. As well as boasting uprated anti-roll bars and sports dampers, it was aided by near-50:50 weight distribution compared to the earlier version's 52:48. No wonder the whole thing felt so good and seemed so well balanced in all conditions at all times.

EARLY UPDATE

So would the new MX-5 continue for as long as its predecessor with little in the way of major updates? Apparently not, for as early as 2000 the Mk2 MX-5 received its first round of revisions, including modified front end styling and what's now referred to as the 'sharknose' look, or sometimes 'Mk2.5'. It was a fairly subtle change but effective nevertheless, and it involved reshaping the MX-5's 'mouth' and giving a more chiselled look to the styling around and beneath the headlamps. It meant more of a family link with the forthcoming RX-8, as well as giving the MX-5 a bit more attitude out on the street. But this latest look wasn't the only change to occur in 2000.

Mazda also took the opportunity to boost the 1.8-litre version's output to 145bhp at a heady 7,000rpm thanks to the adoption of S-VT (sequential valve timing), as well as offering a six-speed transmission for the first time ever. Uprated ABS brakes with Electronic Brake-force Distribution, stiffened suspension, the option of Bilstein dampers, a more rigid bodyshell and a whole host of other changes helped keep the MX-5 ahead of the game, essential in a market where new rivals were fast appearing.

The Mazda MX-5 found itself up against the successful new Toyota MR2 Roadster, and would also face fresh competition with the launch of the MG TF – now with coil-sprung suspension instead of the old MGF's Hydragas set-up. The pressure was on Mazda to maintain the MX-5's dynamics and driving style, a challenge to which the company's engineers rose admirably.

CLEAN SHEET APPROACH

If the Mk2 was going to be as long-lived as the original-style MX-5, it would need to have stayed in production through to the end of 2006. But that was not to be. In fact, another new-generation MX-5 was unveiled to an expectant audience at the Geneva Motor Show of March 2005, the newcomer going on sale in most export markets by the autumn of that year.

And the verdict? Another clever reinterpretation of the MX-5's timeless styling, this time with bulging wheelarches, a dramatic new front air dam and a new look of sophistication about the whole stance. The MX-5's DNA was recognisable even at first glance, but this time in a style far more in tune with 21st century tastes.

Beneath the skin, too, new developments had arisen, most noticeable of which was a choice of 1,798cc or 1,999cc dohc 16-valve power, the latter offering a highly useful 156bhp at 6,700rpm. Even the smaller-engined (124bhp) version boasted a top end of 122mph, hitting 62mph (or 100kph) in 9.4 seconds. Opt for the 2-litre though, and you'd find up to 130mph at your disposal, with the 0–62mph sprint time reduced to just 7.9 seconds. As before, there were quicker sports cars on the market at the same time; but the MX-5's eager nature and all-round fun appeal meant it still felt faster – and was far more enjoyable to pilot enthusiastically – than any official figures might suggest.

Transmission options included five-speed and six-speed manual or six-speed automatic, while the new suspension design (double wishbone front with a multi-link rear) resulted in even more impressive handling and roadholding to cope with the extra power.

Thanks to the clever use of ultra-high-tensile steel, the new MX-5 offered more bodyshell rigidity and strength than just about any rival, while still managing to weigh just 10kg more than the Mk2 model of the late '90s. It meant an MX-5 driving experience that was just as much fun as before, but this time with the rigidity and safety you'd expect from a modern-day design.

UNRIVALLED SUCCESS

By the time the Mk3 model went on sale in the UK in October 2005, more than 730,000 MX-5s of all types had been built, with almost 200,000 of those having found buyers in Europe during the preceding 16 years. In the UK alone at that stage, 67,000 MX-5s had been officially sold, and that's not taking into account the ever greater numbers of second-hand Eunos and Miata grey import models that have arrived over the years. Quite simply, the MX-5 is the most successful open-top two-seater sports car ever produced.

The sports car market has changed immeasurably since 1989, and the MX-5 has changed along with it. That the very latest version retains the same principles and appeal as the first MX-5 ever built says it all. Mazda truly understands what makes a great sports car. And the MX-5 simply goes from strength to strength.

The very latest MX-5 is, of course, a superb machine. But for those who relish the idea of value-for-money sports car motoring, combined with all the fun appeal of carrying out maintenance, repair and restoration tasks themselves (and maybe even a few modifications along the way), there has never been a better time to consider buying an earlier, second-hand MX-5. No matter how small your budget, there is probably an MX-5, Eunos or Miata within your grasp. With the help of this book, you'll be able to make the most of your ownership experience. You're in for a good time.

DID YOU KNOW?

That the MX-5 has been a runaway sales success throughout its life is common knowledge. But the actual production figures that have been achieved make for fascinating reading.

According to Mazda UK, up until July 2005 a total of 724,667 MX-5s/Miatas had been produced. And from the total number of Mazda MX-5s made for Europe (199,542), more than a third (67,079) were sold in the UK, a European figure beaten only by Germany at 83,783 units. In addition, 350,411 were sold in North America, 149,400 in Japan and 11,334 in Australia.

At 431,506 units, the first-generation Mazda MX-5, famous for its pop-up headlights, has had the lion's share of total production. After replacing the first generation at the end of 1997, the second generation car achieved a production volume of 290,123 units. And the 2005-on Mk3 looks like continuing the success story.

Interestingly, out of planned annual production of 40,000 cars for the Mk3 MX-5, Mazda expects to sell 18,000 of those in Europe each year, 14,000 in the USA – but just 4,300 in Japan. Despite that, Mazda still holds – at the time of writing – a healthy 50 per cent of Japan's sports car market, split between the MX-5 and its rotary-engined cousin, the RX-8.

£449

CHAPTER 2

BUYING AND RUNNING AN MX-5

The good news about buying a second-hand MX-5, Miata or Eunos is that there's no shortage of examples at all price levels from which to choose. So, whether it's an early Mk1 that's ripe for some minor renovation work or an immaculate Mk2 that takes your fancy, you'll find a good assortment of models available from a wide variety of sources.

To a great extent, your choice of model will be dictated by the budget you have available. But with early Mk1 examples having never been cheaper than they are right now, even an enthusiast with a meagre budget can afford to join the eager and enthusiastic members of the MX-5 appreciation society.

Your budget, however, isn't the only consideration when deciding which Mazda to buy. Would you, for example, prefer a UK-spec MX-5 to a Japanese-spec Eunos 'grey import'? Will you be insisting on 1.6-litre or 1.8-litre power? And will you automatically opt for the very best example you can afford, or will you choose to spend less, leaving some cash in reserve for a bespoke respray, perhaps, or the fitment of a body styling kit? There's a bit of decision-making to be done before you take the plunge and find yourself driving home in your very own MX-5, Miata or Eunos.

GENERAL ADVICE

Assuming you've already decided which model is top of your list – and, just as important, which you can afford – it's time to get out there and start checking out a few examples for sale. Before you do that, though, you need to know what you're looking for, what goes wrong and how you can best avoid getting ripped off. Despite the inherent reliability of Mazda's famous offspring, there are pitfalls to be aware of during the buying process.

We'll deal with the major specifics of buying a used MX-5 further on in this chapter. First, though, a few words of caution about buying used cars in general. At the best of times it's a minefield of potential dangers and, when you see a car that seems to be exactly the one you've been searching high and low for, it's so easy to get carried away in the excitement and forget some basic procedures. That's when you're particularly vulnerable.

MODEL IDENTIFICATION

MX-5 chassis numbers start JMZ and have 14 characters. **Eunos** chassis numbers start NA for Mk1 cars, NB for Mk2. All UK Mazdas are listed at Mazda UK, and you can call to check on 0845 6013 147.

To begin with, then, when buying any used vehicle, only ever arrange to meet the vendor at their own home – or, in the case of a dealer, at their premises. Meeting 'halfway' or arranging to have the car brought to your address is a classic ploy used by vendors who don't actually own the vehicle in question.

When you get to the vendor's house, ask to see the vehicle's V5C Registration Document and check that the vendor's name and the address shown on it correspond with where you actually are. If you've any doubts or concerns, simply walk away. Should no V5C be available for you to examine ("I haven't long moved house and the log book's still at DVLA," the vendor may claim), don't buy that MX-5 under any circumstances, no matter how tempting it seems.

Checking that a vehicle is genuine goes much further, though. Still with the V5C in your hand, take a look at the Mazda's VIN number; check it with the number that's printed on the V5C and, if there's any discrepancy whatsoever, don't even consider buying the car. It's that simple.

At this stage, and assuming you're examining a UK-spec MX-5 rather than a Japanese 'grey' import (which we'll deal with a little further on), you also need to be looking into the car's service history to check that if the vendor claims the car has a full service history it actually has, as well as using this to help verify the mileage. Never accept a vendor's claim that "... the service book is still at the garage; I forgot to pick it up when I had the car serviced last week." If a service history is boasted about, you want to be able to see it in front of you before you even consider making an offer.

Don't be afraid to spend time carefully studying that service book and any previous MoT certificates that are with the car, too. Check that all the mileages shown on certain dates tally with what's being claimed about the vehicle. You might even want to make a note of the previous owner's name and address, and approach them before you hand over any money, to ensure they can back up what you've been told and that they can vouch for the car's history.

THEFT AND BREAK-INS

Another obvious point when viewing any used car is to look for signs of a forced entry, which relates to the previous point about checking out the vendor's actual ownership. It's a sad fact of life that many thousands of cars get broken into each year, so any signs of a previous break-in may simply have occurred during the current keeper's ownership; don't be afraid to ask, because there's no reason why they should hide this from you. Any soft-top sports car is notoriously prone to break-ins, theft and vandalism; for anybody thinking of owning such a vehicle, it's something to bear in mind.

If you can clearly see that a door lock has been forced, that the steering column shroud looks strangely loose or that there are signs of shattered glass inside the car (although the soft-top roofs tend to be the most vulnerable to break-in damage), you've every right to have your suspicions aroused when the vendor denies all knowledge.

You also need to be on the lookout for signs of previous accident damage, checking for mismatched paintwork (colour, finish and so on, especially making a comparison between wings and doors); ripples in body panels (possible evidence of body filler or poor repair work); signs of overspray; wheels that seem out of alignment; obvious replacement of inner panel work under the bonnet or in the boot. The list goes on, but just a couple of these points should be enough to make you suspicious and question the vendor's claim that "... she's never been in an accident."

It's also not unknown for an MX-5 to be the victim of a 'ringer' exercise, where a stolen example is given the identification (including the registration number, V5C document, VIN plates and more) of a damaged vehicle. It's very easy for even the most experienced car purchaser to be caught out by a 'ringer' and it's something that MX-5 buyers need to be particularly wary of.

DOUBLE-CHECKING

There's one final point worth mentioning before we move on to specifics, and it concerns professional car inspections. You can pay anything between £100 and £200 for an expert to come along and thoroughly examine the Mazda you're thinking of buying. The AA and RAC carry out such inspections, as do many private companies and individuals, and any novice or first-timer thinking of buying an MX-5 should consider paying for an independent inspection. If it shows up any minor faults you might have missed, you'll be able to use this to negotiate the price downwards; and if the examiner discovers something major that makes you think twice about buying the car, that's also money well spent.

If you're an experienced buyer or you're intent on grabbing a cheap and cheerful MX-5 as an ongoing project vehicle, such inspections might not be necessary. But for a large proportion of today's potential purchasers, they make a lot of sense.

Such examinations usually include an HPI (or similar) check to ensure the vehicle in question has never been registered as stolen, previously written-off in an accident or still has any outstanding finance against it. This is essential information, and it's available to anybody with a phone and a credit card to pay for it. Even if you decide against a full independent inspection of a used vehicle, failure to have an HPI check carried out can be a very expensive lesson to learn – no matter how cheap an MX-5 might seem.

The difference in value between a 'clean' MX-5 and one that's been previously written-off and repaired can be 50 per cent or more, so we're talking serious money here. Before you buy any MX-5, give HPI (or the AA or RAC) a call and get all the checks done. If everything is clear, surely that extra peace of mind is worth every penny of the cost?

IMPORT ISSUES

Some – but by no means all – of what you've already read in this chapter won't necessarily apply if it's an unofficially imported Eunos or Miata you're thinking of buying, one that's found its way over, second-hand, from Japan. And with more than 30,000 second-hand cars arriving in the UK from Japan every year these days (among them plenty of Mazdas), there's a lot of 'grey' choice available.

With any 'grey' import, you obviously need to carry out the same checks for accident damage, signs of abuse, VIN number matching and so on; that's logical enough. But such issues as service history and previous MoTs aren't quite so straightforward.

One specialist 'grey' importer spoken to while this book was being written was honest about the fact that he can't always guarantee the mileages of his vehicles. Having said that, 'clocking' (the winding back of a car's mileage) is far less of a problem in Japan than it is in the UK, which means that – as he's a decent trader with a good reputation – there's every chance that the vehicles on his forecourt have never been tampered with in that way. However, not every used car dealer is as honest and, by the time a 'grey' Eunos has been bought and sold a few times, there's no guarantee that its mileage is genuine. So the onus is on the prospective purchaser to verify as much as possible.

The main problem is that a lot of Japanese imports don't come with a service history – and those that do are obviously written in Japanese, which makes deciphering them something of a challenge. Still, even a virtually unreadable service history is better than none, as it still might be possible to see roughly when servicing was carried out simply by studying some of the dates. But it's not always easy.

Similarly, if a Eunos or Miata has only been in the UK a matter of months, there's no way it can come with any previous MoT certificates to help verify its mileage – so bear this in mind and be extra scrupulous when giving the vehicle the 'once over'.

This means that when examining it throughout, not only are you looking for signs of neglect, abuse, accident damage and the like, you're also being vigilant about evidence of non-genuine mileage. If a mileage is indicated at 60,000, for example, you should be happy that the engine is reasonably rattle-free, that there's no excessive smoke when revved, that the interior is tidy and fairly unworn, that the dampers don't feel too soft or wallowy when cornering and that the bodywork's general condition is in keeping with a vehicle of such mileage. If you have any doubts at all, or the odd alarm bell ringing in your head, it's time to look elsewhere – there's certainly no shortage of used Mazdas, 'grey' or 'official', always on sale.

The BIMTA team

The best way of ensuring you don't get stung when buying any 'grey' import is to make sure the supplying dealer is a member of the British Independent Motor Trade Association (BIMTA), an established organisation that, in the event of a dispute between a member of the public and an importer, can get involved and offer a conciliatory service – but only if the company concerned is a current member.

There's more to BIMTA than that, though. When buying from a BIMTA member, make sure you ask them to provide an official BIMTA Certificate of Authenticity specifically for the 'grey' Mazda you're interested in. Every year, BIMTA claims, around 2,000 vehicles stolen in Japan end up being imported to the UK and sold on to unsuspecting buyers. But a BIMTA Certificate of Authenticity (which takes between five and ten working days to produce) will confirm whether or not a vehicle was ever registered as stolen prior to being exported from Japan, and will also prove there's no outstanding finance on it.

BIMTA can also provide odometer checks – and, again, this is a must if you're in any doubt about the imported Eunos or Miata you're buying or the dealer you're buying it from. The vast majority of imports are sold in Japan via one of the country's 140 auction houses, and BIMTA has access to the records of almost all of them. This means an official odometer check can ascertain how many kilometres a vehicle had covered by the time it went under the hammer in Japan, making it easy for any buyer to prove whether or not it has since been 'clocked'.

As long as the 'grey' Mazda you're buying is registered in the UK, has passed an ESVA test (details of which

can be found further on in this chapter), comes with a BIMTA Certificate of Authenticity and appears to be in decent condition, the risks involved are realistically no greater than when buying a UK-spec vehicle. Just don't be tempted to cut corners in the hope of bagging a bargain.

Doing it yourself

Still on the subject of 'grey imports', what happens if you want to bypass dealers and UK-based auction houses in an effort to save money? Is it possible to privately import a used Eunos from Japan yourself? Well, yes, anything is possible; but there are many pitfalls along the way and it's not a route I'd recommend to everyone.

For a start, it's essential that you have a reliable and dependable agent in Japan. Buying a car over there isn't simply a case of catching a plane and heading for the nearest Japanese car auction on your arrival. Most car auctions in Japan are 'trade only', which means a European or American tourist would stand little chance of gaining access. Then there's the issue of what to do with the vehicle once the hammer falls and it's yours.

An agent in Japan should be able to arrange almost everything for you, from attending the auction and bidding on your behalf to such complicated issues as arranging transport to the docks, all the necessary paperwork, the actual shipping process and what happens once your vehicle arrives either in Southampton or Bristol. A good agent is worth every Yen of his commission! However, before you give an agent the go-ahead, make sure you've seen some verifiable references from previous satisfied clients; if he's unable to supply these, don't take the risk.

The arrival of your Mazda in the UK marks the start of another complex process, as you must pay the import duty and VAT that then becomes due. HM Customs & Excise will insist the purchase price of the vehicle in Japan is liable for VAT, as is the cost of the import duties that must also be added. You'll be unable to bring your car away from the UK docks without first paying all the duty and tax that is due; and even then you won't be able to drive your Eunos or Miata home, as it still won't be registered for use on British roads.

Registration itself is relatively straightforward if the vehicle is at least ten years of age. Armed with all the paperwork for your newly-acquired import, you should be able to arrange UK registration fairly easily via your nearest DVLA Regional Office. If your Mazda is under ten years old, though, things get much more complicated.

Any Japanese import less than a decade old must now undergo an ESVA test (replacement for the original SVA test), introduced in 2004. Extra criteria are now part of ESVA, including emissions, noise testing, the fitment of suitable alarms and the suitability of a vehicle's instrumentation for British usage. Within ESVA is the requirement for a Model Report, applicable to most Japanese imports manufactured from 1 January 1997 onwards.

The Model Report is a tool developed and produced by the Vehicle and Operator Services Agency (VOSA) from information supplied to it by official test centres. Its examiners then use the information on the Model Report to satisfy themselves that the vehicle being presented for ESVA testing is the same as a model originally tested.

Oh, and just because your vehicle has passed an ESVA test, don't assume it's automatically legal to use on the road once it's registered. ESVA is not a test of roadworthiness, so – assuming your Mazda is at least three years old – it will still need to pass a standard MoT test, too.

The cost of getting a Japanese import through an ESVA test varies hugely from model to model. However, most importers reckon on spending anywhere between £700 and £1,500 per vehicle simply to meet ESVA criteria, before they could even think about trying to register the vehicles in the UK.

Do you still want to arrange your own 'grey' import? Perhaps not.

WHERE TO FIND THEM

Narrowing down your choice of a second-hand MX-5, Eunos or Miata isn't the only major decision to be made. You also need to consider whether you'll be buying privately, from a trader or even via a car auction.

Buying a used car from a dealer certainly brings the greatest consumer rights, with more comeback available to you if things go wrong. Buying from a dealer means you're covered by the Sale of Goods Act, which essentially means the MX-5 you're spending your hard-earned cash on must meet an acceptable standard. It's also a relatively simple way of buying, as you can see several vehicles on one dealer's forecourt without the need to travel great distances viewing cars that have been advertised privately.

This applies whether you're considering paying a visit to an official Mazda dealership or one of the many independent MX-5 specialists that can be found throughout the country. Remember, though, that most Mazda dealers won't consider retailing a car more than four or five years of age, which means that for older models (and Mk1s in particular) you'll have little choice but to visit a specialist if you want to buy from a trader.

There are some excellent specialists in used MX-5s, Eunos and Miatas throughout the world, most of them offering a superb service. Not only do they usually have cars for sale, they also offer spares, repairs, servicing and upgrades once you've bought the vehicle of your choice. The MX-5 scene is thriving – and that's to the benefit of owners and potential owners everywhere. Check out the listing of all the major Mazda specialists in Appendix 2.

Of course, there's always a chance you could simply come across a suitable MX-5, Miata or Eunos on a general used-car dealer's forecourt. As ever, though, there are pitfalls to be aware of. First of all, you need to ensure the dealer you're talking to is a member of a trade association, such as the Retail Motor Industry Federation in the UK; and, second, you need to ensure you understand exactly the terms under which the vehicle is being sold to you.

For example, is the dealer claiming some kind of warranty is included in the sale – and, if so, has he given you an opportunity to study the small print, the various exclusions and, of course, confirm the timescale of the warranty? Some dealers offer their own one- to three-month all-inclusive warranty, while others will try to sell you a one-, two- or even three-year independent used car warranty – on which they will obviously be earning commission. Use a warranty as a useful haggling tool, but make sure you understand exactly what is and isn't part of its coverage.

You also need to be realistic about the age of the Mazda you're buying from a dealer, as your consumer rights are, in essence, affected by this. You have every legal right to expect a 12-month-old MX-5 purchased from a dealer to be in superb condition throughout, unless he stipulates otherwise. But a 10- or 15-year-old example will inevitably have experienced wear and tear – which means that if the exhaust fails, the brake pads need replacing or the battery dies after a few days of ownership, you'll have very little cause for complaint. It's an older vehicle and, quite simply, parts do wear out. It's a fact of life.

ALTERNATIVE ROUTES

Buying privately can be a risky business, too, although it can save you money. The only real legal obligation of a private seller is that the vehicle must be sold 'as described' – and that's about it. The seller isn't obliged to offer any kind of guarantee, you won't get a warranty and it's unlikely you'll be able to part-exchange your old car. On the other hand, a private seller doesn't have the overheads of a trader, which means that, bought this way, a used MX-5 should, in theory at least, cost you less.

The most effective way of taking the risk out of buying privately is to ensure you get an HPI check carried out, as detailed earlier in this chapter. And, as already mentioned, it's worth considering a professional car inspection by an independent expert. It could save you a considerable sum in the long run.

The third major source of used MX-5s is a car auction – although you could be waiting a long time for the Mazda of your dreams to appear at your nearest auction house. Car auctions in general bring their own set of rules and consumer rights, of which you should be aware before you attend. For a start, there's usually no opportunity to test drive any vehicles being sold at auction, as the sales process happens so quickly. Also, those auction houses offering any MX-5s with what they call a 'Trial' will be giving some kind of guarantee on the condition of the engine and transmission only – with absolutely nothing else included.

Most older vehicles are 'Sold As Seen', which means no comeback whatsoever. Bear in mind, too, that an auction house will charge a buyer's premium on top of what your winning bid is, and VAT added to the premium, so you need to find out how much this is before you bid. Don't forget that your winning bid is legally binding and means you have entered into a contract with the auctioneers from which you are then unable to withdraw.

Interestingly, there are now several auction houses in the UK that specialise in freshly imported second-hand vehicles direct from Japan. One of the most popular is Motor Way auctions, located in Southampton – but there are others out there. So what happens at such auctions?

It's pretty much the same as an ordinary car auction, apart from the fact that all the vehicles being sold have recently arrived in the UK and have yet to undergo ESVA testing or the registration process. It's a way of locating a vehicle that you can actually see before you buy, without having to pay any kind of a dealer's premium. However, as with importing a vehicle yourself, you then have to go through the ESVA (a compulsory test for all 'grey imports' under ten years of age), MoTing and registration procedures before you can use the vehicle in the UK.

If the idea of that appeals, there are some good buys to be had. But, if buying a second-hand Mazda needs to be as hassle-free as possible for you, there's still little substitute for buying your Eunos or Miata from a BIMTA-affiliated specialist dealer. It may not be the cheapest option, but it's certainly the least risky.

What many people don't realise is that similar rules and regulations apply to Internet auction sites just as they do to traditional auction houses, so don't be tempted to enter a bid on a vehicle listed on eBay 'as a bit of a laugh' unless you're serious about buying it. If you win the online auction and don't proceed with the purchase for any reason, the vendor has every right to take legal proceedings against you.

BUYING SPECIFICS

Whether you're buying a British-market MX-5 or an unofficially imported Eunos or Miata, you can take comfort from the fact that these cars have reliability and robustness built in as standard. When Mazda set out to launch a fun and funky two-seater convertible, it was also determined to make it practical and durable in long-term usage. Happily, the company achieved this brilliantly.

That's not to say that things don't go wrong or that you don't need to give any used MX-5 a seriously close inspection before you buy. No car is perfect, so it still pays to be vigilant when buying. And it all starts with the MX-5's bodyshell.

We've already mentioned the fact that you need to be on the lookout for signs of previous accident damage or repair work, but it's worth repeating here. Many MX-5s have been driven hard and worked their way through several owners by now, and such treatment can take its toll. So pay particular attention to paint finish, panel fit and so on.

From the factory, Mazda's paint finishes were traditionally excellent, although some of the earliest examples suffered from 'thin' paint that, after a few years of being polished, could actually wear through to the primer in parts. If you come across a used example with a suspiciously orange-peel finish, differing shades on adjacent panels, evidence of overspray, localised lack of shine or simply a poor finish, there's every chance some respray work has been tackled by someone with little expertise.

You also need to check that the gaps and shut lines between all the panels are even and that, as you look down the flanks of the car in daylight, there are no suspicious ripples, indents or creases. Minor damage could have been previously repaired with body filler, so be on the lookout for this.

Any MX-5 showing the odd rusty panel or two will almost certainly have had post-accident work carried out, and maybe at least one panel replaced and not properly protected against the elements. A hastily applied replacement might not have been undersealed properly and may now be suffering from the ravages of the British winter. Is an MX-5 that's had such work carried out really the kind of car you want to be buying?

Rust can occur on early MX-5s that have never had bodywork repairs carried out, though it's fairly rare and tends to be restricted to specific areas. The most common place for an MX-5 to rust is at the bottom of the sills at the rear **01/02** after the drain tubes have blocked and overflowed. If holed, this is a difficult and expensive repair, so avoid cars that have gone there. You need to check any early MX-5's floorpan and box sections to make sure there are no early signs of rot, because the chassis rails are thin in the middle and vulnerable to damage. It's not unknown for rust to break out at the rear of the boot floor, and wheelarch lips **03**, and the front bottoms of the front wings **04** also start to go on older cars. Generally, Japanese imports that have seen fewer British winters than their MX-5 contemporaries will have fared better.

01

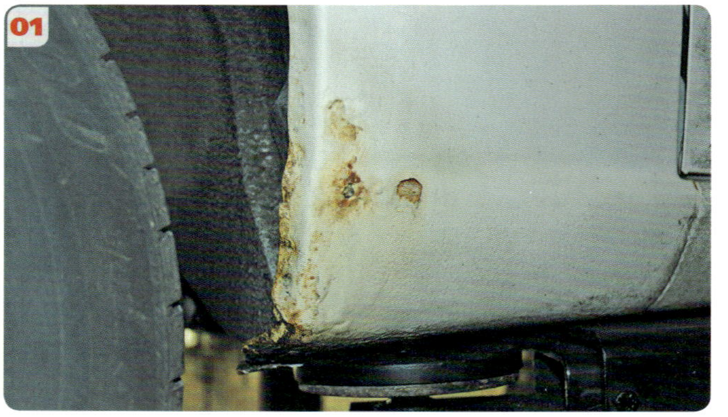

02

03

04

05

06

07

08

It also pays to check the aluminium bonnet and the pop-up headlamps on Mk1 cars, as these can show signs of corrosion, as well as being prone to stone chips which can soon spoil the overall look.

Generally, though, it's pretty good news when it comes to the MX-5's bodywork. This is one of the most well built, most robust sports cars of its era and it's a tribute to its overall quality that so many examples still look superb.

Hood and interior

Like any other convertible, an MX-5's hood is prone to wear from a combination of age and misuse, so it's important you check it carefully for signs of damage. A hood that needs replacement isn't always a major problem, as there are plenty of MX-5 specialists around that offer a same-day fitting service; and, of course, you can use a tatty hood as an excellent bargaining tool when you're buying the car.

A new hood, fitted, starts at around £250 for a standard black vinyl type with a plastic zip-out window. If you decide to take your hood requirements to another level, you can easily spend more than £500 on a mohair hood with a heated glass rear window.

When examining any hood for signs of wear, make sure you look for scratches, creases or tears on the plastic rear window **05**, and pay attention to the zip as this is often frayed or has missing teeth. The zipped section needs to be unzipped before the hood is lowered and, if owners ignore this, damage begins. On the hood itself, look closely for rips, tears, repairs and any signs of misuse **06/07**. If it has already started deteriorating, it will only get worse and you need to be prepared for some expense over the coming months.

If a hardtop is fitted, check that the rubber seals are in good order and seem a tight fit; also look inside the car for evidence of previous leaks. Also check for signs of rust or mould around the roof seating at the rear of the body **08**.

Early MX-5 interiors weren't always a stylish place to be, thanks to Mazda's odd choice of fabrics and colours over the years – and that's why many examples have had upgraded interiors installed, often in leather. Assuming the original upholstery is in place, look for signs of 'bobbling' of the fabric, and also for wear on the edges of the cushion. A tatty interior can again be replaced, and costs vary according to the specification you expect; but in 2005 we were quoted around £500 for a full leather re-fit, which again can be used as a haggling tool when buying a car.

You also need to check the carpets in any MX-5, feeling for signs of dampness caused by hood leaks and condensation. Beneath the wet carpets, are the floor sections free of rust? It's also worth checking for rust creeping from under the sill kick plates (if fitted), easily spotted when you open the doors. MX-5 carpets are made in one piece and even specialists hate fitting them, some even cutting them in half lengthways to fit them in two sections.

Inside any MX-5 you need to ensure everything's working

as it should. If electric windows are fitted, do they operate smoothly and reasonably quietly? (they are always relatively slow). Does the air conditioning (standard on the Eunos) function as it should? Are all the lights and the stereo in working order? It's easy to miss such areas, though they can indicate whether or not a car's been meticulously maintained.

Under the bonnet

We've already said in this chapter that an MX-5 is one of the most reliable sports cars you can spend your hard-earned cash on. But that doesn't mean there aren't some obvious checks you should carry out before agreeing to buy.

Any well-maintained MX-5 engine is tough, reliable and will have no problem achieving a six-figure mileage with ease – it's not unknown for early MX-5s to still be running well with nearly 200,000 miles on the odometer. Even so, don't assume all is well under the bonnet without checking for yourself – and that means taking a test drive from cold.

Check the oil and water levels first – if they are low, that's a possible sign of neglect. Both oil and antifreeze should be clean; if the antifreeze is grey and the oil black and sludgy, it's been a while since they were changed. The MX-5 needs regular oil changes to stay healthy. Remove the oil filler cap, on the left front of the engine. Are there any signs of mayonnaise-type gunk on its underside? This, or a similar sludge in the cooling system (press, twist and lift the radiator cap with the engine COLD – see photo on left) could point to cylinder head gasket failure – rare on an MX-5, but you should be aware of the possibility when buying any used car.

On start-up, is the engine fairly quiet and not suffering from excessive tappet noise? Mk1 cars have hydraulic tappets, and they sometimes rattle for a short time, but they should settle down as the engine warms through. Are there any plumes of blue smoke from the exhaust? (These might point to a high-mileage engine burning oil.) Is the engine misfiring? (Sometimes caused by faulty spark plugs or leads, or by a basic lack of maintenance and regular servicing.) Has the cam belt been changed recently? (Ask for proof of this; it should be changed at least every 60,000 miles or five years, whichever comes sooner.)

If the MX-5 you're inspecting will shortly be due for a service or a new cam belt, make sure you build the cost of this into the price when you're negotiating. Both jobs together cost anywhere between £200 and £400 (at 2006 prices), so it's an important consideration.

Exhaust-wise, it's pretty much the same as for any car – which means being on your guard against a failed catalytic converter (a fairly expensive item to replace), so make sure you check the most recent MoT's emissions readings carefully. Examine the entire exhaust system for signs of corrosion,

although most of the aftermarket replacements tend to last well these days, and are available in stainless steel.

Transmission checks

MX-5 gearboxes tend to be as reliable and durable as the engines, although they're not all without faults. Gearchanges should be smooth and quiet, so any major clunking or whining noises should immediately arouse your suspicions.

If you're trying out an early MX-5, make sure it's a long enough test drive for the car to warm up fully. Up until around 1992, MX-5s employed a single-cone synchromesh on second gear, which made the first-to-second change a bit notchy; this should fade though, once fully warmed through, so again be on the lookout for this. A failing clutch slave cylinder, a known MX-5 weakness, can prevent the clutch from fully disengaging, and make this problem worse. You can just see the cylinder through the right-hand front wheelarch (see photo above), and if it's wet, most likely it's been leaking.

Clutches tend to last a long time, although much depends on the abuse a car has experienced and, of course, its mileage. Watch for signs of a slipping clutch, but don't be too concerned about a noisy clutch release bearing; most MX-5s suffer from this.

Brakes

The all-disc system is simple and easy to maintain, and any problems usually centre around the rear calipers (right). They tend to seize with lack of use in winter (there's often not enough grease on the slider pins even from new), and not everybody knows that the rear pistons need adjusting when new pads are fitted. So if the handbrake lever feels firm but provides little effect, suspect one or the other. Luckily, the calipers are simple to adjust, and not too expensive to replace.

Looking elsewhere

All else mechanical is pretty good news when buying just about any MX-5, Miata or Eunos, as the cars' steering, suspension and most of the braking system all tend to be long-lived and durable. Basic maintenance and repairs will be covered further on in this book, at which stage we can take a closer look at exactly what can go wrong and what may need doing to put it right. Rest assured, though, that the MX-5 is a reliable piece of kit compared with just about any other sports car at any price. For that to be the case on a used sportster offering such great value for money really is the icing on the cake.

The question of value and pricing, however, brings another obvious question: just how fussy should you be about the cosmetics and overall appearance of a second-hand MX-5? The answer lies in what you have planned for your new acquisition.

Increasing numbers of MX-5 buyers are now deliberately choosing to buy less than perfect examples, safe in the knowledge that the money they save can go towards the full respray, the new hood and the upgraded interior they have in mind. Mk1s, in particular, are now looked upon as modern classics – traditional sports cars with few of the foibles and problem areas of some of the older rivals out there. And that means more enthusiasts are now willing to buy a solid but cosmetically drab example, going on to personalise and improve it to their own specification.

This can bring good news, as it means you'll end up spending less buying your MX-5 than you might otherwise. Two words of warning, though. First, you need to ensure your MX-5 is as rust-free and as mechanically fine as it's possible to be within your budget. And, second, it's imperative you price up the cost of all the work you want carried out before you actually take the plunge into ownership. Failure to do this could result in you spending far more in total than the finished 'product' is actually worth.

If carrying out your own renovation or upgrade isn't part of your agenda, you really need to be looking for the very best (cosmetically, structurally and mechanically) example of an MX-5 your money will stretch to. Even such basic tasks as having the alloy wheels refurbished can easily set you back a couple of hundred pounds or more, so being vigilant and haggling hard at the pre-purchase stage will be time well spent.

RUNNING AN MX-5

Another great bonus of owning an MX-5, Miata or Eunos is that its running costs are so competitive. In fact, driving an MX-5 every day need cost no more – and realistically could cost significantly less – than driving about in a very mundane hatchback.

Assuming you can live with a two-seater sports car with a small boot on an everyday basis, an MX-5 is the finest choice on today's used market. Its inherent reliability (combined with fantastic driver appeal) makes it an unrivalled proposition. And that's equally true when it comes to the cost of keeping it on the road.

Insurance groupings vary according to the engine size and exact specification of the model you own. Remember, though, that many classic car insurance specialists now offer cover for just about all the Mk1 models, which can bring costs down considerably – particularly if you can agree on a limited-mileage, agreed value policy for peace of mind on both sides. The MX-5 Owners' Club will also be able to help with sourcing insurance, while owners of later models can turn to brokers and insurance companies that specialise in sports and performance cars. Unless you're an 18-year-old with a poor driving record and an ungaraged MX-5, you shouldn't be too shocked at the sort of quotes you'll get.

The cost of parts and accessories can also work out cheaper than you might expect, aided by the plethora of MX-5 specialists that now exists. Servicing via a specialist rather than an official Mazda dealer can work out significantly less expensive, as can such tasks as having a new hood fitted, having the cam belt replaced, installing a new clutch … and so the list goes on.

There's another crucial area where an MX-5 can save you money, however, and that's in its residuals. Compared with a mainstream and rather boring car of similar value wearing, say, a Ford badge, an MX-5 of any age will almost certainly depreciate at a far slower rate. Early examples have already lost most of their value, of course, and now represent seriously good value for money. But later Mk1s and even the Mk2s are still worth a far greater percentage of their when-new prices than most dull hatchbacks that originally cost the same.

Given the age and current values of the earliest MX-5s, there's never been a better time to buy. These models are already being accepted as modern classics and are appearing regularly in the classic car press; it can't be too long before values of the finest examples start to rise.

Over the years, the Mazda MX-5, Miata and Eunos have established themselves as the fun and funky sports car choice for owners who don't want to spend every weekend wielding a spanner or who don't want to endure rusting bodywork, interior flooding and dodgy durability. It's one of the most sensible sports car designs the world has ever seen; and it just so happens to be one of the most entertaining, too.

CHAPTER 3

PREPARING FOR WORK

Before you start, you'll need tools, somewhere to work – and an idea of what you can accomplish. Luckily, the MX-5/Miata/Eunos is essentially a simple, reliable car, and most of the jobs you'll need to do are simple servicing tasks, or possibly improvement and embellishment projects that won't take too much time or occupy too much space.

Most of the jobs described in this book can be accomplished with a decent socket set and a good set of hand tools, with a few significant additions, but there's absolutely no shame in farming out jobs that you feel are too difficult, or which need expensive tools that you'll use only rarely.

There is, however, a joy in doing things for yourself, not least in the knowledge you gain – and the money you save over garage labour prices. Be aware that the MX-5 has been around since 1989 and there's nothing new – many owners have carried out these jobs before, all the car's secrets are known and most are reproduced in this book. But if you want to find out the possible pitfalls of a particular job, there are plenty of Internet discussion forums where you can ask advice from others, usually club members, who have done the job before.

Club membership is one of the most useful 'accessories' you can buy when owning any car that is even vaguely interesting, and there are plenty of thriving owners' clubs for the MX-5. Apart from the camaraderie and plenty of meets and social events with like-minded people, club membership can steer you towards great deals on parts and insurance, and advice is free. A simple Internet search will find the best club for you.

Most important to consider before you start any work, there are some basic safety procedures that you need to follow. Accidents are called that for a reason, however unlikely their possibility sounds, but they do happen. Be properly prepared, and enjoy getting to know your MX-5. We'll look at tools first, then workshop practices, and finally safety.

TOOLS

The general rule when buying tools – as with any equipment – is buy the best you can afford, and look after them. There's no need to go for a full set of Snap-On tools costing thousands if you're not working on your car every day, but get decent kit – it's cheaper in the long run. Luckily some of the companies producing tools at the cheaper end of the range have raised their game in recent years, and there are some good finds to be had from specialist tool suppliers, or offers through magazines.

Clean the tools after use, and put them back in their respective slots and holders in their boxes, or back in the main toolbox so you can find them again. Cleaning also helps you to note any wear or damage that might make a spanner or socket slip off a nut or bolt, either cutting your knuckles or rendering the fastener impossible to undo without butchery or a nut splitter.

Socket set and accessories

Your most useful piece of kit, without which it's impossible to operate, will be a decent socket set – ⅜in drive is the most useful for the limited space in modern cars. Most of the nuts and bolts on an MX-5 are 12, 14, or 17mm – the distance across the flats on the hexagonal heads – with the occasional 19mm, 21 or 23mm for drain plugs.

You will need extra extensions and a universal joint: a mechanic friend once observed that the main difference that marked out his tool kit from an amateur's was access – he had a multitude of ratchets and extensions to cover every eventuality, meaning he could reach the parts others couldn't – any nut and bolt, however inaccessible.

On the MX-5, there are a few places that are really hard to get into, and are a few extra tools will make your life easier. One place is the alternator clamp bolt on 1.6-litre Mk1s. It's most easily reached with a very short ratchet drive that most of us don't have, but the cheaper alternative is a cut-down 12mm ring spanner – it's worth buying one especially to shorten, or cut down an old one. Make sure you round off the cut end with a file. If the alternator bolt is tight, you can apply extra leverage by slipping another ring spanner over the end at a 90° angle, and applying extra leverage with that.

Reaching the exhaust manifold flange joint bolts needs 360mm (14in) of extensions, so buy extras. A universal joint comes in handy there, so if you're planning to tackle the exhaust, buy one if your socket set doesn't already include one. The clutch slave cylinder is a bit of a stretch, as one of the bolts needs undoing through the right-hand wheel arch, though you can see it easily enough. Also, if you ever plan on removing a front wing, under the wing there's a 10mm bolt set well back inside the wing that you undo from within the wheelwell after removing the liner, and this demands at least 250mm of extensions.

Also very useful for nuts and bolts under the car is a breaker bar – to 'break' the initial resistance of a tight fixing. It's simply a long bar with a pivoted square end that attaches to your sockets and provides lots of extra leverage. Cheapskates like the author just use a short length of scaffold tube slipped over the ratchet handle to increase leverage – but you're risking damaging the internal ratchets if you do.

Small spark plug socket

The MX-5 has slim 10mm spark plugs. Make sure you have the right-sized socket to fit them, with a rubber liner that holds the plug while you lower it down its bore – it's impossible to do this with fingers, though you can, as an alternative, push the plug into a length of 3/8in heater hose and screw it in with that, tightening it with a socket afterwards.

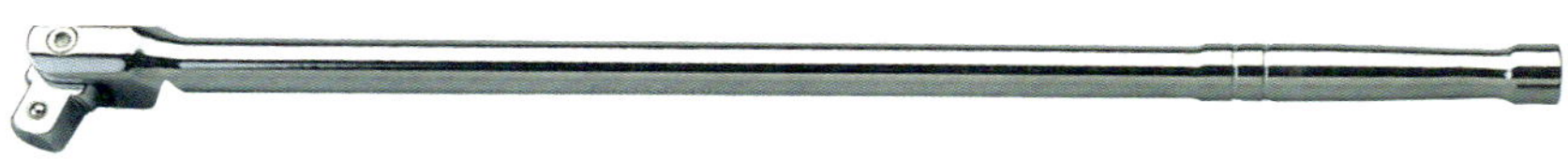

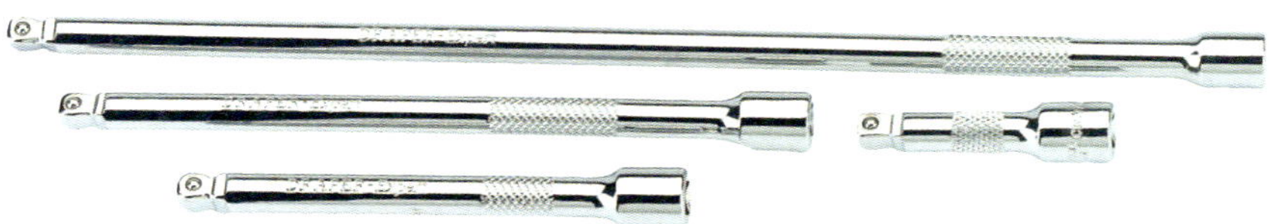

Torque wrench

Many older mechanics used to claim they never used a torque wrench in their life – and that was fine in the days of over-engineered, cast-iron sports cars. The MX-5 by comparison is a precision piece of kit with many aluminium parts. While well-engineered and pleasant to work on, certain torque settings are demanded, and if they are not adhered to it's very easy to strip threads. There are super (and expensive) digital readout torque wrenches available, but the best bet for home use is the pre-set type, where you wind a collar up to the desired setting, and the wrench clicks when it gets there – they only cost £50 or so: do the car a favour and get one. You should really torque up your road wheel nuts too – all conscientious tyre fitters do – and, if you plan to sprint or hillclimb the car, it looks cool in the paddock when you do your bolt checks before your runs. (You mean, you've driven the car to the venue, and you're not going to check the tightness of vital, life-preserving nuts and bolts before you go out and drive it as hard as you can? Crazy.)

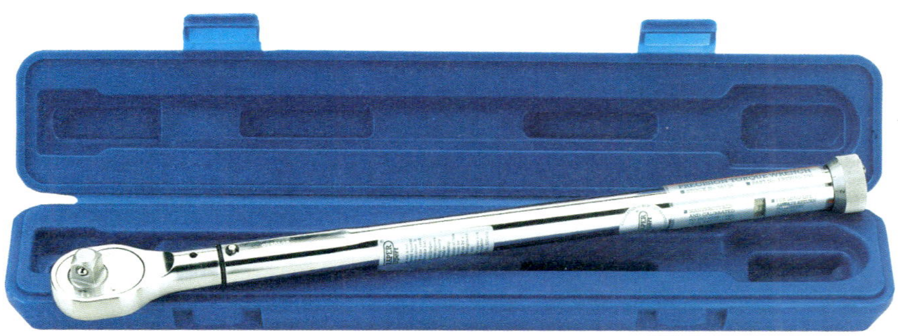

Decent hand tools

A selection of screwdrivers, both cross-head and flat. There are many different profiles of cross-head screws and drivers, and they don't all mate perfectly with each other. Some socket sets come with a small selection of interchangeable bits that can be used in conjunction with a small ¼in drive ratchet handle.

Please don't ever use screwdrivers as chisels or drifts – you'll ruin them. There are lovely and inexpensive drift/punch/cold chisel sets around for that.

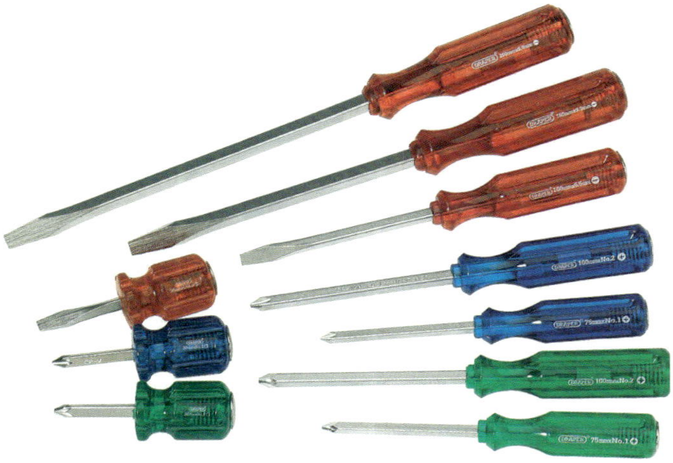

Must-have hand tools include a selection of spanners, both open-ended and ring or, combination. Try to find slim, not chunky ones – access in some parts of an MX-5 is tight. You'll need 8mm–19mm range at least.

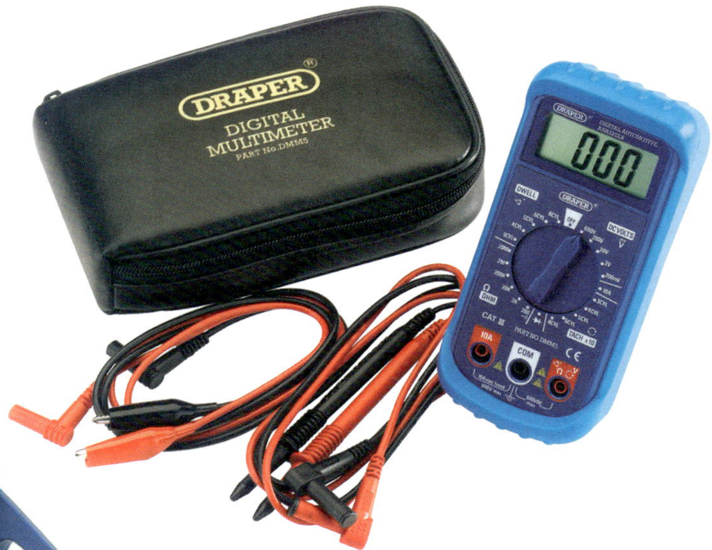

Pliers

You'll need a decent pair of these for releasing the spring clips on the coolant hoses – proper hose clip pliers are available, but a large pair of square-jawed pliers – or even a self-locking (Mole) wrench will do the job just as well. A small pair of needle-nosed pliers is useful for bending your bridging wire to shape, for grabbing things through small holes or for picking up nuts and washers that you've dropped in inaccessible places (we all do it, even after 30 years' wrenching). Get the type with rubber-insulated handles just in case you're working near electrical systems.

Test lamp or multimeter

Vital for finding out if electrical power is arriving at a connector: for example, when troubleshooting an electric window. Multimeters are cheap, give you voltage readings and also can be used to check for continuity: for example, when suspecting a broken wire. (You can also use them to test dry-cell batteries from your torch, camera or TV remote to check if they're used up.)

Useful tools that will help with the MX-5

Old car aerial with ball end

Useful for cleaning out the hood drains from the top. Don't use a screwdriver – it could tear the rubber tubes.

Hammer and brass drift

Using these is the kindest way to knock tight bolts out of the wishbones when changing springs and or dampers. Don't use your nice new screwdrivers.

Oil filter wrench

Vital if the filter won't unscrew by hand (they usually don't). Get the three-legged type that grips the filter harder the more you turn it. There isn't room to use a strap-type wrench.

G-clamp

Just the thing for pushing back the pistons in the front calipers to make room for new, thicker pads. Professional garages use a special expander tool that fits within the caliper jaws, but a large clamp works just as well. It's possible to use large pliers or a self-locking (Mole) wrench but you run a very good chance of damaging the piston's protective rubber gaiter. If that lets in moisture, the caliper will soon seize.

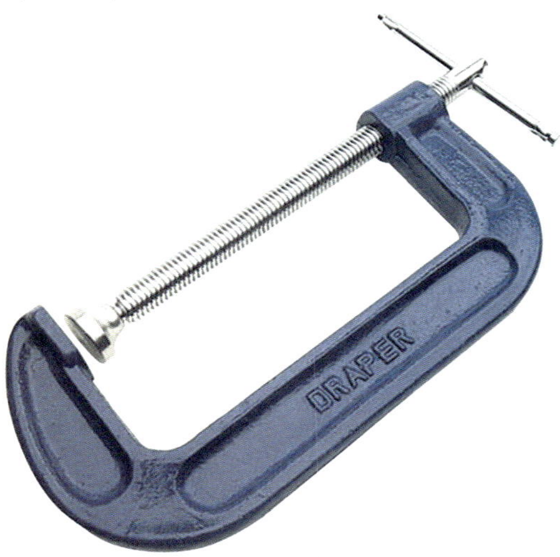

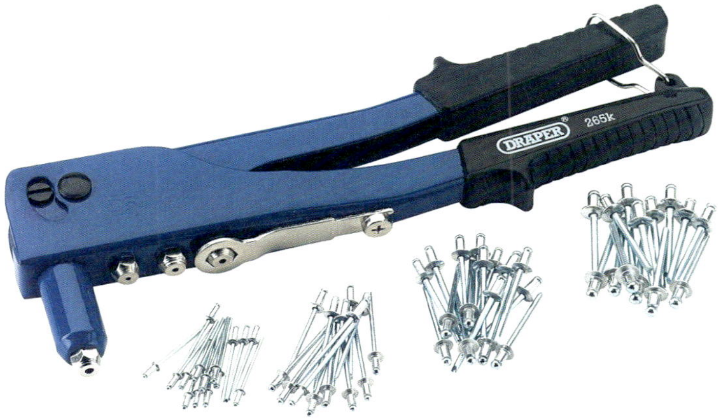

Electric drill and rivet gun

If you plan to change the hood, you won't get far without these. Rechargeable battery-powered drills are the most convenient, and very cheap if you buy them at a home DIY store rather than a specialist tool shop. Basically, the higher the voltage the more use they will be.

You don't need the best rivet gun in the world – you won't be using it very often. The cheapest place to buy one of these is at one of the tool stands in the autojumble section of classic car shows. Both also come in handy for riveting repair straps/panels across things like broken fridge shelves.

Good practice with tools

Keep them clean, and put them back where they belong. Wiping the oil off after every use means they will be ready next time. Having a home for every tool means you can find it when you want it. If they get wet, which does happen from time to time if you're working outside, wipe dry and spray lightly with WD-40 or rub with an oily rag to preserve them.

Regular cleaning means you can check for damage, such as damaged jaws or rounded-off sockets and ring spanners. If a tool is damaged, throw it away and buy a new one. The nut or bolt heads it rounds off will always be the ones you can't reach by any other means, which means a lot more dismantling to get the parts undone and then maybe a trip to your local engineering shop. For the same reason, get into the habit of changing rounded-off or damaged fasteners for new ones – aside from the fact that you'll be able to undo them more easily in future, they look neater too.

Generally, pull spanners towards you when loosening or tightening fasteners – otherwise you're guaranteed slashed knuckles when the fastener suddenly loosens or slips. If you have to push, do it with the heel of your hand and an open palm to minimise the risk of injury.

Don't use pliers, self-locking (Mole) wrenches, or even an adjustable spanner, on nuts or bolt heads. Mole grips are for butchers and adjustable wrenches are for plumbers. Use the right tool. If you don't have it, buy one and it's yours forever.

Don't use your lovely new torque wrench as a breaker bar for more leverage on tight nuts and bolts. It's an expensive, precision bit of kit. Breaker bars are comparatively cheap.

INDOORS OR OUTDOORS?

Few of us have the luxury of a fully-equipped workshop and plenty of room to move around the car. Not all of us even have a lock-up garage. But luckily the MX-5 is a smallish car; so many operations can be accomplished in a small garage.

Your working environment will to a large extent dictate the kind of jobs you want to tackle. You wouldn't change a hood outside in the rain, but then it's a job that's easier in summer, anyway, because the hood material stretches better. You wouldn't really want to change a clutch or exhaust at the side of the road (although some of us have).

But, even if you have limited access, many jobs may be possible under some cover. If changing dampers and springs you could, for example, work on one end of the car at a time, with some shelter under your up-and-over garage door.

If you are working on the floor, a sheet of cardboard (or an opened-out cardboard box) contributes to comfort, and also catches accidental spills. When leaning over the car, always protect bodywork and paint with an old blanket or sheet. Exposed zips can make a real mess of paintwork, which is why proper mechanic's overalls don't have them.

BASIC WORKSHOP PRINCIPLES

Damaged threads

Stripping internal threads is one of the biggest dangers when working on aluminium parts. Luckily, most of the external fixings on the MX-5 engine are studs and nuts, but still a word of caution. Overtightening until the spanner 'gives' and the fastener turns some more brings on that sickening feeling – 'I know I shouldn't have done it, but I thought I'd just do it a little tighter' – a feeling that gets worse when you unscrew a bolt and it brings the aluminium threads out with it. You can sometimes get away with chasing out the threads with a plug tap of the right size and then using a slightly longer bolt or stud, but taps aren't cheap and there is no guarantee of success.

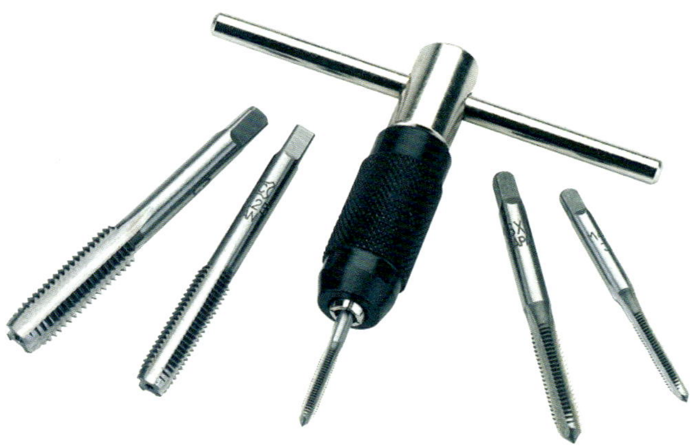

Helicoiling is the next solution, a kit you can buy that involves drilling out the hole larger, re-tapping it with the tap supplied and then winding in a steel coil that forms a new thread of the original size. Or it's a trip to the machine shop so they can do it for you.

If you're lucky, and you strip the threads in a nut but the threads on the bolt look all right, clean out the bolt threads with a wire brush and use a new nut. These are available in various grades from tool and bearing shops. It's good practice to renew self-locking nuts (the ones with the coloured plastic insert) every time anyway.

Electrical testing

Warning: *Be very careful not to short the probe across electrical terminals, or you'll blow fuses or relays.*

You can check whether electrical current is arriving at a component using a test light – usually looking like a small screwdriver with a pointed end and a lead coming out of the handle with a small alligator clip on the end. Connect the alligator clip to earth (ground). With the ignition and the electrical component switched on, touch the probe to the terminal where the power is meant to arrive – say the centre terminal of a suspected faulty indicator, with the bulb removed. If it lights, then power is arriving and the bulb or component is faulty. If not, then work back down the wire at various connectors until you find power.

If the bulb doesn't light, there could be a broken wire, and the only way to check this is with a multimeter, for continuity.

WITH THE IGNITION OFF set the meter to the ohms (Ω) scale. Touch the probes together to first check if the meter is working. If so, the needle will read full deflection, or if digital the display will quickly read zero. Then touch the probes to the ends of the suspect wire. If the wire's good, you'll get the same zero reading – if there's no deflection or change then the wire is most likely broken.

You can also use a multimeter to read the amount of power arriving at individual components. Set it to the most suitable DC scale – usually 20 volts – and first check across the battery terminals to see how much power it is producing: typically near 13 volts. By connecting between various components and earth (ground) you can see how much power is arriving at the relevant component or being lost.

Oil catch tanks – and oil/antifreeze/brake-fluid disposal

You need to catch old oil, antifreeze and brake fluid and dispose of it safely and responsibly. All these fluids are toxic, if not carcinogenic, and it is illegal to pour them down the drain. Find your nearest recycling centre and pour your old oil away there instead.

BUYING PARTS

There are four main sources of parts for your MX-5: motor accessory stores; motor factors; marque specialists, often taking orders on the Internet; and main/authorised dealers. There's a fifth alternative that could also be handy.

The first (general motor parts and accessory stores) are generally the cheapest and useful for buying consumables such as oil, filters, bulbs, belts, plus touch-up paint, accessories and useful tools such as brake bleeders and rivet guns. Their advantage is that they can be found in every town and often keep long hours, sometimes including part of Sunday and evenings. They can also source slower-moving items such as clutches and timing belts, but are unlikely to hold them in stock and may well have to order these from a motor factor… so you might as well cut out the middle man and save money.

Motor factors are fewer and further between, usually located in industrial areas on the outskirts of town and keeping basically office hours. But many offer small discounts, even to private individuals. Always phone first, though, to make sure they have what you need, or find out how long it will take to order it in.

Marque specialists can usually supply parts from stock; ordered either on the phone or via the Internet. As well as spare parts – often in the case of body panels these will be genuine Mazda parts – they usually sell tuning and modification goodies.

The main dealer is the place to go for all those parts nobody else carries – such as master cylinders, or small items of trim, for example – or if you decide to stick to all genuine Mazda parts.

There is an alternative source of parts, and that's to buy second-hand – particularly useful for high-value parts such as tail light clusters, alternators and starter motors, although these rarely go wrong. Though you can still find the traditional old-style breaker's yard complete with fierce dog, where you have to remove the parts yourself, you won't find too many MX-5/Miatas there.

Much better to consult one of the online parts finder services. Tap in the details of the part you want and very soon, breakers from around the country will contact you by either e-mail or text message to offer parts and their price. Very often they will have the part on the shelf, delivery is usually next day and the author's experience is that they often turn out cheaper than the traditional breakers.

SAFETY

Even experienced mechanics find it's very hard to work on a car without drawing blood from sliced fingers and grazed knuckles. This is almost inevitable, though you can minimise the risk by wearing disposable latex gloves. We know it's hard to resist the old 'bend over' jokes when first snapping them on – but they stop you getting in contact with used engine oil, which is carcinogenic, and keep you clean, at least until you hole them. Most important, they're cheap – a box of 1,000 is usually less than £10 – so use them.

But the main thing we are trying to prevent is the car falling on us, or any heavy bits falling and crushing digits. Don't use the car's own jack for raising and lowering – it's for emergency wheel changes only. Use a trolley jack instead, which can be bought very cheaply. These also have the advantage that you can lift one complete end or side of the car at a time. Always chock the front wheels or apply the handbrake before lifting the car.

Lifting the car

Don't ever get under a car supported only by a jack. Lower it on to axle stands. Where to jack? At the rear, the best place is under the differential **01**. Trolley jacks usually have a lifting cup in which the diff sits snugly. At the front, jack under the crossmember, protecting the metal with a piece of wood, and making sure you're not actually lifting under the sump, which is alloy. You can't hammer dents out of these, unlike pressed-steel ones.

Jacking under the chassis rails is OK, as long as you jack only at the ends of the rails where they are double skinned, and use a wood protector **02/03**. The single-skinned sections in the middle are fragile, and many MX-5 are quite well scuffed here.

01

02

03

04

Once you've got the car in the air, you're going to want to keep it there. For this you need axle stands, which again are quite cheap. The traditional type is telescopic with holes and pins to set the height, but the ratchet type is more convenient to use. Once you have jacked up the car – AND WITHOUT GETTING UNDER IT – raise the stands to the desired height, insert wooden packing pieces to protect the metal and then gently lower the car on to them **04**. For many jobs on the MX-5 – such as removing the exhaust and gearbox to get at the clutch – you'll need to have the whole car clear of the ground, so you either need four stands, or two stands and a pair of ramps. You could drive the car forward up on to the ramps, then pick up the rear with a trolley jack and support it on the stands.

Why the packing pieces? Axle stands tend to have V-shaped support brackets to retain things like axles and wishbones, and if you place them under the sills or frame rails, they could damage the metal. Using protectors gives the underside of the body an easier ride.

Battery

Never smoke near a battery, especially one that's charging. Batteries emit flammable hydrogen gas when they're working or charging.

To make things really safe, it's recommended that you disconnect the battery whenever you're working on the electrical, ignition or fuel systems. Always disconnect the battery negative (earth, or ground) lead – this is the awkward one to reach – but first make sure you know the security code for the radio/stereo, which will need resetting before it will work again.

Fire

Rare, but remember a car is full of both flammable fluids and vapours and the potential for electric sparks. Car fires generally take hold very quickly, and are very frightening – you want to do everything you can to avoid a fire.

Fuel vapours, when allowed to build up in confined spaces, are both highly toxic to humans, and highly explosive. If you've got fuel or solvents about, make sure the area you are working in is well ventilated, and never smoke or have any kind of open flame around when working on a vehicle. Before working on the fuel system, always disconnect the lead from the battery negative (earth/ground) terminal.

Always keep a fire extinguisher handy, of the carbon dioxide, powder or AFFF type suitable for electrical or fuel fires, and never try to put out an electrical or fuel fire with water.

General safety rules

The chance of things going wrong always seems so remote, but remember they're not called accidents for nothing. When working on cars, always follow some simple rules and you shouldn't go wrong.

Tell someone

If you're working alone and out of sight, make sure someone knows where you are and what you are doing, and get them to check up on you periodically.

Long hair/loose clothing

Want to get scalped? No? Make sure everything loose is tied or tucked up out of the way when working on moving parts. The same goes for watches and jewellery – it's a shame to spoil them but, more important, they can cause an electrical short circuit.

Eye protection

Always wear some, such as safety glasses, when using power tools – electric drills, grinders and the like. A trip to casualty is very time-consuming – and who's going to put away your dismantled car and all your tools?

Radiator cap

Don't remove the radiator cap from a hot cooling system – let it cool down first, or cover it with a thick cloth and release the pressure slowly.

Heat

Engines, radiators and exhausts are HOT. Even if the sump feels cool the oil inside may be scalding. And don't put your fingers near the fan blades of a hot engine. It could just spin up at any time.

Oil and solvents

Fuel (especially modern unleaded), solvents and brake fluid are toxic and/or carcinogenic. So never siphon them by mouth, and wipe them off if they get on your skin. Better still, wear latex gloves for the oily stuff.

Keep chemicals, solvents, oil and other harmful fluids out of reach of animals and children, and with the lids screwed on tight.

If you're not sure about something, don't do it. Remember your vehicle's safety affects others as well as yourself, so if in doubt get professional advice.

H29 GNF

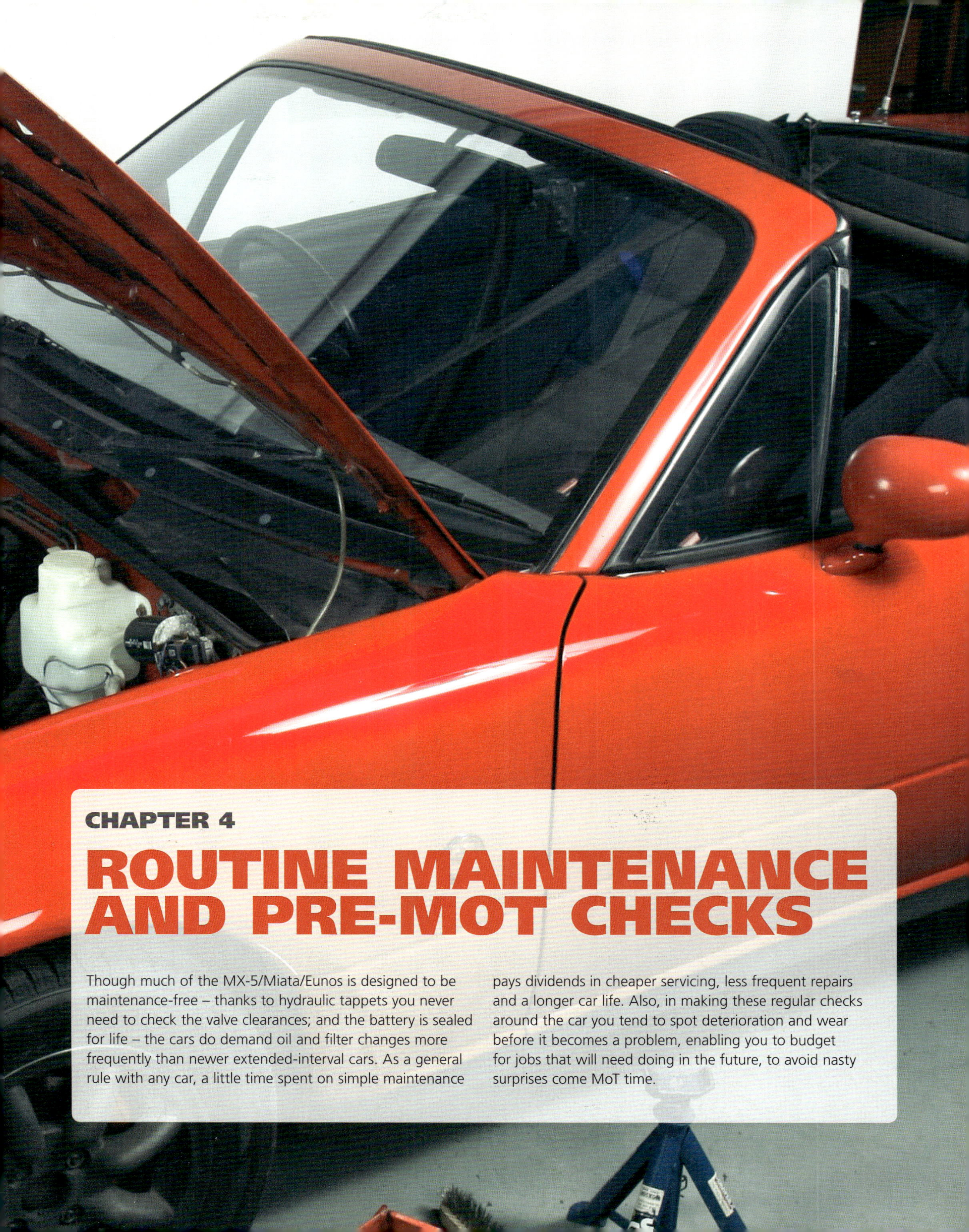

CHAPTER 4

ROUTINE MAINTENANCE AND PRE-MOT CHECKS

Though much of the MX-5/Miata/Eunos is designed to be maintenance-free – thanks to hydraulic tappets you never need to check the valve clearances; and the battery is sealed for life – the cars do demand oil and filter changes more frequently than newer extended-interval cars. As a general rule with any car, a little time spent on simple maintenance pays dividends in cheaper servicing, less frequent repairs and a longer car life. Also, in making these regular checks around the car you tend to spot deterioration and wear before it becomes a problem, enabling you to budget for jobs that will need doing in the future, to avoid nasty surprises come MoT time.

ROUTINE MAINTENANCE SCHEDULE

EVERY 250 MILES OR WEEKLY
- Check the engine oil level
- Check the engine coolant level
- Check the windscreen washer level
- Check the brake/clutch fluid level
- Check the tyres and pressures

EVERY 3,000 MILES
- Change the engine oil and filter

EVERY 7,500 MILES
- Check the power steering fluid level
- Check the automatic transmission fluid level (where fitted)
- Check and top up the differential oil
- Check the manual transmission oil level
- Check the brake pads and discs
- Check and adjust if necessary the engine drivebelts

EVERY 15,000 MILES
- Change the air filter
- Inspect the steering and suspension parts, plus the driveshaft boots

EVERY 18,000 MILES
- Change the spark plugs

EVERY 30,000 MILES
- Check and if necessary change the spark plug HT leads
- Change the transmission lubricant (manual and auto)
- Drain, flush and refill the cooling system

EVERY 60,000 MILES
- Change the cam belt and ancillary drive belts
- Change the fuel filter
- Renew the differential oil

TORQUE WRENCH SETTINGS

	Nm	lbf ft		Nm	lbf ft
Roadwheel (lug) nuts	88–118	65–87	Differential filler plug	39–53	29–39
Spark plugs	15–22	11–16	Differential drain plug	39–53	29–39
Sump drain plug	30–41	22–30	Automatic transmission oil pan	6–8	4–6
Gearbox filler plug	25–39	18–28	Brake caliper sliding pin/lockbolts	78–88	58–65
Gearbox drain plug	25–39	18–28	Brake caliper bracket retaining bolts	49–69	36–51

RECOMMENDED LUBRICANTS AND FLUIDS

Engine	Semi-synthetic 10W/40 engine oil to API SG or higher
Cooling system	2/3 antifreeze to 1/3 water for most territories
Manual gearbox	SAE 75W90 gear oil, or synthetic equivalent, to API GL–5 or higher
Automatic transmission	Dexron II or equivalent automatic transmission fluid
Differential	SAE 80W90 gear oil to API GL–5 or higher
Power steering	Dexron II or equivalent automatic transmission fluid
Braking system	Brake fluid to DOT 3 or higher

EVERY 250 MILES OR WEEKLY

ENGINE OIL LEVEL CHECK

The oil level is shown on the yellow-handled dipstick at the rear left corner of the engine **01**. With the car parked on level ground, and allowed to stand for a few minutes to let the oil run back down into the sump, pull the dipstick and wipe it on a clean rag. Reinsert the dipstick and pull it back out again **02**. The oil on the dipstick should be between the upper and lower (F and L) marks **03**. If it's not, top up to the maximum mark through the filler at the front left of the cam cover at the top of the engine **04**. The difference between the maximum and minimum marks is 0.8 litre (1.4 pints).

While you're checking the oil, have a general look around for leaks. The most likely place for an MX-5 engine to leak is where the camshaft sensor bolts to the back of the cylinder head – that's what Mazda called it even before it began fitting position sensors at the crankshaft nose with the Mk2 1.8. A leak from here can very often be misdiagnosed as a leaking cam cover gasket or even a failed cylinder head gasket, because the oil runs down the back of the block and manifests itself as dripping from the right rear of the sump.

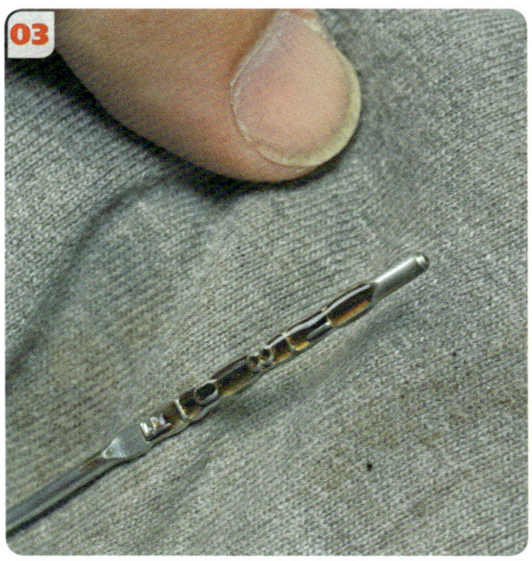

■ EVERY 250 MILES OR WEEKLY

COOLANT LEVEL CHECK

Only do this when the engine is cold – before you've driven the car. You can take a visual reading of coolant in the expansion (header) tank mounted on the right-hand inner wing and connected to the radiator filler neck by a thin hose; but it's best to peer into the radiator to check the level in there too. The MX-5/Miata uses a smaller radiator cap than most cars; push down and turn so you can lift it off **01**. Hold a rag over it in case there is still pressure in the system. You should be able to see coolant covering the tops of the tubes in the radiator – if not, top up with antifreeze or a mixture of water and antifreeze **02**.

While you're there, check the condition of the sealing rings on the radiator cap carefully, especially if the car has been overheating but still retaining coolant in the header tank. The lower, smaller seal sometimes swells up and covers the overflow outlet in the filler neck. Pressure in the cooling system pushes expanding coolant out past the O-ring, up the pipe and into the header tank **03**, but the suction when the engine cools is insufficient to bring it back past the swollen ring. The result is that the engine eventually evacuates its cooling system through the header tank, and overheats. The simplest cure is a new radiator cap, which needs to hold between 11psi and 15psi.

■ EVERY 250 MILES OR WEEKLY

WASHER FLUID LEVEL CHECK

Remember that in the UK it is an offence to drive a car with inoperative windscreen washers. The reservoir is mounted on the bulkhead (firewall) at the back of the engine bay – the bottle is translucent white plastic so you can see at a glance if the level needs topping up **01**. On ABS-equipped cars the bottle is under the closing panel in front of the radiator. In either case, the flexible lid simply pulls off, so top up with the appropriate mix of water and screenwash fluid for your climate **02**. Never use antifreeze, as it can discolour or damage paintwork.

■ EVERY 250 MILES OR WEEKLY

BRAKE AND CLUTCH FLUID LEVEL CHECKS

These are white translucent plastic, so again you can perform a visual check without removing the covers – there are maximum and minimum level lines moulded on the outside of the reservoirs. To top up, first clean up the reservoirs and lids **01** to stop any dirt or grit falling in, then unscrew the lids **02** – the clutch reservoir has a subsidiary bung under the screwed cover that you have to lift out too **03**. If the reservoirs need topping up, pour in new hydraulic fluid from a container you've just opened **04**. Hydraulic fluid absorbs moisture from the atmosphere, which lowers the boiling point of the fluid, and in extreme cases this can be either very unnerving, affecting braking efficiency, or at worst disastrous.

The fluid in the brake reservoir should be clean, about the colour of honey – if it's dirty it needs changing (see Chapter 7). Clutch fluid always seems to get dirty more quickly.

■ EVERY 250 MILES OR WEEKLY

TYRE CHECKS

Check pressures weekly with the tyres cold. Though fuel station air pressure gauges are getting better, there's no guarantee of their accuracy – visit a few on the same day and you'll find many vary by a few psi – so it's a good idea to check pressures with your own hand-held gauge which can be bought inexpensively from auto accessory stores.

Working on one wheel at a time, remove the valve stem cap and simply press the gauge firmly on to the valve – some electronic types will bleep when they have taken a reading, which will be shown digitally. The recommended pressures will be shown in the car's manual, or on a sticker on the driver's door pillar, and vary according to tyre type and size, though it's 26psi all round for standard-size tyres.

When adding air and rechecking pressure, remember that each check takes about ½psi out of the tyre. The spacesaver spare in the boot needs to be inflated to a much higher pressure – 60psi.

While checking pressures, take a good look at the tyres to make sure there are no nails or large stones embedded in the tread, that the sidewalls are free from cuts and bulges (if there's any significant damage, such as metal cords showing, junk the tyre) and that the treads are wearing evenly – odd patterns suggest misaligned steering or suspension).

■ EVERY 3,000 MILES

ENGINE OIL AND FILTER RENEWAL

01

02

The oil drain plug is on the lower right of the finned aluminium sump **01**, and has a 17mm hexagonal head. Apply the handbrake and jack the car up using either the jacking points or a trolley jack under the ends of the chassis rails, where they are double-skinned and at their strongest, or under the front crossmember, and support the car on axle stands, using wood packing pieces to protect the car's chassis. DON'T jack the chassis rails anywhere other than at their double-skinned ends – they crush easily (see Chapter 3).

Remove the oil filler cap to prevent air locks from 'holding' oil in some of the passages inside the engine.

With a suitable container ready to catch the oil, unscrew the drain plug **02**. Ideally, wear latex gloves to stop carcinogenic compounds getting on your skin. Keep a firm hold of the plug to avoid dropping it into the oil container, and, unless you like oil up your sleeve, try to hold it tight to the sump plug hole until it is fully undone, whipping it away quickly to keep the job as clean as possible.

Removing the oil filter is one of the few horrible jobs on an MX-5. Before you start, move the oil catch tank under it, or use another if the sump oil is still draining, to avoid a horrible mess. The filter is buried under the inlet manifold on the right-hand side of the engine **03**, so the only option is to roll up your sleeve, feed your arm in over the top of the fuel pipes, grab hold and unscrew it anti(counter)clockwise. It's a small filter that you can get a grip of easily and, if you're lucky, it won't be too tight. If it is tight, you'll have to use a three-legged claw wrench, an inexpensive investment for next time the job comes around.

The job's not over yet: access is tight, and the only way out for the filter is to bring it forward and up past the alternator **04** – try to keep it upright to avoid spilling oil.

Clean up the filter mating face on the engine block with a clean rag, and wipe up the inevitable spillage down the side of the block and sump, which sometimes also gets on the crossmember (subframe). Lubricate the sealing ring of the new filter with clean oil and screw it on, taking care not to overtighten it – ½–¾ turn (some filters are marked) after the rubber O-ring touches base is enough.

Once all the old oil has drained, refit the sump plug – be careful not to overtighten the plug into the aluminium sump threads: the specified torque is enough – then return the car to the ground and pour in new semi-synthetic oil. When you're pouring from a 5-litre bottle, using a clean funnel is the best way not to slop oil all over the engine.

The 1.6 engine takes 4 litres (1.8 takes 5 litres) of oil from completely dry, so try about 3.5 litres at first, wait a minute or so and check the oil on the dipstick, adding more until it's at the max mark. Then run the engine for a minute or two to fill the filter and oil galleries and circulate oil around the system. The oil light should go out within a second or two. If it doesn't, stop the engine before serious damage results, and check the oil level again. If the oil light still won't go out, you might have got a faulty filter.

Check for leaks while the engine is running. Switch off and wait a couple of minutes to let most of the oil drain back into the sump, then check the oil level and add enough to bring the level up to maximum. Have a last check for oil spills, and wipe up before going out on the road.

TIP

Professional garages use a mesh-filter catch tank on a telescopic mounting to reach up under the sump and avoid spilling any oil. Because you'll most likely be working closer to the ground, you can achieve the same effect by using an oil catch tank available from car accessory shops. The oil can then be poured into an old oil bottle for later disposal, or straight into a recycling tank. Even cheaper, make your own catch tank by cutting the side out of an oil bottle. Transfer the old oil to another bottle for disposal as soon as possible.

■ EVERY 7,500 MILES

POWER STEERING FLUID LEVEL CHECK

The power steering fluid reservoir is made from black plastic, and is located at the left front corner of the engine compartment, in front of the air filter

The level is shown on a small dipstick located in the top of the reservoir that has upper and lower marks – check with or without the engine running after twisting and pulling the dipstick to remove it. Topping up is done though the dipstick housing.

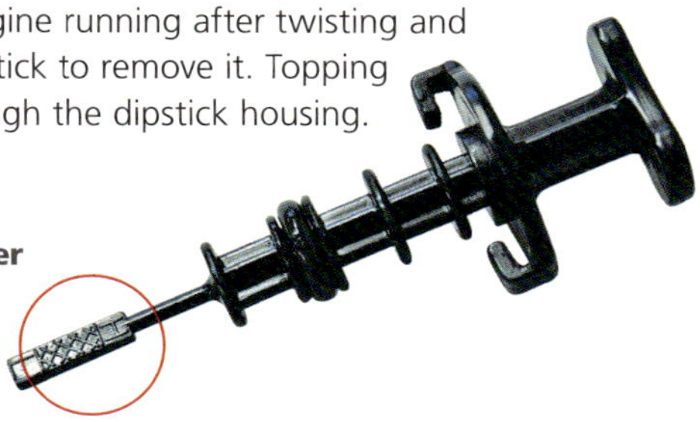

Upper and lower levels on the power steering dipstick

■ EVERY 7,500 MILES

AUTOMATIC TRANSMISSION FLUID LEVEL

CHECK

You don't have to get under the car for this one – you can check the auto fluid level from under the bonnet because it has it own dipstick – at the back of the engine bay on the right-hand side. The dipstick top may be black or orange **01**.

Check the level with the engine warm and running, and the car parked on level ground. If the transmission is hot, such as after crawling through traffic for an hour, it will be too hot and will give a false (too high) reading. Holding the car on the footbrake, run the transmission selector (shifter) slowly through its range of positions, then return to P (park) and leave the engine idling. Pull out the dipstick, and first examine the fluid on it – it should be clean and pink. If it's discoloured or smells burnt, then either the transmission is on the way out or the fluid is badly in need of changing, but try changing the fluid before you condemn the transmission. To check the level, wipe the dipstick, reinsert it, and pull it out again **02**. If the level is far under the maximum mark, add fluid to bring it up. It takes a pint between the minimum and maximum marks.

RENEWAL

On automatic gearboxes, it is recommended that you change the fluid every 30,000 miles, and it's best to do this with the transmission warm, because the fluid will drain better and more quickly – but be warned – transmission fluid can get very hot. There's no drain plug, so to empty it you have to unbolt the oil pan, the large flat pressed-steel sump forming the bottom of the transmission – you'll need a larger catch tank for this, or use a deep drip tray. Undo the bolts evenly a few turns, then remove the front bolts, prise the pan off the bottom of the transmission (it may be stuck on by the gasket), then gently lower the pan, letting the fluid drain into the tray. Once the oil has drained, remove all the bolts and remove the pan. Carefully clean off what's left of the old gasket on the mating faces on the bottom of the transmission.

Then unbolt the strainer/filter housing and lower it from the transmission – be careful because it contains more fluid, which may be hot. Bolt up the new filter, then, using a new gasket, bolt the oil pan back on to the bottom of the transmission, torquing the bolts to the specified torque. The transmission takes 4 litres of Automatic Transmission Fluid (ATF) which you pour down the dipstick tube. Warm the engine and go through the checking procedure again, then add a little more fluid if necessary to bring it up to the maximum mark. Don't overfill!

01

02

■ EVERY 7,500 MILES

DIFFERENTIAL OIL LEVEL

CHECK

This is checked via the smaller of the two plugs in the back of the differential housing. Jack up the car and support it securely on axle stands, keeping it as level as possible. Undo the plug, halfway up the cover – it might be quite tight **01**. If so, don't swing on it with a huge breaker bar – the casing could crack, or the threads could strip. Instead, clean around the plug head with a wire brush, then trickle some penetrating oil – if you've none, vinegar works well – into the joint between the head and the casing, then wait a while. Once you've got the plug out, if a little oil trickles out and then stops, the level is fine. If there's not even enough oil to coat the threads in the bottom of the drain hole, slowly add hypoid 80W90 oil until it trickles out, then refit the plug when it has stopped.

RENEWAL

The differential oil needs changing every 60,000 miles, and the differential holds 1 litre of SAE 80/90W gear oil. Drain while warm, using the larger plug at the bottom of the casing **02**, then replace the plug and fill. Check the level as described previously.

01

02

■ EVERY 7,500 MILES

MANUAL GEARBOX OIL LEVEL

CHECK

The level/filler plug is the square-headed one half-way up the gearbox casing on the left side **01**. You'll need to lift the car to reach it, so jack it up and support it on axle stands, keeping it as level as possible. Have a catch tank or bowl ready and, using an open-ended spanner, unscrew and remove the plug and see if any fluid comes out **02**. If not, slowly add 75W90 oil – only a little to begin with – from a squeezy bottle, using its long flexible neck. When you've added enough it'll begin to dribble out of the gearbox hole, so catch the excess oil in the bowl, wait until it's stopped dribbling, screw the plug back in and wipe up.

01

02

RENEWAL

There's another plug at the bottom for completely draining the oil. The gearbox uses 2 litres of AAPI GL-5/SAE 75W90 gear oil, or a synthetic equivalent.

■ EVERY 7,500 MILES

FRONT AND REAR BRAKE PAD AND DISC CHECK

Unless your car wears massive aftermarket wheels featuring few spokes and lots of fresh air (please don't do it – it spoils the steering feel, one of the MX-5/Miata's best features), you'll need to remove the road wheels to check the pad wear. Front pads generally wear more quickly than rears, so check these first.

Apply the handbrake (parking brake), then loosen the wheel nuts, jack up the car and support it on axle stands (see Chapter 3). Remove the front wheels. The pads are visible through a rear-facing window in each caliper **01**, and you can see how much friction material is remaining between the pad's steel backing plate and the brake disc. New pads have about 10mm of friction material. If yours have less than 2mm, change them (see Chapter 7).

Rear pads can be checked in the same way, except that the window is at the front because the calipers lead rather than trail **02**, and you need to chock the front wheels before jacking up the car.

This is also a good time to examine the state of the brake hoses and pipes – corrosion or cracks on the outside are an MoT failure. Remember to torque the wheel nuts after you refit the road wheels and lower the car to the ground.

TIP

There's a quick check to tell you when the pads are almost used up – the brakes are designed to squeal, so if you hear this warning the pads are almost completely worn out and need to be changed very soon, certainly before undertaking the next long journey. Sticking out of the inner lower pad locating clip on the front brakes is a small metal tang. When the pad is well worn (about 1mm left), this tang rubs gently on the disc when you apply the brakes and produces a squeal that's designed to make you investigate. When the squealing starts, this means the pads are very low and need changing without delay, otherwise metal-to-metal contact will eventually ruin the discs.

■ EVERY 7,500 MILES

AUXILIARY DRIVEBELT CHECK

Most MX-5/Miatas have two auxiliary drive belts: one for the water pump and alternator, and one for the power-steering pump and/or air-conditioning compressor. With the bonnet open, the belts are at the front of the engine, behind the main air trunking. Looking towards the back of the engine compartment, the alternator belt is the one on your left, and the power-steering belt is the one on your right. In the rare event that you find a car without either power steering or aircon, it'll just have the one belt. On cars with two belts, the alternator/water pump belt runs rearward of the power-steering and aircon belt, so if the alternator belt breaks, the other one has to come off too to replace it.

INSPECTION

Make regular checks on the state of the belts, so you don't get caught out with one breaking or being thrown off. If you hear a squealing from the front of the engine as you accelerate, it's a sure bet one of the belts, probably the alternator drive, is loose and needs retensioning.

With the engine stopped, twist each belt to examine all round. Light cracking on the inner ribs of a polyvee belt, as used on the steering-pump side, is acceptable, but belts that have begun 'stringing' or delaminating, or which have threads showing out of the sides are not, and need changing. The same goes for a belt that's oil-soaked, glazed or has cracks running around its flat back side.

■ EVERY 7,500 MILES

ADJUSTING THE ALTERNATOR BELT TENSION

To check the tension, push the belt down with moderate pressure mid-way along its top run. It should deflect no more than 10mm – measure with a ruler if you like. If it's more, or less, you'll need to adjust it. A loose belt slips, causing overheating and loss of electrical power, but a belt that's too tight will wear out the bearings of the ancillaries it drives.

To adjust the alternator belt, first loosen the clamp and pivot bolts that hold the alternator to the engine. On 1.6s, the clamp bolt **01** is very inaccessible and can only be reached from behind the alternator – you'll need a short spanner or ratchet wrench. On 1.8s, the clamp bolt points forward and you can see it under the air trunking. Turn the adjuster bolt – that's the one that faces out away from the engine towards the right-hand side of the car **02** – until the slack in the belt is about 10mm on the top run. Tightening the bolt moves the alternator away from the engine and tightens the belt; turning it anticlockwise loosens it – though you'll have to push the alternator back towards the engine, as the adjuster only pulls 'one way'. When you're happy with the amount of slack in the belt, retighten the clamp and pivot bolts and recheck the tension.

■ EVERY 7,500 MILES

ADJUSTING POWER-STEERING/AIR-CONDITIONING COMPRESSOR BELT TENSION

For the power-steering/air conditioning compressor belt **01**, the procedure is the same as that described previously for the alternator belt, except that first you undo the clamp bolts, pivot bolt **02**, and two locknuts facing forwards near the adjuster. Use the adjuster to tension the belt, then tighten the bolt and locknuts and recheck the tension. Repeat until you're happy with the amount of slack in the belt.

On cars that have air conditioning but no power steering, the belt is adjusted by an idler pulley mounted above the compressor. This has a screw adjuster like the alternator and power-steering pump, and is adjusted in the same way.

■ EVERY 15,000 MILES

STEERING, SUSPENSION & DRIVESHAFT GAITER CHECK

Rubber bushes in the suspension refine the ride, and flexible gaiters keep lubricants inside steering racks, driveshaft constant-velocity joints and suspension balljoints **01**. Over time these flexible protectors deteriorate, and it's a good idea to check them periodically.

Perishing rubber bushes allow slop to develop in the suspension and take the edge off the car's fine handling – which is the point of having an MX-5/Miata in the first place. And gaiters, as well as keeping lubricant in, keep out dirt and grit, both of which accelerate wear when they get in the wrong places, especially after all the grease has been flung out. Though rear drive shaft joints and gaiters are not part of the MoT test, as front ones are, a failed gaiter eventually costs money in the shape of a new joint or driveshaft being needed. Left to its ultimate conclusion, a flailing driveshaft, the result of a failed joint, is potentially disastrous – and long before this will make the car unpleasant to drive.

With the car jacked up and secure on axle stands, start by examining the boots and gaiters visually – if there's any dampness, oil or grease on the outside, chances are it's come from inside.

In the case of steering rack gaiters **02**, extend the steering to the extremes of lock to fully extend one gaiter then the other

– this will help expose any perishing or cracks. With driveshaft gaiters, leave the transmission in neutral and the suspension on full droop so you can rotate the wheels and driveshafts and see right around the gaiter **03**.

Next, flex, squeeze and stretch the rubber to see if there are any tears or cracks – cracking usually happens in the 'troughs' of the boot **04**, and you won't make matters worse by giving a good tug with your fingers – gaiters and boots are tough and if you can make any impact on it, it's a goner anyway. Squeezing the gaiter sharply may produce a hiss that helps track down pinholes.

If there's a leak, but the gaiter appears intact and you are lucky, then it might be just that one of the clamping bands at the ends of the gaiters have come adrift. If so, you can replace them with Jubilee clips, or, in the case of CVJs (constant velocity joints), the biggest zip tie that will fit in the securing band groove. But first pull back the gaiter, clean the joint and apply new lubricant – special graphite grease for CVJs, a smear of ordinary grease for unassisted steering racks – before refitting the gaiter or boot and securing it with the zip tie. Cars with power steering won't need lubricant added direct to the rack and joints, but may need to have the steering fluid reservoir topped up afterwards.

On the track rod ends, prod the small rubber boots with a finger to detect splits and perishing.

If the gaiters/boots are split, then replacement is the only solution. Driveshaft gaiter renewal is described in Chapter 6, while a steering gear gaiter can be renewed by removing the appropriate track-rod end, as described in Chapter 7. Release the securing clips to remove the gaiter, and always fit new clips when fitting the new gaiter **05/06**.

The last type of boots you'll find under an MX-5/Miata are the concertina gaiters on each suspension damper. These protect the damper rod and seals, and often split and fall down on to the spring pan. This isn't an MoT failure, unless the damper is leaking, which will eventually happen after grit gets into the seal. The boots are cheap to buy (£11 each at UK rates in 2006), but to replace them means removing and dismantling the spring/damper units, so it's best left until you are changing springs, dampers or bushes. Always use new gaiters here if you are rebuilding the suspension – it's a false economy not to.

While you're under there, give all the rubber suspension bushes a visual check **07** – if you suspect any of going soft, gently levering with a small pry bar or large screwdriver between the two suspension parts they separate will soon tell you if they are tired – there should be hardly any movement.

The last suspension check is for excessive rust on the wishbones, plus the rear crossmember on early cars. If they're badly corroded, then renewal is the only solution. For suspension dismantling, see Chapter 7.

02

03

04

05

06

07

■ EVERY 15,000 MILES

AIR FILTER RENEWAL

Note that for clarity we have removed the black plastic air trunking, after releasing the large hose clip that secures it to the mass airflow unit **01** on top of the air box – but, unless you need to remove the trunking for any other reason, such as changing the cam belt, you can leave it in place.

Unscrew the four 10mm hex-headed setscrews that join the top and bottom halves of the air-filter box together **02**, lift off the top of the box, taking care not to pull on the airflow sensor wires, and lift out the old filter element. If there's any dust, dirt or leaves in the bottom of the filter housing, vacuum the debris out. Wipe out the inside of the airbox with a damp cloth **03**. Fit the new filter **04**, making sure the lips of its flexible gasket, top and bottom, fit properly into the grooves in the plastic housing. Carefully fit the housing top back on, then fit and tighten the setscrews.

■ EVERY 18,000 MILES

SPARK PLUG RENEWAL

WARNING *Don't crank the engine over with the HT leads disconnected from the plugs, or with the plugs out of the engine and not earthed, or damage to the igniters and coils can occur.*

The MX-5 uses slim 10mm plugs buried deep in the alloy head, so you'll need the correct small plug socket and a medium extension bar to reach them. Boots at the ends of the plug leads seal the tops of the plug bores, and a long plastic section reaches down to each plug. If the leads are not already marked, label them before you disconnect them to make sure they go back in the right order, though their lengths should make it obvious. Then pull each one out of the cam cover, pulling on the plastic boot rather than the lead.

Unscrew and remove the plugs **01** and check them for wear and colour – they should be cleanish/light brown and the electrode should have defined edges. If not, fit new plugs – they are relatively inexpensive and you'll probably feel a benefit in easier starting and better performance afterwards.

Set the electrode gaps to 1.1mm **02**, carefully bending the electrodes to suit if necessary, and fit the plugs to the engine. Pushing them into the rubber of the spark plug socket will hold the plug as you feed it down the bore and locate it in its threads, but be very careful not to cross-thread the plugs into the alloy head, because the threads are soft and easily damaged. Another way to get them in is to push the plug into a straight length of ⅜in heater hose, and use that as an extension to twirl each plug in before tightening it with a socket.

These plugs do not need to be very tight – tighten to the specified torque. Refit the plug leads, in the correct order.

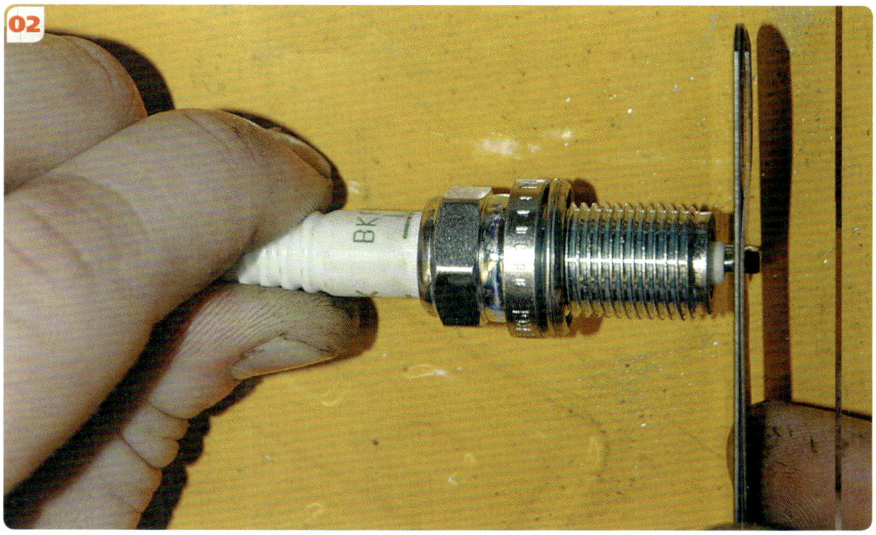

02

■ EVERY 30,000 MILES

SPARK PLUG HT LEAD CHECK AND RENEWAL

WARNING *Don't crank the engine over with the HT leads disconnected from the plugs, or with the plugs out of the engine and not earthed, or damage to the igniters and coils can occur.*

MX-5/Miatas are hard on their HT leads, and it's recommended you change them at least every 30,000 miles. If the car is misfiring and the spark plugs look in reasonable shape, suspect the HT leads first. It makes sense to change the plugs at the same time, however, because they are inexpensive and you have to disconnect the leads to get at them.

The leads are a simple push-fit into the coils, mounted at the rear of the engine, and on to the spark plugs which live in deep tunnels in the top of the engine. When disconnecting the leads from the spark plugs, pull the plastic boot instead of the lead – twisting the boot slightly from side to side helps. The leads will pull straight out of the ignition coils, bolted to the back of the cylinder head on the left of the engine on 1.6s and at the right rear on 1.8s.

With the leads pushed home into their connectors, secure them in the plastic clips along the top of the cylinder head, and you're done. Start the engine and test drive the car to make sure the misfire has disappeared.

TIP

Each coil fires two plugs simultaneously – one fires Nos. 1 and 4 cylinders, the other looking after Nos. 2 and 3. As long as the lead from each plug is connected to the correct coil, it doesn't matter which of the coil's two terminals you use. On a 1.6, the coils are on the left side of the head, and cylinders 1 and 4 run from the left coil. On a 1.8, the coils are on the right of the head, and cylinders 1 and 4 run from the right-hand coil.

■ EVERY 30,000 MILES

COOLANT RENEWAL

Antifreeze loses its effectiveness after a while, and, though it's possible to test its strength with a hydrometer, the easiest way to ensure continued protection from both freezing and internal corrosion of the engine's waterways is to replace the coolant at the recommended 30,000 miles or two-year intervals, whichever comes sooner – especially if it's dirty. It should be a clear blue/greenish colour not unlike diluted washing-up liquid.

Remember antifreeze is poisonous, so try not to get it on your skin, don't swallow it and, if any splashes into your eyes, flush it away immediately with lots of cold water.

To drain down the cooling system, there's a plug in the bottom of the radiator, accessible through a hole in the engine undertray **01**. (The cooling system holds 6 litres, so make sure you have a large enough container.) Open the drain plug with a large cross-head screwdriver and let the old coolant drain out **02**. Dispose of it safely in the same way as you would with waste oil – DON'T pour it down the drain: apart from being environmentally harmful, it's illegal.

It's now a good idea to flush the cooling system to get rid of any silt, rusty water and gunge.

This involves running water through the radiator and/or cooling system at mains pressure with a hosepipe. If the old coolant isn't particularly dirty, there's no need, but if you want to have a go, stick a hose in the radiator neck and blast water through it until it runs clear out of the bottom. It helps to wrap some rag around the hose nozzle so it fits better and avoids spray.

Replace the drain plug, then, using a pre-mixed container of antifreeze and water to suit your climate (follow the instructions on the side of the antifreeze bottle), refill the cooling system, with the help of a funnel, through the radiator neck **03**. MX-5s aren't prone to any airlock problems, and the heater's a constant-flow type, so it doesn't matter if the temperature control is set to hot or cold.

When the radiator is full – be careful not to splash any antifreeze and wipe it up quickly if you do – refit the cap, then top up the header tank **04**. Run the engine with the radiator cap off until the top hose is warm, topping up the coolant as necessary, then stop the engine, refit the cap and recheck the coolant level when cold.

01

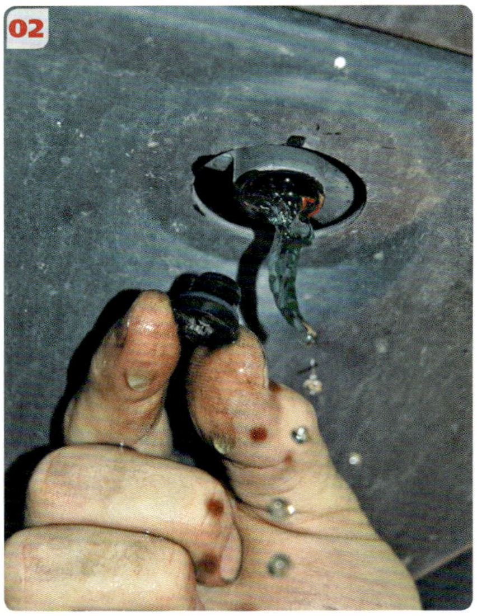
02

03

04

■ EVERY 60,000 MILES

CAM BELT AND ANCILLARY DRIVE BELT RENEWAL

Like most cars today, the Mazda's camshafts are driven by a toothed belt, even if the engine's outward appearance might suggest otherwise. In this case it needs changing at least every 60,000 miles, or immediately if you buy a car with more mileage and there is no evidence to show how old the belt is. On the MX-5 it's a far more straightforward job than on most cars, and it's a job that can be easily tackled at home with no special tools.

To reach the cambelt, the drive belts for the water pump and alternator and for the power steering pump and air conditioning compressor (if fitted) need to come off first, so it makes sense to change these at the same time if they need replacement. Full instructions for these jobs are given earlier in this Chapter.

■ EVERY 60,000 MILES

FUEL FILTER RENEWAL

WARNING *The fuel delivery and injection system maintains a high residual pressure even when the engine's not running. To avoid petrol spraying everywhere when you disconnect the fuel pipes, first you have to relieve the pressure from the system (see main text).*

Always disconnect the earth (ground) lead from the battery negative terminal before disconnecting any pipes in the fuel system, but first make sure you have the access code for the radio/stereo to ensure it'll work again afterwards. Just in case, have an appropriate fire extinguisher nearby. And, because unleaded petrol is truly nasty stuff and highly carcinogenic, wear latex gloves so you don't get any on your skin – a little fuel will inevitably spill when you disconnect the rubber fuel hoses and remove the filter.

The fuel filter lives under the back of the car behind the fuel tank, protected by a cover **01**, and is a throwaway metal canister type that Mazda recommends you change every 60,000 miles. However, if you have ever run the car out of fuel, the fuel pump might have blown sediment into the filter and clogged it.

01

02

RELIEVING FUEL PRESSURE

Relieving the pressure in the fuel system is simple – the engine does it for you. Under the steering column, find the connector for the circuit opening relay (1993 and earlier models) or the fuel pump relay (1994 and later models). Unplug the connector **02**, remove the fuel filler cap and start the engine. When the engine stops (runs out of fuel) the system is depressurised. Turn off the ignition and replace the fuel cap.

REMOVING THE FILTER

Find the fuel filter behind the fuel tank at the right rear of the car, protected by a plastic cover. It's possible to reach the filter by lying on your back under the rear of the car but, if you find you need more space to work, jack up the rear of the car and support it securely on axle stands.

Undo the fixings that hold the cover – these look like cross-head screws but work a little differently, and are the same type as those holding the front of the nosecone. You need to unscrew the middle cross-head section until it sticks out. This shrinks the outer plastic plug so you can pull the whole fastener out – there are four – and lift the cover away **03**. NB (Mk2) covers are a little smaller than NAs, but the principle is the same.

With the filter exposed **04**, use pliers to squeeze the hose clips, move them down the hoses away from the metal filter stubs and pull the hoses from the stubs – they might be stuck, so twisting them gently will help, or levering with a thin screwdriver. Temporarily plug them with pencil stubs or golf tees to reduce spillage.

Your new filter should have come with a bracket already fitted. If, so, undo the two 10mm bolts that hold the old bracket to the car, and remove the filter, bolting the new one in its place. If not, undo the clamp bolt that pinches the filter into the bracket (it's got a captive nut on the back of the bracket so you'll only need one spanner or wrench), remove it and clamp in the new filter.

Push the hoses all the way on to the pipes, and refit the hose clips, then refit the plastic cover – remember the fasteners will only fit if the centres are extended – screwing in the centre expands the whole fastener to keep the cover tight.

REPRESSURISE THE FUEL SYSTEM

When you've finished changing the filter, and the hoses are both on and tight, you need to reprime the fuel system to prevent unnecessary engine cranking – Mk1s have small batteries.

Reconnect the battery negative lead and the fuel pump connector you removed earlier. Under the bonnet, find the diagnostic connector (it's on the left towards the rear of the engine compartment, near the bonnet shut – see photo 04 on page 84), and connect the ground (GRD) and fuel pump (F/P) terminals with a short piece of wire – the locations of the terminals are marked clearly on the underside of the diagnostic connector cover. Turn on the ignition for about ten seconds but don't crank the engine. Turn off the ignition and remove the wire, and shut the lid on the diagnostic connector. The system is now primed and back up to pressure. Have a last check under the back of the car to make sure nothing is leaking, then lower the car to the ground.

03

04

ADDITIONAL RECOMMENDED SERVICING JOBS

The following tasks aren't part of the manufacturer's recommended service schedule, but they're all worthwhile, and some of the suggested jobs will help to avoid known MX-5 problems.

Making sure drain holes are clear is essential with any MX-5 and it's also worthwhile, with the help of the section on brakes, checking from time to time to make sure the rear calipers are operating freely.

ADDITIONAL SERVICING JOBS

WIPER BLADES CHECK AND RENEWAL

Change these once a year, preferably every six months, and wipe the rubber blades clean every time you wash the car.

It's best to take old wipers with you when buying new ones, to make sure you get rubbers of the right length.

To change the blades, lift each wiper away from the windscreen and rotate the blade so it's at an angle of about 90 deg – you'll see then that this gives enough room to separate the blade from the arm **01**. The plastic connector unhooks from the arm after you have pressed down the plastic tang that locates in a hole in the hook of the arm – press it down and push the blade and connector out of the hook **02**. The new blades will probably come with a selection of connectors, though if there's not one suitable you can re-use the old one – it's just clipped on to the cross-pin on the blade. Push the blade and connector back into the hook of the arm until the securing tang clicks into place. Return the wipers to the screen and make sure they don't hit each other in operation.

If you wish, you can buy the rubbers separately which saves money – the fixings vary, so you just need to use common sense and sometimes a small pair of pliers to fit them.

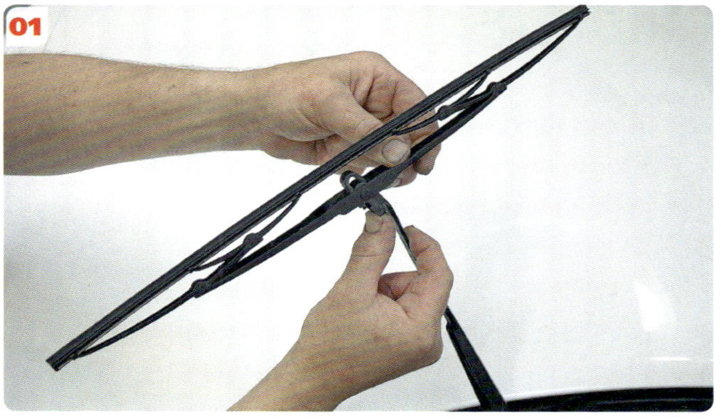

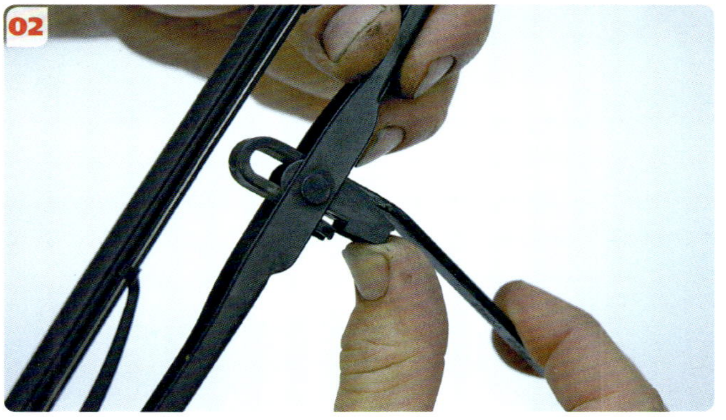

ADDITIONAL SERVICING JOBS

HINGES, PIVOTS AND DOOR CHECK STRAPS

Periodically oil or grease these to prevent them seizing up – spray grease is good for this, as it gets the lubricant exactly where it's wanted **01**. On Mk1s, periodically oil the pivots on the headlamp lifters **02**.

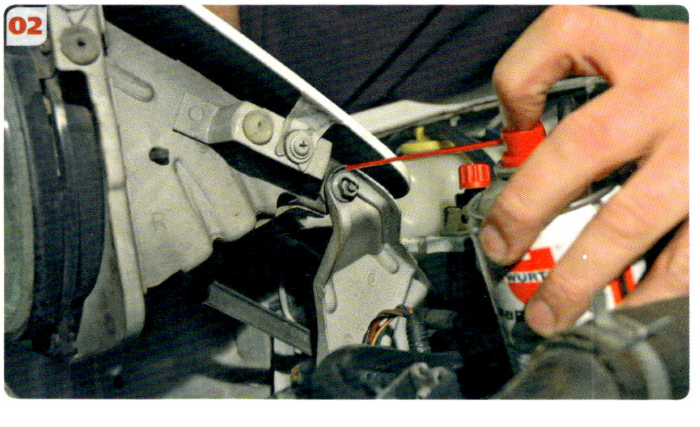

■ ADDITIONAL SERVICING JOBS

CHECKING THE BATTERY

The original battery is gel-filled and maintenance-free, and you can't top it up. Do make sure, however, that its drain/vent tubes are present and correct to avoid corrosion in the boot (trunk).

If your battery has covers or removable screws in its top, then remove these to check the electrolyte level – it should be 5mm or so above the top of the plates inside the battery (the battery is inaccessible, so you can if necessary check by shining a torch into the hole to help you see better (NOT a naked flame – batteries are potentially explosive). If you can't reach to top it up, first remove the battery (see Chapter 9).

If you have a later battery, it's even more crucial that the drain tubes are in place, to prevent any spills or overflow creating massive and rapidly-blooming corrosion in the boot.

Corrosion on the battery terminals can restrict the amount of current the battery can supply, possibly giving starting problems, and the MX-5/Miata uses quite a small battery anyway. So if there is any corrosion on the terminals or clamps, undo the clamps, negative side first (the inaccessible one nearest the outer skin of the car) clean it up with a wire brush, then smear with petroleum jelly (Vaseline) and reclamp. If there's not enough room to clean up the terminals, remove the battery first (see Chapter 9).

■ ADDITIONAL SERVICING JOBS

CHECKING DRAIN HOLES FOR BLOCKAGE

Blocked drain holes can kill an MX-5 structure in a couple of years, but only take minutes to keep clear. The main drains are located at the front of the parcel shelft behind the seats. First, make sure that nothing has fallen into the plastic catch tanks and blocked the outlets. Then, using a suitable probe (an old car aerial is ideal, because it has a ball end that won't damage the rubber drain tubes), 'rod' the pipes to make sure they are clear. You can also clear the outlets from underneath, in front of the wheel housing **01**, and a satisfying amount of water and gunge should come out.

There are also some smaller drain holes near each of the jacking points on the sills' lower seams, so poke these through to make sure they are clear **02**.

■ ADDITIONAL SERVICING JOBS

CHECKING THE PCV VALVE

The Positive Crankcase Ventilation system reduces emissions by scavenging crankcase vapours. It does this by circulating fresh air from the air cleaner through the crankcase and burning the resulting vapour in the engine by feeding it into the inlet manifold. The PCV valve is mounted in the right-hand side of the cam cover **01**, and can get blocked up with oily gunge.

To check it, gently pull the valve out of its grommet in the cam cover **02**, and shake it. It should rattle. If it doesn't, change it for a new one. As a further check, start the engine and allow it to idle, then put your finger over the valve opening. You should feel a vacuum. If not, it's probably blocked, so change it. If you had to replace the valve, its hose may well be clogged up too, so remove it and clean it out before connecting it to the new valve.

■ ADDITIONAL SERVICING JOBS

WINDOW CHANNELS

MX-5 windows are sluggish, so give them every chance by making sure the channels they slide in are clean and the glass is free from binding. A gentle spray of WD-40 into the channels, concentrating the spray using the thin red pipe provided, helps still further.

Use the red pipe provided to concentrate the spray into the channels

PRE-MOT CHECKS

As well as all the obvious items – making sure the tyres aren't bald and that all the lights work – there are a few other items that you should check before taking the car for an MoT.

New MoT rules (now the whole system is computer-controlled by VOSA) mean that the car has to be logged in on the garage's terminal for the entirety of the test. If it fails, a full retest needs to be carried out – at the full fee. There are no half-price or free retests any more, so it's worth making sure everything is right before you go.

Have a good look underneath, specifically at rubber parts. Split gaiters on the steering rack **01** or CV joints spell failure, as do perished or cracked brake pipes. Check the exhaust and its mountings, too, preferably with the engine running **02/03**. A minor blow is permissible, at the tester's discretion, but nothing more. You can't easily check emissions levels at home, but if there's visible smoke, forget it.

Check for excessive corrosion on suspension components and their mounting points **04**. Have a close look at the chassis rails and the backs of the sills. Chassis rails get a hammering on the MX-5 – they're low to the ground and quite thin, so they often get scraped or crushed. This in itself isn't a failure, but if rust has set in badly the car won't pass. The backs of the sills are where water collects if the hood drain holes have blocked up, and the joint between the inner halves is where they rust through **05**. If there's a hole here, get it welded or you're wasting your test fee. While you're

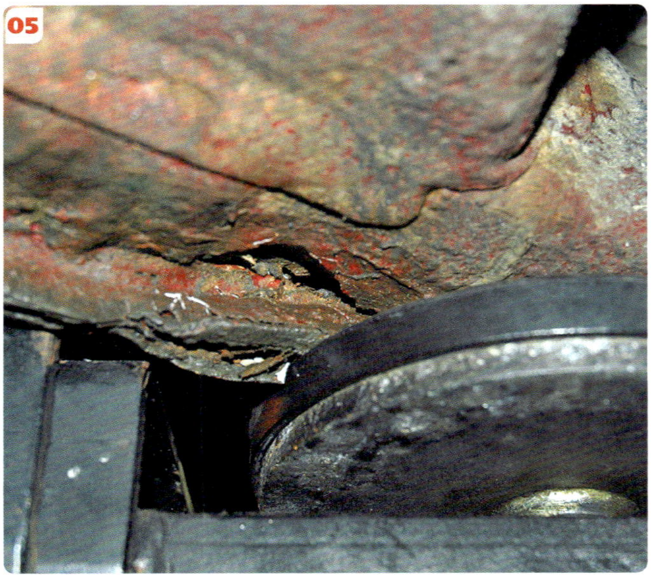

05

06

under there, take a look at the dampers – they don't want to be leaking **06**.

Headlights need to be correctly aligned – get an idea of this by aiming the car square on at a wall or a garage door, on level ground, at night, with the lights on dip. You'll be able to see if the tops of the beams line up. If you're following a car at night, the tops of the beams on dip shouldn't shine above the boot lid.

Split wiper blades or a cracked or damaged windscreen will fail the test. You're allowed small chips, but big ones (more than 10mm in diameter) in the driver's line of sight, and cracks need to be outside the approximate area shown **07**. Various companies can visit to fix stone chips, plus there are some inexpensive DIY kits available at car accessory shops.

Inside the car, check the seat belts aren't frayed, the seats aren't loose and the door handles work. And check that the handbrake actually holds the car on a hill – it's tested separately from the service brake, on rollers.

07

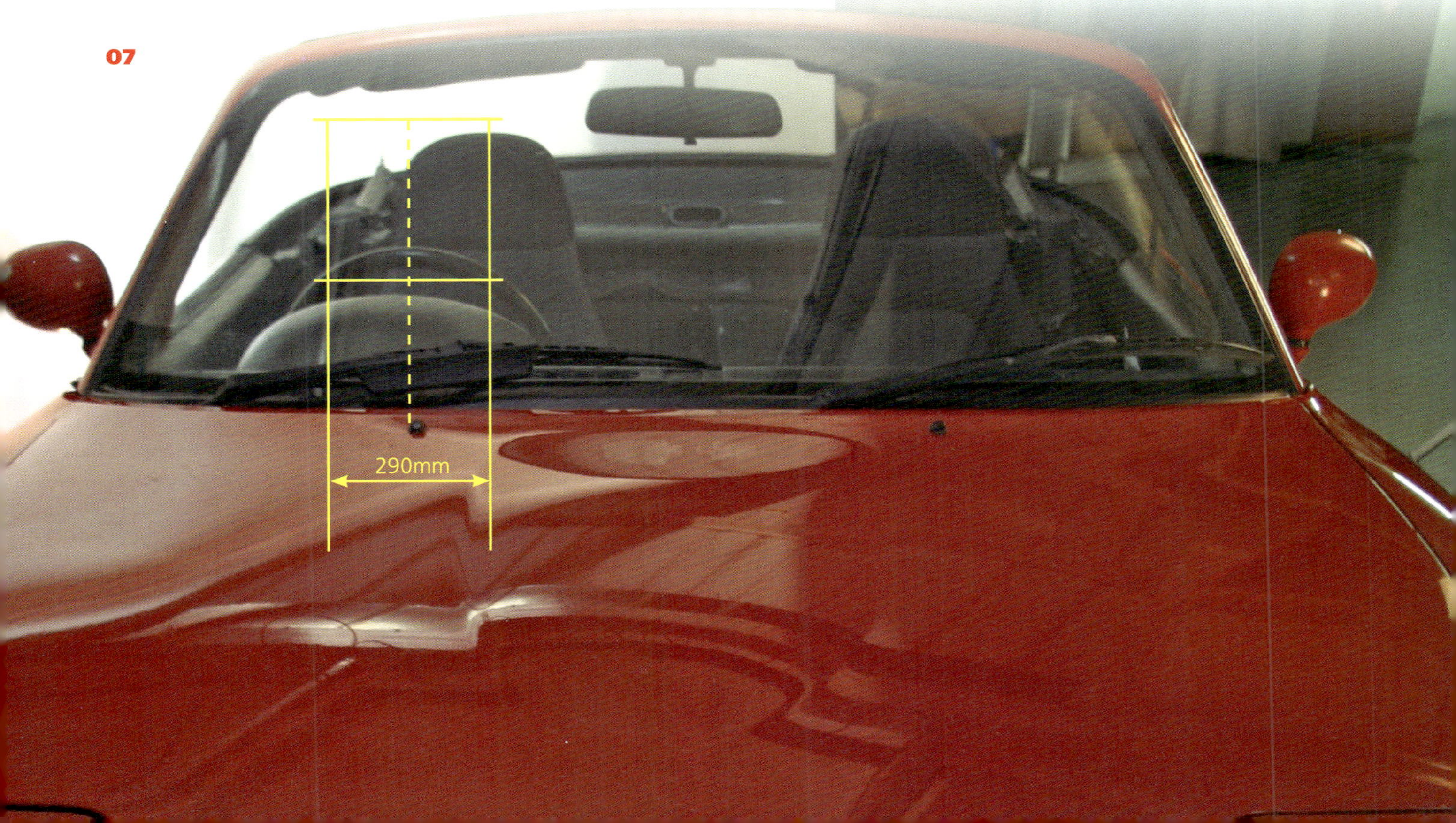

DOHC 16-VALVE
注意
CAUTION

CHAPTER 5

UNDER THE BONNET

INTRODUCTION

The MX-5's engine is a neat double-overhead-camshaft design that superficially resembles the power unit of the classic Lotus Elan that some like to believe the MX-5 was copied from. With its single alloy casting for the cam cover, it was even stylised to look like the classic '60s sports car units it emulated.

But there the similarities end. The MX-5/Miata engine runs hydraulic tappets (lifters), unheard of in a '60s sports car, and opens its four valves per cylinder via a toothed rubber belt. Instead of a big pair of twin-choke Webers, there's fuel injection.

With a cast-iron block and alloy head, it was based on the existing Mazda four-cylinder unit from the Familia (323) but with nearly every detail changed to suit the characteristics of a sports car, and with a new rev limit of 7,200rpm thanks to detail attention to the crankshaft and flywheel. Coded B6-ZE (RS), it was originally available as a 114bhp 1.6-litre (1,597cc) **01** or, from 1993, as a 130bhp 1.8-litre (actually 1,839cc) and coded BP-ZE (RS) **02**, though in 1995 an 88bhp 1.6-litre was reintroduced to the UK as a base model. Spot an 1800 Mk1 by the lettering standing proud rather than recessed into the cam cover.

The engine has a free-flowing exhaust manifold fabricated from large-diameter stainless steel tube rather than the usual cast iron, and a finned alloy sump (another feature harking back to '60s classic Alfa Romeos). More than half of the engine is behind the front axle line, giving the even weight distribution required of an agile sports car.

All MX-5/Miata/Eunos models are fuel-injected. Early 1.6-litre models had L-Jetronic fuel injection with a flap valve to measure airflow **03**; later cars got more complicated, having a hot-wire air mass sensor. Mk2 1.8s have a Variable Intake Control System, or VICS – a set of butterflies in the intake tract that

01

02

TORQUE WRENCH SETTINGS

	Nm	lbf ft
Spark plugs	15–22	11–16
Cam cover bolts	6–8	3.5–6.5
Cam belt cover	hand tight	hand tight
Power steering pump clamp nut	19–25	14–18
Power steering pump pivot bolt (through pulley)	38–51	27–39
Power steering pump pivot bolt (on engine)	32–46	24–33
Water pump pulley bolts	8–11	6–8
Alternator clamp bolt	19–25	14–18
Alternator pivot bolt	38–51	28–38
Cam belt tensioner bolt	38–51	28–38
Crankshaft pulley outer bolts	13–17	9–13
Crankshaft pulley centre bolt:		
Early models	108–118	80–87
'Long crank' post-1991 cars	157–166	116–122
Starter motor bolts	38–51	28–38

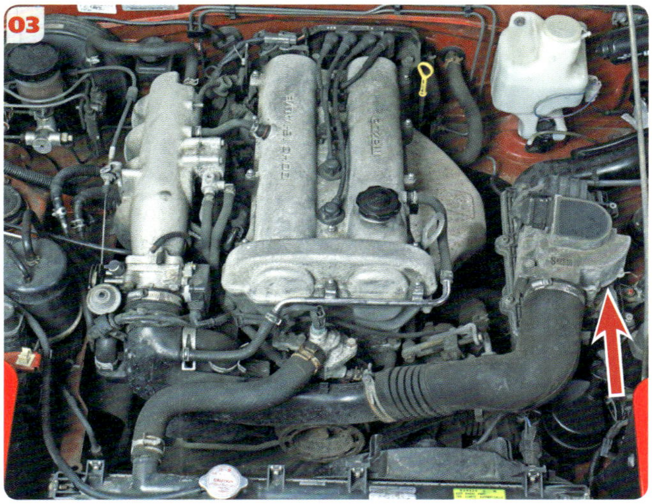

03

04

open at 5,700rpm to alter the breathing characteristics, and later examples also have variable valve timing.

Though those smooth aluminium covers hint at chain drive for the overhead cam layout, the camshafts are driven by a toothed belt which needs changing at least every 60,000 miles. To minimise maintenance, hydraulic tappets are fitted, meaning the valve clearances never need to be adjusted.

For the MX-5, the Familia's distributor was also ditched, as it would have fought for space with the wiper motor, and instead a compact camshaft angle sensor and ignition/coil pack was substituted. On 1.6s the sensor is driven off the back of the inlet cam and the coil pack is on the left **04**; on 1.8s the layout is reversed **05**.

The engine functions, including the ignition system, are run by a 'brain' or, in Mazda-speak, PCM (Powertrain Control Module). This includes an On Board Diagnostic system that illuminates the engine warning light on the instrument panel if any faults are detected, and which can be interrogated by Mazda service tools. But, on early cars, by simply bridging two terminals with wire, you can check for fault codes by counting the number of times the engine warning light flashes, and make a basic analysis of the problem.

All you need to service this engine is a set of normal hand tools, sockets and spanners – nearly all nuts and bolts are 10, 12, 14, 17 or 21mm – plus a long breaker bar to undo the crankshaft pulley bolt. Normal servicing is limited to changing the oil and filters, but even changing the cam belt is simple, requiring no special tools, just a methodical approach. The oil filter is inaccessible, and may be tight, so have a three-legged claw wrench handy in case it won't come off by hand – you can't reach it with the strap type. The recommended oil is a 10/40 semi-synthetic, so have a fresh 5-litre can, filter and belts ready before you start servicing work.

TIP

Don't disconnect the battery without checking first that you have the individual stereo activation code for your car. The stereo is fitted with an anti-theft feature that will render it inoperative if the power supply is interrupted – this is meant to act as a disincentive to theft. Even if you reconnect the battery immediately after disconnection, the sound system won't work without first having the right code entered.

05

CAM BELT (TIMING BELT) RENEWAL

This job needs doing at least every 60,000 miles, though some owners like to change the belt more often to bring peace of mind. Compared with most cars, it's quite a simple job, and most of the time taken is in removing hoses and covers to reach the belt. If you buy a car that has covered a higher mileage and there is no proof of the belt having being changed, change it immediately. Unusually, standard MX-5/Miata engines are 'safe' – that is, if the cam belt breaks or slips, the pistons won't hit the valves and destroy the engine (though we can't guarantee they won't touch lightly if the belt breaks at high revs) – but the belt will still need changing to get you going again, and a breakdown is always inconvenient, sometimes expensive.

Before you buy the parts, check the state of the drive belts for the alternator and, if fitted, power steering pump and air conditioning compressor – these have to come off to reach the cam belt, so it makes sense to change them at the same time if they are worn or cracked.

Start by removing the air trunking that runs across the front of the engine **01** – there are hose clamps at each end, plus a 10mm locating bolt just in front of the inlet (right-hand) camshaft. On 1.8-litre cars the trunking is in front of everything else and can simply be undone and lifted away once the two smaller air pipes are disconnected from it **02/03**.

On 1.6-litre cars, the trunking is the 'wrong' side of the radiator top hose, so temporarily disconnect the hose from the thermostat housing **04** – to do this you'll need hose-clip pliers – you can get away with big pliers or Mole (self-locking) grips to release the tension on the spring clip. Slide the clip down the pipe a couple of inches and release it, then pull the hose from its stub

02

01

03

04

05

– twisting it will help release it if it is stuck. As it releases, try to hold the free end up in the air to minimize coolant loss, then withdraw the air trunking from behind it and pop the hose back on to the thermostat housing – not all the way because it's coming off again soon.

Release the tension on the power steering pump belt (where fitted) by slackening off the in-line adjuster – and loosen the pump's fixing bolt and nuts. These face forward and you'll find, if you turn the engine over slowly via the crankshaft pulley bolt, slots in the pulley will line up with the lower nut to allow you to undo it **05**. Lift the belt off the crankshaft pulley.

Next is the alternator belt. Its adjuster, pointing to your left, is a fiddle to get to and, on 1.6s, the clamp bolt is hidden behind the alternator (see photos on page 57). It will be tight, and access is poor. If necessary, use a 12mm ring spanner cut down to fit behind the inlet manifold. On 1.8s, the clamp bolt is accessible from the front, and is much easier to undo. Slacken off the alternator and lift the belt off the pulley, leaving it loose at the front of the engine.

Remove the water pump pulley (dead centre at the front of the engine) by undoing the three 10mm bolts and lifting it off **06**. Pull the small bypass hoses from the thermostat housing one at a time after squeezing and sliding back their spring clips, so that you can pass the alternator belt over the

06

thermostat housing and then remove it. The hose clips are small and easily damaged, so have at least one small Jubilee clip ready as a replacement on reassembly.

Next, remove the camshaft cover. It's aluminium, and held by 10mm bolts **07/08**. First you'll need to disconnect the spark plug high-tension leads, by pulling them vertically out of the plug holes by their boots, marking them first to enable you to refit them in the right order. It's a good idea to remove the spark plugs too (see Chapter 4) because it makes it easier when you later come to rotate the engine. Before you lift the cam cover, disconnect the PCV valve piping from the right-hand side of the cover – it simply pulls out of a rubber grommet.

Now remove the cam belt middle and lower covers. The covers are plastic, and each is held on with four 10mm bolts. Make a drawing of the wiring clips behind the bolts, so you get them back in the right place.

Now remove the crankshaft pulley – on early short-nose cranks, (four slots in crankshaft pulley: see sidebar) the recommended method is to undo the four 10mm bolts recessed in the front of the pulley and remove it, leaving the pulley plate attached to the crankshaft. But this is fiddly so you might prefer to undo the crankshaft front bolt (21mm) and remove the whole pulley, which you'll need to do on long-nose cranks (eight slots in pulley) anyway. The bolt will be very tight, so you'll need a long breaker bar and a close-fitting socket

09. There's no provision for locking the engine, so you may have to get a helper to put the car in gear and stand on the brake to hold the crankshaft still via the transmission. Once the bolt is out, remove the crankshaft pulley – if it's tight on the nose of the crank, tapping it back and forth with a small hammer will help free it. Removing the pulley may dislodge the Woodruff key that locks the sprocket in place on the nose of the crankshaft, so be very careful not to let this fall out, and if necessary tap or push it back into place **10**. Unbolt and remove the cam belt lower cover, which is secured by four 10mm bolts **11**. CAREFUL, these corrode in place and are very easy to shear off, so use plenty of penetrating oil or WD-40.

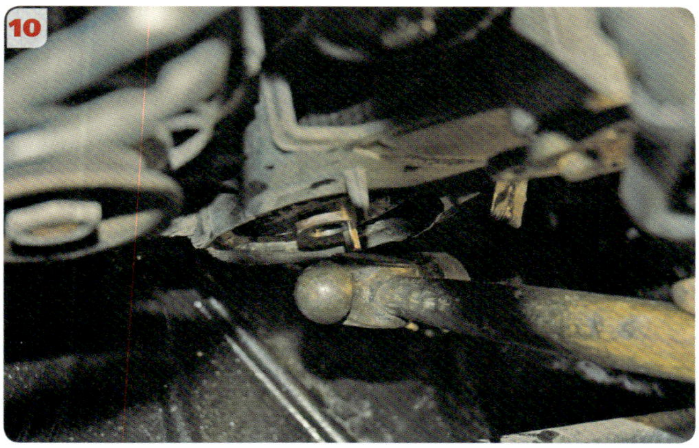

LONG-NOSE AND SHORT-NOSE CRANKSHAFT

Mk1 and 2 MX-5s used two designs of crankshaft. The first, called the short-nose, used a small Woodruff key and keyway to locate the crankshaft sprocket and pulley, and these are prone to wear if the bolt comes slightly loose, sometimes allowing the pulley and sprocket to slip out of alignment and reduce performance by affecting valve and ignition timing. In mid-1991 Mazda redesigned the crankshaft, using a larger bolt and keyway, tightened to a higher torque to fix the problem. The later arrangement has a much larger shoulder on the bolt. Another way of telling them apart is to check the front pulley. Early (short-nose) engines have four slots in the front of the pulley; later cars have eight.

If, on a short-nose crank, the bolt is loose, or the Woodruff key falls out when you remove the crankshaft pulley, you could have problems, so pull off the crankshaft sprocket and have a look. If the keyway in the crank is worn wider than the Woodruff key, you can fill it with an epoxy liquid metal – Loctite 660 'Quick metal' is recommended – but don't start the engine for 24 hours after reassembly to give the epoxy a chance to harden. It is also recommended that on earlier cars you use a new bolt and key whenever they are removed. And it's important that the key goes the right way – tapered end facing in towards the engine.

Next, the camshaft and crankshaft timing marks must be aligned. Rotate the engine clockwise using a socket spanner on the crankshaft pulley bolt, temporarily refitted if you removed the whole pulley. Looking at the engine from the front, the inlet cam is on the left and the exhaust on your right. Each sprocket has a groove on its lip that should point vertically when the engine is at top dead centre **12**, when the grooves on the lower sprocket and/or pulley plate are topmost and lining up with a small pointer sticking forward from the engine **13**. As a further check, the secondary grooves in the cam pulleys – 'E' on the inlet sprocket and 'I' on the exhaust sprocket – will line up with pressings in the steel cover behind them.

14

15

Undo the cam belt tensioner clamp bolt using a 14mm socket, lever the tensioner pulley towards the inlet cam using a screwdriver or flat bar behind it **14**, then nip the clamp bolt back up. This gives enough slack in the belt to pull it forward off the cam sprockets and remove it **15**. To completely remove it from the car and fit the new one, you'll need to temporarily once again remove the top and bypass hoses **16**.

At this stage, check the engine for fluid leaks. The inside of the cam belt housing should be quite clean and dry. Oil leaks from the camshaft front seals are almost unheard of, but also check to make sure there's no evidence of water escaping from the pump **17**, or oil getting past the crankshaft front seal

16

18. If there are any leaks, you'll need to deal with them first, for example by fitting a new water pump.

Fit the new cam belt over the crankshaft sprocket first, then the exhaust cam sprocket, keeping it as tight as possible, then fit it over the inlet cam sprocket and behind the tensioner pulley **19** – you can use small bulldog clips to hold the belt to the cam sprockets if you want, and a further tip here is that turning the inlet cam a few degrees clockwise will help get the belt teeth on the sprocket. Then, when you have pushed the belt fully home, turn the cam back anticlockwise. As the belt comes tight, all the marks should line up. If they do, undo the tensioner clamp bolt to tension the belt, then retighten it. If not, adjust the position of the belt on the sprockets until all the marks line up as described previously.

TIP

As a final confirmation to make certain the cams are timed correctly, rotate the engine two turns and then make sure all the marks line up again. If you wish you can make a final check on tension by once again loosening the tensioner clamp bolt and then retightening it and ensuring that the marks still align.

20

21

Refit the lower and middle cam belt covers **20**, remembering to fit the clips behind two of the bolts **21**. Then refit the cam cover, first checking that the rubber gasket is in good condition. It's quite complicated and delicate, and should be supple to the touch **22**. If not, change it. With age and heat this gasket goes brittle, first around the spark plug holes **23** and the first you will know if it has failed is that the spark plug bores fill with oil.

Tighten the cam cover bolts evenly a little at a time, working from the centre out in an anticlockwise spiral fashion. These bolts only need to be done up gently finger-tight using a short ratchet handle – overtighten them and the gasket will leak.

Depending on how you took it apart, either reassemble the crankshaft pulley by bolting the pulley back to its plate with the 10mm bolts, or by removing the crankshaft pulley bolt again, refitting the pulley and bolting it up to the specified torque, locking the transmission with the brakes with the car in gear if necessary. Refit the water-pump pulley with its three 10mm bolts, and the alternator belt. Tension the belt using the screw adjuster so that there is about 10mm of slack in the top run **24**. Then tighten the alternator clamp bolt (behind on a 1.6, in front on a 1.8). Put on the new power-steering belt, where fitted, tension it with the threaded adjuster so there's about 10mm of slack, and tighten up the pump clamp bolts.

Refit the air intake cross-pipe trunking (on 1.6s, temporarily

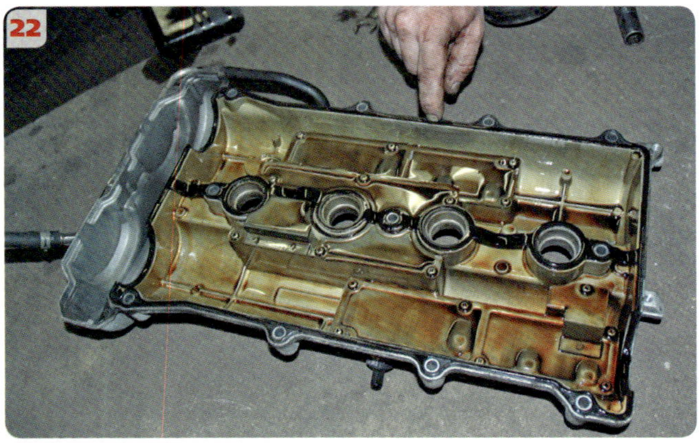
22

23

24

25

26

27

disconnecting the top hose from the thermostat housing to pass the trunking into position). Push the pipe into its housings at each end, then tighten up the large-diameter hose clips that secure it. Don't forget the 10mm bolt on the left-hand end, just in front of the inlet cam, that helps hold the pipe in place. If you haven't yet done so, push the radiator/coolant hoses fully back on to their stubs and refit the spring clips where they belong – bear in mind that one or both small hose clips may need replacing with Jubilee clips.

On 1.8s refit the air intake cross-pipe last **25**. Then remove the radiator cap **26**, top up with coolant (see Chapter 4), and, if necessary, also top up the header tank mounted on the right inner wing **27**. The tank is translucent with level indicator marks on the side, and the plastic cap simply pulls off.

STARTER MOTOR REMOVAL AND REFITTING

The starter motor is inaccessible, buried under the inlet manifold on the right-hand side of the engine. Unlike most starters that are held into the bellhousing by three bolts, the MX-5 has an extra bracket to secure the tail of the starter to the engine block. You'll almost certainly have to go under the car to reach two of the mounting bolts, so apply the handbrake, chock the rear wheels, jack up the front of the car and support it on axle stands. You might find that removing the right front wheel gets you a little more access.

Removal

Isolate the battery by disconnecting the lead from the negative terminal. Working in the engine bay, disconnect the two leads from the starter motor – one pulls off its terminal, while the larger battery cable is held by a 12mm nut under a pull-off plastic cover.

01

Unbolt the starter motor bracket **01** from the engine block – it's held by a single 14mm bolt. Then there are three more 14mm bolts that clamp the starter motor into the bellhousing. The top two are threaded into the bellhousing, pointing forward and reached from under the car, beside the gearbox. The lower bolt has a nut on the back – you'll have to get a helper to hold the head of the lower bolt through the wheelarch while you undo its nut. Then undo the top two bolts – you'll need plenty of extensions. Both of these top bolts hold brackets that secure wiring and hydraulic pipes, so tie these out of the way. Back in the engine bay, remove the starter by pulling it forward out of the bellhousing, and manoeuvre it out of the engine bay.

Refitting

If you've got an exchange starter, it probably won't come with a mounting bracket, so you'll have to transfer the old one to the new motor. The bolt holding the bracket halves together needs to be tightened to the specified torque.

Wiggle the starter under the inlet manifold and back into place in the bellhousing. Fit the top two bolts loosely, not forgetting the cable and pipe clips that go under them, then fit the lower bolt and nut, followed by the bracket-to-engine bolt. Tighten all these to the specified torque if you can get a torque wrench near them – if not then moderately tight with a ratchet wrench is near enough. Reconnect the cables, and clip the plastic cover back over the main lead when you have tightened its 12mm nut. Finally, reconnect the battery and make sure the starter cranks the engine over.

ALTERNATOR REMOVAL AND REFITTING

Checking, removal and refitting of the alternator is covered in Chapter 9.

EXHAUST SYSTEM REMOVAL AND REFITTING

Removal

On catalyst-equipped cars remember first to disconnect the oxygen sensor wiring. The sensor is in the side of the downpipe just below the manifold flange. Later cars may also have a second sensor in the top of the pipe just behind the catalytic converter. The wires to the sensors are permanently attached, so trace the wiring back from the sensor(s) and separate the two halves of the wiring connector(s). Catalysts run extremely hot, so don't begin work until the system has completely cooled.

On later cars, you'll also need to unbolt the braces that run across the bottom of the transmission tunnel.

Release the downpipe from the bottom of the manifold by undoing the three bolts at the flange joint near the sump – you'll need socket extensions of at least 360mm (14in) to reach them **01**, and a universal joint makes life easier. Then unbolt the downpipe bracket attached to the bellhousing, and the clamp that secures it to the exhaust. Working from the rear of the car, prise off the rubber exhaust hangers – there are three supporting the silencer (muffler), hanging transversely below the boot floor **02**, and one on each side of the pipe about half-way down the car **03**. You should then be able to lower the exhaust and pull it out rearwards.

Refitting

Refit the system using a reversal of the removal procedure, but make sure that any sealing gaskets between components are renewed, and renew any rubber hangers that are worn or perished.

01

02

03

DIAGNOSTIC CONNECTOR AND IGNITION TIMING

MX-5s have a diagnostic connector mounted on the left inner wing in the engine bay, so that Mazda agents can plug in their testers to interrogate the engine brain while investigating any problems. But, if you have a pre-1996 car, which uses the original On Board Diagnostics system, you can use this socket to set the car up for performing basic checks, or for checking the ignition timing with a strobe light.

If the car's on-board computer – Mazda calls it the Powertrain Control Module (PCM) detects anything wrong based on the information it receives from various components and sensors around the engine, it will store a fault code, so it can later 'tell' the tester there's a problem. If the computer detects a fault, it will illuminate the 'check engine' light in the dashboard. This comes on when you turn on the ignition, but should go out when the engine starts. If it stays on, you have a problem. Some of the minor faults are hard to notice in normal driving, but economy and emissions will suffer. More serious ones may prevent the engine from starting.

If your car is a later (post-1995) model with the OBD-II system, or has a serial data communications port, then a special code reader connected to a computer is needed – that means a trip to your Mazda dealer or specialist.

If you are investigating problems, before starting make sure the engine has decent compression, and that the ignition and fuel systems are all in order. If the engine won't start at all, first check the main fuse, plus the two fuses that feed the engine control unit, or PCM. One, labelled BTN, is in the main fusebox under the bonnet **01**, and the other, labelled 'Room' (in Japanese on Eunos Roadsters) is in the fusebox in the driver's footwell **02/03**. If either has blown, the engine will not run.

Also make sure the spark plug leads are in good order. They need replacing every 30,000 miles or so, so if the engine is misfiring, that may well be the cause.

Changing them every 30,000 miles is a good idea. Don't crank the engine over with any of the leads or plugs disconnected, or damage to the igniter and coils can occur.

Reading fault codes

Before checking for faults or setting ignition timing, you need to set the diagnostic connector to test mode. For this, connect an insulated wire, stripped at the ends, between the GDN and TEN terminal in the connector **04** – early cars have the terminals labelled on a sticker on the inside of the connector lid.

Switch on the ignition but don't start the engine. Miata models have an engine check light, and on these models the light should illuminate for three seconds, then go out. (MX-5 models don't all have a check light, and on these you'll have to use an LED, as described later in this section.) This means the self-diagnosis system is working. If there are no more flashes, there are no fault codes stored. If the light flashes again, carefully count the flashes. A long (1.2 second) flash counts as 10, and a short (0.4 second) flash means 1, so a code 14 is one long flash followed by four short ones. There is a four-second pause between each set of flashes, so you can check them again. If there is more than one fault code stored, they are flashed in sequence, each separated by one long flash. So a 15 and 17 would be one long flash and five short ones, one long, seven short, one long, before the sequence repeats.

If your car has no check engine light, or it's blown, you can still read the codes using a 12-volt LED (light emitting diode, with built-in resistor) at the diagnostic connector. Insulate the LED's short leg with black sleeving or plastic and the longer leg with red, leaving about 5mm of bare wire at the end.

Plug the short leg (insulated in black) of the LED into the terminal marked 'FEN' and the long leg (insulated in red) into the terminal marked +B **04**. This is connected directly to battery positive and will deliver many amps, so be careful not to touch it with any metal object apart from the leg of the LED. Then by switching on the ignition, you can read the codes from the LED in the same way as counting the flashes of the engine check light.

04

The check light reports up to 16 codes (more can be picked up with a Mazda special service tool), and these mean:

Not all codes apply to all models, and the engine will still run, though not at peak performance, while displaying some of these codes		
code	**effect**	**suspect/diagnosis**
1	engine will not run	ignition system – igniter coils and wiring
2	engine will not run	no signal from camshaft angle sensor
3	engine will not run	no signal from camshaft angle sensor
4	engine will not run	no signal from camshaft angle sensor
8	runs badly	airflow meter or connections
9		coolant temp sensor or connections
10	engine seems 'flat'	intake air temp sensor or connections
12	lack of performance	throttle position sensor or connections
14		atmospheric pressure sensor (inside PCM)
15	high fuel consumption	oxygen sensor output too low
17	too lean or too rich running	oxygen sensor or problem with fuel injection or ignition
16/28/29		exhaust gas recirculation system (1.8s)
25		PRC solenoid valve (1.8)
26		purge solenoid valve (US models)
34	erratic tickover	idle speed control valve

Resetting fault codes

Before you start: *Make sure you have the radio code handy. You'll need to reset it afterwards because removing the BTN fuse has the same effect as disconnecting the battery.*

Once you have retrieved the codes stored, and the problem has been fixed, possibly by a specialist, they can be erased from the memory by pulling the fuse marked BTN from the main fuse box, and pressing the brake pedal for more than five seconds. Refit the fuse and switch on the ignition, but wait for at least six seconds before starting the engine. Then run the car, making sure it exceeds 2,000rpm for at least three minutes. Retest, to make sure the codes have disappeared.

Checking the ignition timing

Before you start: *The timing marks on the crankshaft pulley, far down at the bottom of the engine, are hard to see, and it'll be much easier if you first pick them out in white paint or correction fluid. The timing needs to be checked with the engine at normal operating temperature, so take the car for a run first to warm it up.*

Connect your bridge wire between GND and TEN in the diagnostic connector **01**. Using a 12V strobe light, clip the positive wire to the blue socket behind the left-hand headlamp **02**. This supplies a standing 12 volts whenever the ignition is switched on. Clip the other wire to a suitable earth point in the engine bay – a bolt head on the engine, for example. Connect the light's induction loop around the No.1 (front) HT lead.

Because you'll be peering down into the engine bay when the pulleys and belts are whirling round, take off loose clothing and necklaces. If you have long hair, tie it up out of the way. With the engine warmed up to normal operating temperature, start it and let it idle, then aim the strobe light at the front pulley and pointer **03**. The light should 'freeze' the timing marks, ideally when the notch on the crankshaft pulley is opposite the 10-degree mark **04**.

If the marks don't line up, you'll need to adjust the timing using the camshaft angle sensor on the back of the engine. This is mounted on the back of the inlet cam on 1.6s, and on the back of the exhaust cam on 1.8s. Each sensor has a long single clamp bolt with an extended head that you can reach with an open-ended, or ring, spanner passed down the back of the engine.

If the timing needs adjusting, loosen the clamp bolt and, with the engine running, gently rotate the sensor housing until the timing marks line up, then reclamp the sensor. Experts say MX-5s perform better with 14 degrees of advance, so you might want to try a little more than 10 degrees. But if there's any suggestion of pinking (pinging), or a light rattling when you accelerate, then revert to 10 degrees because pinking heralds the onset of detonation, which ultimately will blow holes in the pistons – and that's going to be expensive.

Rev the engine a little to check the timing advance – the timing mark will move away from the pointer as revs rise. Once you're happy, turn the engine off, disconnect the timing light – and don't forget to remove your bridging wire from the diagnostic connector.

CHAPTER 6

TRANSMISSION

Early MX-5s use a lightweight five-speed manual all-synchromesh gearbox, with a six-speed offered in Japanese-market face-lifted 1.8s from 1997. This had more closely-spaced ratios than the five-speed, and a higher final drive, though European-spec cars are taller-geared than their Japanese or American equivalents.

The clutch is a conventional diaphragm spring single dry-plate unit, larger on the 1.8 at 8.5in diameter as opposed to 7.9in on the 1.6, and hydraulically operated. One of the MX-5's few inherent glitches is the clutch slave cylinder, mounted on the right of the bellhousing, that often springs leaks and is a fiddle to replace.

The Vehicle Identity Number (VIN) appears on a plate riveted to the gearbox casing on the exhaust (left) side, so you can tell by comparing with the number on the plate riveted to the dashboard and visible through the windscreen, and the one stamped in the centre of the scuttle, whether or not your car has had a gearbox change. A four-speed automatic was optional, though not originally sold in the UK, so any pre-1995 car so fitted is an import.

The manual MX-5 gearbox has a very short throw – the movement at the knob is about 100mm between gears – and this can make the box feel notchy, though the very positive 'rifle-bolt' feel was engineered in to the shift at the design stage. If the change is actually obstructive, this might be because of a failing clutch slave cylinder (an MX-5 weak point, as mentioned previously) which fails to disengage the clutch properly, making the 'box 'hang on' to the gears and eventually wearing out second gear synchromesh. If the synchromesh has worn and you can live with it, it's best to leave it alone, or drive around it (by changing gear into second more slowly, or even double-declutching on downchanges), but if you can't, the most effective solution is to fit a good second-hand gearbox, available for £250–£350.

The factory recommends that the gearbox oil is checked every 15,000 miles and changed every 30,000 – automatics need the level checking every 7,500 miles and the fluid changing every 30,000.

TORQUE WRENCH SETTINGS

	Nm	lbf ft
Driveshaft centre (hub) nut	217–293	160–216
Driveshaft-to-differential flange bolts (early cars)	54–64	40–47
Upper wishbone-to-hub carrier pivot nut and bolt	46–67	34–49
Clutch cover bolts	19–26	14–19
Bellhousing-to-engine bolts 17mm	64–89	48–65
Bellhousing-to-engine bolts 12mm	38–51	28–38
Propshaft-to-differential flange nuts and bolts (use locking compound)	28–30	21–22
PPF mounting bolts	104–123	77–91
PPF angle bracket bolts	37–53	27–39

DRIVESHAFT REMOVAL AND REFITTING

Driveshafts rarely fail, but when they do it's usually because the rubber gaiter protecting one of the constant velocity joints (CVJs) has split, letting the grease out and allowing grit and moisture in. Wear manifests itself as clunking when beginning to accelerate or decelerate, or as a clacking sound. If you grab the driveshaft and shake it, any notchy movement indicates serious wear.

If a gaiter has split, but there is no noticeable wear in the joints, you can get away with just replacing the gaiter. Only the inner CVJ comes apart, so both gaiters have to be removed and replaced from the inner end of the driveshaft.

If the outer CVJ has worn, you'll need a whole new driveshaft – but whether replacing the inner joint, the gaiters or the whole shaft, the whole shaft has got to come out of the car, a job that is of similar difficulty to changing a damper. You'll need a hub puller to separate the driveshaft from the hub and a breaker bar, because the hub nuts are done up very tight.

Before you buy new driveshafts, find out about exchange, rebuilt units – which will be a lot cheaper.

Removing a driveshaft

If the design of the wheels allows you to reach the central hub nut, loosen this first – it's easier with the wheels on the ground because the friction of the tyre on the road stops the

wheels and hub from turning. Before you can loosen the nut you'll need to unstake its crown where it's peened into the driveshaft, using a hammer and punch.

Using a breaker bar and possibly an extension tube, undo the nut – it'll be tight. Chock the front wheels, loosen the rear wheel nuts, jack up the car and support it on axle stands. Remove the rear wheels.

If you can't reach the hub nuts with the wheels on, lift the car first. Chock the front wheels, loosen the rear wheel nuts, jack up the car and support it on axle stands, then remove the rear wheels.

If you didn't get the hub nut undone, now is the time to tackle it. The car must be securely supported on axle stands, because you'll be applying considerable force via the breaker bar. The easiest way to stop the hub turning is to jam a large lever, or prybar, between two of the wheel studs, and wedge the other end of the bar against the ground. Unstake the hub nut and undo it.

Remove the pivot bolt that holds the upper end of the rear hub carrier to the top wishbone. This will allow clearance to remove the driveshaft **01**.

Push the driveshaft out of the hub splines with a puller that bolts to the wheel studs. If you don't have one, they are available for hire.

Pull down the top of the hub carrier to make room to separate the outer end of the driveshaft from the hub, then you can release its inner end from the differential. On later cars, you just 'pop' the inner CVJ out of the differential housing by levering between the diff housing and the inner CV joints with a couple of screwdrivers or levers. On older cars, the inner ends of the driveshafts are secured by four bolts, which you have to undo first **02**. Before you undo the bolts, mark the relationship of the driveshaft housing to the differential housing, to make sure they go back the right way.

When you finally pull the driveshaft out of the differential housing, have a catch tank ready underneath because oil will spill out.

Refitting a driveshaft

If you have a new or replacement driveshaft ready to go, then refitting is a reversal of removal – make sure there is a new circlip (snap ring) on the inner end of the shaft, and use a new outer hub nut. Lubricate the splines on the inner end of the shaft with molybdenum grease, and push the shaft into its splines sharply to engage the snap ring with grooves in the differential gears. Take care not to damage the oil seal as you introduce the splined end of the shaft.

Fit the outer end of each shaft into its splines in the hub, and pull the shaft through the hub with the large nut. On early cars, tighten the driveshaft-to-differential flange bolts to the specified torque. Rebolt the hub carrier to the top wishbone and tighten to the specified torque, and, finally, tighten the hub nut to the specified torque and 'stake' the crown portion into the slot on the driveshaft using a hammer and punch, or drift. Don't forget to top up the differential oil afterwards (see Chapter 4).

If the shaft and joints are sound but you need to change a gaiter, there's a bit more dismantling to do (see below).

DRIVESHAFT DISMANTLING AND GAITER RENEWAL

Dismantling

With the driveshaft removed from of the car, as described in the previous section, and on a workbench, you need first to dismantle the inner CV joint so you can slide the gaiters off the shaft. Hold the driveshaft in a vice, using wood packers to protect it.

Prise up the ends of the steel bands that hold the gaiters, and remove the bands. Slide the gaiter off the outer joint and back on the driveshaft, and prise the wire ring ball retainer out of the inner joint outer race. Wipe off as much grease as you can and mark the relationship of the outer race and the driveshaft with paint or correction fluid (DON'T scratch marks in them), then pull the outer race off the inner joint assembly.

Mark the inner race, ball-bearing cage and the shaft to make sure they go back together the same way, then remove the circlip from the inner race, and slide the joint off the driveshaft.

Checking the joints visually

You can dismantle and examine the inner joint after popping the balls out of the cage, using a small screwdriver, but be careful not to mark them – and don't drop them: even big ones like this are almost impossible to find when they roll away. Then remove the inner race from the cage – it comes out when its lands (the pointy-out bits) line up with the windows in the cage. Clean all the parts and examine them for wear – shiny polished spots are normal but grooves, pitting, cracks or score marks are bad news.

On the outer joint, pull back the gaiter, clean the grease off the joint and examine for wear in the same way as the inner joint. It doesn't come apart, but you should be able to articulate it enough to see all the working parts. If any parts are damaged or significantly worn, you'll need a new driveshaft.

Renewing the gaiters

If the joints are OK, go ahead and change the gaiters by carefully slipping the old ones off the driveshaft and sliding on new ones. Don't tighten the securing clips to attach them to the CV joints yet.

> **TIP**
>
> When sliding the new gaiters on to the shafts, cover the splines with tape to avid damaging the gaiter. Remove the tape once the gaiter is in place.

Reassembly

Reassemble the inner joint by fitting the inner race into the cage, and pressing the balls back through their holes in the cage – thumb pressure should do it. Then slide the joint back on to the shaft and fit a new circlip. Note that the larger, bulged end of the bearing cage goes nearest the end of the shaft. Make sure that the circlip is correctly seated by pushing the joint firmly against it. Pack the joints with the grease that came with the gaiters, and squeeze any surplus into the gaiters. Fit the inner joint back into its outer race, following the alignment marks you made, and refit the wire retaining ring.

Seat the gaiters into the recessed grooves on the driveshaft and outer races. Before fitting their retaining bands or clips, lift each gaiter off its seal face to let out any pressure that may have built up inside.

Once the gaiters are in place, correctly seated and their bands or clips are secure, refit the driveshaft according to the previous section.

REMOVING AND REFITTING THE PROPSHAFT

Removing

To make the job easier, remove the exhaust system, as described in Chapter 5.

The propshaft is splined into the tail of the gearbox at its front, and four bolts at the back hold it to the differential flange. Mark the position of the propshaft and this flange before you start, so you can refit it in the same position.

Undo the four 14mm bolts and nuts holding the propshaft to the flange. These will be tight and it helps to apply the handbrake to lock the rear wheels, and therefore the differential. If this doesn't work, use a large screwdriver or socket extension across two of the other nut heads to hold the flange in place while you undo each bolt. For this reason, it's best to loosen each nut and bolt before you remove any of them. Push the propshaft slightly forward to disengage it from the differential flange, then lower the rear of it, and gently pull the front end out of the gearbox. Some oil will come out, so be ready with a drip tray, and then wrap a plastic bag and big rubber band around the tail of the transmission to catch the rest of it.

Refitting

Wipe clean the front of the propshaft, push it back into its splines in the back of the gearbox, then bolt the rear of it back to the differential flange, making sure the marks you made earlier line up. Use a locking compound such as Loctite on the bolt threads, then tighten them evenly, to the specified torque.

MANUAL GEARBOX GEARSTICK (GEARSHIFTER) REMOVAL AND REFITTING

Removal

If you're removing the transmission, first you'll need to remove the gearstick. Inside the car, unscrew the gear knob, by twisting anti-clockwise, then lift out the ashtray, held in by spring clips. Unscrew the retaining screws holding down the centre console and lift it out.

Underneath this you will find a rubber boot around the gearstick held down by four 10mm bolts. Remove these, then lift up the boot around the gearshift and undo the three bolts holding the stick at its base. Lift the gearstick out of its housing, but have a rag ready to wrap it in – it will drip oil and you don't want it on the seats or carpets.

Refitting

Use a new gasket underneath the nylon bushing that lives in the shift lever turret, because the upper remote control housing contains oil and will leak otherwise. The three 10mm bolts need to be little more than finger tight, or just tweaked up with a ratchet or short 10mm spanner. Pull the rubber gaiter back down over the gearstick and bolt it back down to the transmission tunnel with its four 10mm bolts and straps, then refit the centre console, ashtray and gear knob – if the gear knob doesn't want to stay tight, or facing the right way, remove it and try using a little locking compound on the threads at the top of the gearstick. Leave the locking compound to set before trying to move the gearstick.

MANUAL GEARBOX REMOVAL AND REFITTING

This is an operation you'll need to carry out to reach the clutch, or to swap the transmission. Whatever the reason for removing the gearbox, it's a complex, heavy job you really don't want to repeat, so it makes sense to change the clutch at the same time. Fitting a clutch yourself saves at least £100 over the price at the cheapest clutch replacement specialist chains.

One of the features of the MX-5's design is the Power Plant Frame (PPF) transmission brace which ties together the driveline, an almost unique feature (the only other contemporary sports car to use the same idea was the Dodge Viper) which contributes to the car's refinement and agility. This supports the back of the engine/transmission and stops the differential from rotating under torque loadings – but it also means one more stage to get through in removing the transmission **01**.

How you work depends on how high you can get the car. Lifting it above your head on a proper garage hoist makes unbolting everything easier, but few home mechanics have access to this kit. Also, you'll need another strong pair of hands to help you lift the gearbox in and out.

If, as is likely, you are working with the car raised 0.5m off the ground on four axle stands, you will be able to lower the gearbox on a trolley jack, letting it do the heavy work lifting the 'box in and out of the car – but you'll have less room to move and you'll be lying on your back during all of the unbolting work. To remove the transmission you will have to remove the exhaust system first.

Before you start

MX-5s in good order don't leak much, so everything underneath tends to be bone dry and, on older cars, fixings may be corroded into place. This certainly goes for the bolts holding the exhaust pipe to the manifold flange, and the ones securing the Power Plant Frame that ties together the gearbox to differential (these are the large 17mm bolts that point upwards). So, before you start, get under the car, wire brush all the dirt and rust away from the bolt heads, and threads where visible, and give them a good spray with penetrating oil. Life will be even easier if you can spray them a couple of times, starting a few days before you begin the job, to allow the oil more time to penetrate.

Gearbox removal

Before the gearbox can be removed, first disconnect the battery, then remove the gearstick, clutch slave cylinder, starter motor, exhaust system and propshaft. The gearbox oil should then be drained.

Under the car, once the gearbox has finished draining, refit the drain plug to stop the last few drips of oil from leaking out and messing up the floor.

Release the speedometer cable from the gearbox – the cable outer is held into the right-hand side of the transmission with a large knurled nut that you may have to slacken with a large pair of pliers, or Mole grips, before unscrewing it with your fingers. Pull the cable out of the transmission and tie it up out of the way.

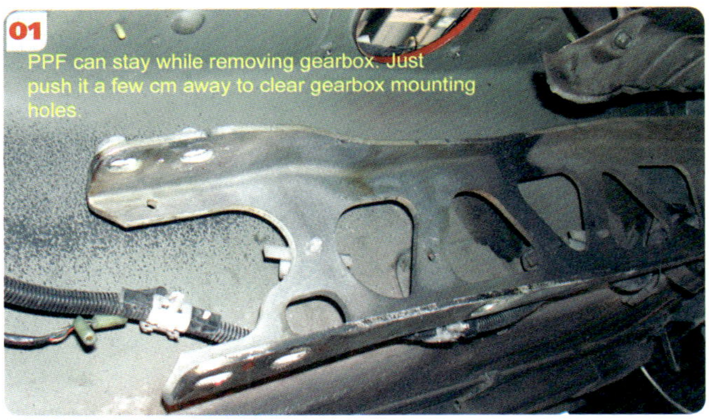
01 PPF can stay while removing gearbox. Just push it a few cm away to clear gearbox mounting holes.

02

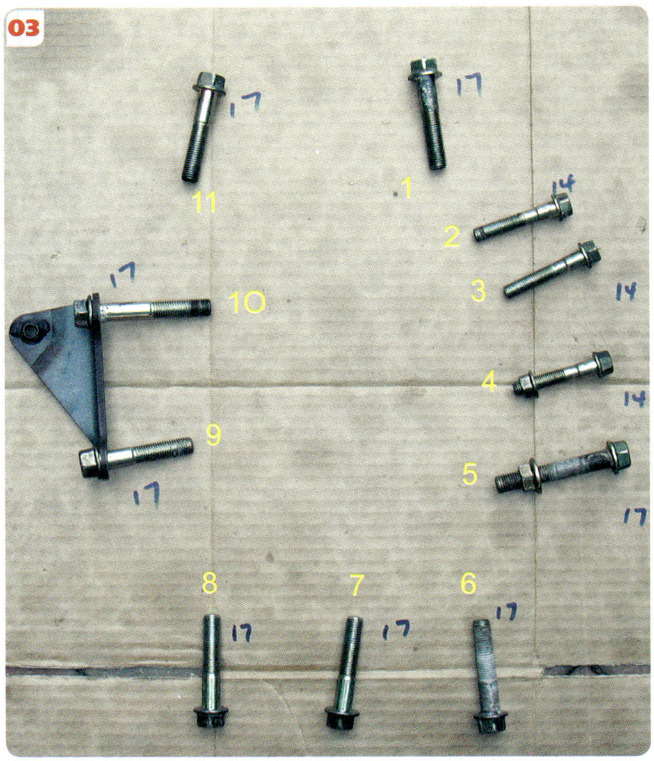
03

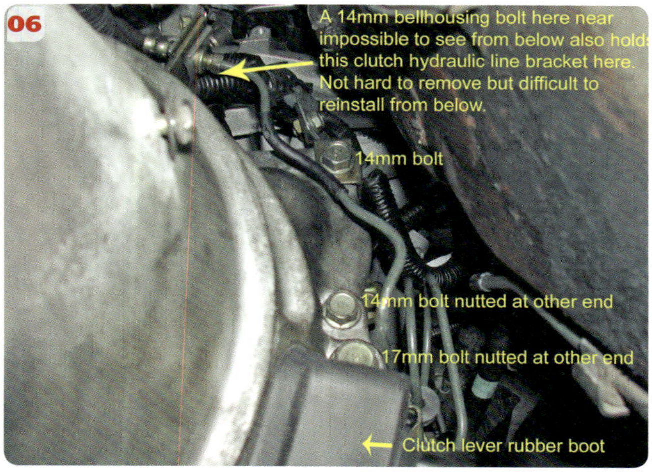

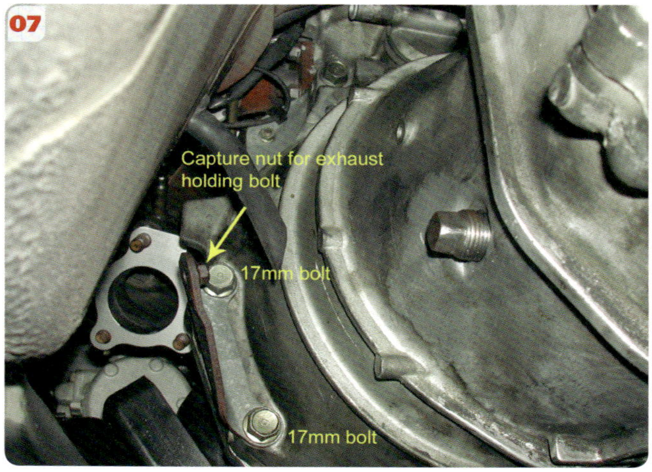

Disconnect the wiring from the reversing-light switch. There are connectors a couple of inches from the switch – if you can't quite reach them, wait until you have lowered the transmission slightly before removing it (see below).

The PPF transmission brace (the deep aluminium stamping along the right-hand side of the driveline) effectively forms the rear gearbox mounting and also carries a part of the wiring loom, so carefully unclip this plus the earth (ground) strap that's attached near the back of the PPF by a 10mm bolt.

The brace is attached to the side of the gearbox with one angled bracket held by three bolts, plus two 17mm bolts at the front, bolted up from underneath. Support the tail of the transmission with a trolley jack lined up with the car, so that you can wheel it out later, then unbolt the bracket from between the PPF and the transmission, and undo the PPF front 17mm bolts. These are 200mm long. The PPF front holes are oval so it's essential to mark the bolts' positions first, to ensure perfect alignment when you put it all back together.

You can leave the PPF in place and just push it sideways out of the way for more clearance, but if you want more space to work, undo the rear PPF bolts **02** – don't mix them up, because the front one is accurately machined to fit its hole for perfect location. Prise out the plastic spacer that was under the forward bolt head – but don't remove the upper spacers.

Unbolt the differential mounting spacer/bracket and you can lift the PPF out from under the car – this gives more room to remove the transmission.

Lower the trolley jack supporting the gearbox slightly to give more clearance, and undo the 17mm bolts that hold the transmission on to the back of the engine, but leave two bolts in place to stop the gearbox from sliding away from the engine. There are six around the bottom, and one at the top on each side. Also unscrew the three 14mm bolts, which also hold various brackets to the bellhousing **03–07**. If you need to remove the jack to create more room to work, tie a loop of rope around the back of the transmission, pass it up through the gearstick hole in the transmission tunnel, and tie it to a stout piece of wood or bar resting across the hole so the gearbox is supported from above.

Leave two bolts until last, then resupport the gearbox on a trolley jack positioned towards the front of the gearbox, remove the last two bolts and pull the gearbox off the back of the engine in a straight line – *don't let it fall on you*, because although it's a comparative lightweight at about 36kg, it can still do serious damage. Don't let it dangle either, or its weight could bend the input shaft. If you need more clearance, lower the transmission a little more and help with another jack lifting under the front of the engine (take care not to damage the sump), but be careful not to stretch any hose in the engine bay. If you're working on a pre-'97 car, be very sure not to damage the camshaft angle sensor bolted to the back of the cylinder head. If you're over-enthusiastic in jacking under the front of the engine you can crush it against the bulkhead (firewall).

Once the input shaft is clear of the clutch, lower the trolley jack to the floor and use it to wheel the transmission out from underneath the car. There will probably be some oil left in the remote gear linkage housing on the top rear of the manual transmission, so keep the assembly upright until it's out from under the car, then, with a helper, tip it sideways over your oil container to catch the rest of the oil. The clutch release bearing will have come away with the transmission, but leave it there until you have inspected the clutch, flywheel and spigot bearing.

If the oil seal for the propshaft and/or the small O-ring that seals the speedometer drive have been leaking, it's much easier to change them on the floor before you refit the transmission to the car.

Renewing the manual gearbox oil seals

Drive out the old rear seal with a light hammer and a small chisel or drift behind the flange of the seal, working evenly all round so it comes out easily. Then clean up the oil from the area, lightly lubricate the lip of the new seal with clean transmission oil and tap it into place using a wooden block or large tube that matches the diameter of the seal's metal rim to keep it straight.

Gearbox refitting

Now you can refit the gearbox, by offering it up to the back of the engine on the trolley jack. The rules are the same as for taking it off – keep it in line with the engine, don't let it dangle on the input shaft before it gets fully home and don't force anything, though be prepared to put in a bit of effort to push the box the last inch home. If it proves difficult to fit, try rotating the tailshaft a few degrees either way as you offer the box up, to help the splines in the input shaft and the clutch engage (make sure that the clutch friction disc is centred, as described in the 'Clutch renewal' section).

Once the gearbox is in position, get some bolts in to hold it to the engine as soon as you can. Then you can relax a bit, and put in the rest of the bolts. This is a good time to do something for a bit of light relief, such as reconnect the reversing-light switch wires, before lifting the engine and transmission back into their proper alignment so you can bolt the PPF transmission brace back on. Remember to refit the 'reamer bolt' and its spacer back in the front hole at the back of the brace. Tighten the PPF bolts to the specified torque, noting that the torques for the main bolts and angle bracket bolts differ.

Refit the clutch slave cylinder using its two 12mm bolts, and refit the starter motor; then you can refit the exhaust.

Refit the gearstick and console.

> **TIP**
>
> **To minimise fluid loss from the clutch fluid reservoir when you disconnect any hydraulic pipe, unscrew the lid, top up the fluid then stretch a plastic bag over the open reservoir and screw the lid back on. This stops the reservoir from breathing though its tiny air hole, and helps retain the fluid by vacuum.**

CLUTCH SLAVE CYLINDER REMOVAL AND REFITTING

Removal

Remove the securing clip and disconnect the slave cylinder pushrod from the clutch release lever.

Unbolt the clutch slave cylinder from the side of the gearbox – there are two 12mm bolts and the lower one is easy to get to **01**. The top one is inaccessible but can be reached using a slim socket on a long 360mm/14in extension through the right-hand front wheelarch. Take the wheel off and you'll just be able to see the top mounting bolt past the top of the subframe. Check the cylinder carefully for leaks because a new one is relatively cheap and this would be the most logical time to change it. Unless you're going to change the cylinder there's no need to disconnect the hydraulic hose and thereby spill fluid everywhere, so hang it out of the way on a piece of wire. But don't press the clutch pedal when the cylinder is unbolted from the car, otherwise the actuating rod will pop out, create a mess and possibly destroy the cylinder's hydraulic seal.

If you need to change the slave cylinder for a new one, it is easiest to undo the hydraulic pipe while the cylinder is still attached to the gearbox.

01

Refitting

After fitting the new cylinder and reconnecting the hydraulic pipe, you will need to bleed and top up the system. The bleeding procedure is similar to the brake hydraulic system bleeding procedure described in Chapter 9 The bleed nipple is located at the rear of the slave cylinder.

CLUTCH RENEWAL

Removing the clutch

Once the gearbox has been removed, as described previously, the clutch can be removed as follows.

The clutch is held to the back of the flywheel by a ring of six 14mm bolts. Undo these evenly, turning the engine to bring the uppermost bolts within range – you should be able to turn the engine with both hands on the flywheel.

With all but one of the bolts out, support the clutch with one hand in case it falls, while you remove the last one. Lift the clutch off the back of the flywheel, put it to one side, and examine the clutch mating face of the flywheel. If it is badly uneven, scored or the cracks are more than surface-deep, you will need to fit a new one. Also check the friction material on the friction disc to make sure that the clutch does indeed need to be renewed **01**.

Crankshaft spigot bearing inspection and renewal

The spigot bearing supports the front of the gearbox input shaft in the back of the crankshaft. It's greased at the factory and doesn't need any more lubrication. However, if any of the rollers look damaged or have come out, or the bearing has damaged the nose of the gearbox input shaft that mates with it, you'll need to change it – and removing it can be tricky. There are two methods: with grease or with a puller.

To try the first, fill the bearing with grease, then insert a close-fitting rod or ferrule and whack it with a hammer. If you're lucky the grease will 'hydraulic' the bearing out (I never believed this until I tried it for the first time more than 20 years ago, but it works – just a matter of physics).

Otherwise, you'll have to hire the correct tool, a slim-jawed internal slide hammer that should bring the bearing out with a few impacts. Fit the 'legs' down inside the bearing until they are located behind it, give the stop a few whacks with the slide and the bearing should pull out in a very satisfying manner. Clean up the housing in the end of the crankshaft, then gently tap the new bearing into place, making sure it is absolutely square. Lubricate the bearing with a little-finger-full of high-temperature grease before you refit the gearbox.

> **TIP**
>
> **Clutch alignment tool**
>
> This is a universal tool available from motorists' discount stores and tool shops, having a main ferrule or rod on to which various sleeves of different sizes fit. Find the two that closely fit the inside of the splines on the clutch pressure plate and the inside of the spigot bearing in the end of the crankshaft, slide them on to the tool and use it to hold the clutch in line when you fit it. If you don't centralise the clutch before you tighten the pressure plate, the gearbox will either be impossible to fit because the spines don't line up, or the clutch will judder if you do get it on.

Refitting the clutch

The clutch friction plate is marked engine side and gearbox side – so make sure you fit it, sandwiched between the flywheel and the pressure plate, the right way round.

With the flywheel clean (and making sure the spigot bearing in the end of the crankshaft is intact: if not, renew it as described previously), fit the new

01

clutch friction and pressure plates loosely in place, and push in the clutch alignment tool (see 'Tip') **02**, wiggling it if necessary to pass right through the centre of the clutch and into the spigot bearing. Make sure it is in line with the crankshaft, then bolt up the clutch evenly, working in a diagonal fashion around the bolts a little at a time until they are nipped up to the specified torque.

02

Renewing the clutch release bearing

Whether you are fitting a replacement transmission or the original, the last clutch component to change is the release bearing which lives inside the bellhousing at the front of the gearbox **03**. First, remove the release arm by disengaging it from its ball mount (you can see the socket location – indicated by the bump on the front of the release arm); pull on its retention spring so it lets go of the ball. The outside end of the release lever will pull through the rubber boot that keeps grit and dirt out of the bellhousing – inspect this and renew it if it is cracked or damaged. Unhook the old bearing and, before you refit the release lever, apply high-temperature grease to its pivot **04**. Push its outer end back through the protective rubber boot, then clip on the new bearing, using a little high-temperature grease on the fingers that contact the bearing. Use a little more grease on the gearbox input shaft splines, but not too much or it might get on the new clutch and make it slip.

The gearbox can now be refitted, as described earlier in this chapter.

03

04

CHAPTER 7

SUSPENSION, STEERING AND BRAKES

SUSPENSION AND STEERING

The MX-5 owes its delightful handling to a stiff, well-balanced structure that uses a classic suspension layout to achieve its combination of suppleness and chuckability.

Technically, the layout is unequal-length double wishbones (or A-arms) all round, which locate the wheels well and whose geometry provides the best compromise of camber and track change on bump, and gives the best handling. It's the same basic layout used by just about all Formula One cars, and all the best sports cars, since the '60s.

TORQUE WRENCH SETTINGS

Front suspension	Nm	lbf ft
Top mounting plate-to-damper rod nut	31–46	23–34
Top mounting plate-to-body nuts	29–36	22–27
Bottom damper mounting nut and bolt	73–93	54–69
Bottom balljoint vertical mounting bolt	73–93	54–69
Bottom balljoint horizontal mounting nut and bolt	73–93	54–69
Anti–roll bar drop link nut and bolt	36–54	27–40
Track-rod end-to-steering arm	29–44	22–33
Upper wishbone-to-body pivot bolt and nut	118–137	87–101
Lower wishbone-to-body bolts and nuts	94–112	69–83

Rear suspension	Nm	lbf ft
Top mounting plate-to-damper rod nut	31–46	23–34
Top mounting plate-to-body nuts	29–36	22–27
Bottom damper mounting bolt	73–93	54–69
Upper wishbone-to-upright pivot nut and bolt	46–67	34–49
Lower wishbone-to-upright pivot nut	63–75	46–54
Lower wishbone-to-upright pivot bolt	63–75	46–54
Anti–roll bar drop link nut and bolt	36–54	27–40
Upper wishbone-to-body pivot bolt and nut	46–67	34–49
Lower wishbone-to-body nuts and bolts	73–93	54–68

All the major suspension parts are carried by steel crossmembers, or subframes, one front and one rear, that are bolted to the body. At the front there are conventional wishbones made of pressed steel, and a measure of anti-dive geometry is built in by the top arm's pivot being tilted slightly off horizontal. At the rear there are wide-based lower wishbones (A-arms), with an upper link running in front of the spring/damper units to locate to brackets on the crossmember.

Springing all round is by coil springs mounted concentrically on telescopic dampers, connected between the lower wishbones and the body and passing through the top arms at the front, and behind the upper link at the rear. Anti-roll (stabilizer) bars are fitted to both front and rear, connected to the lower wishbones by rubber-mounted drop links. The lower wishbones at all four corners are adjustable via eccentric mountings holding them to the chassis, the front ones for camber and trail, the rear for toe-in/toe out. In the modern idiom of fine-tuning the suspension behaviour via flexible bushes, those locating the forward ends of the lower rear wishbones are designed to deform slightly on cornering, giving a measure of toe-in on roll for stability and to reduce excessive oversteer – though not much: one of the joys of an MX-5 is that the rear end can be tweaked sideways at will. Especially when it's wet.

Because the MX-5 suspension is adjustable at all four corners, correct wheel alignment is essential, and needs checking after any major suspension operation – or even if the car has been 'kerbed' and certainly if the tyres are wearing oddly or unevenly.

The most common revival jobs will be changing used dampers, worn balljoints and, sometimes, wishbone bushes.

BRAKES

The braking system uses ventilated discs all round with two separate hydraulic circuits sharing a common reservoir, vacuum assistance, plus optional ABS **01**, though it's uncommon to find a later car without it. A proportioning valve on the front bulkhead (firewall) adjusts the relative level of braking between front and rear circuits.

Most of the attention needed to the brakes will be to change worn-out pads and discs, though older cars may have sticking calipers or even corroded hydraulic pipes that need replacing. Flexible hydraulic pipes between the car's structure and the brake calipers deteriorate over time: when they show signs of cracking it's time to change them, as this is an MoT failure point.

Another common fault on imported cars that would be an MoT failure, but is often picked up at the SVA (Single Vehicle Approval) test when the cars first come into the UK, is braided brake hoses that do not flex neatly on wheel bounce and steering, and foul the tyre tread on full lock.

01

DAMPER (SHOCK ABSORBER) REMOVAL AND REFITTING AND GAITER RENEWAL

Front dampers

Caution: *There's a great deal of energy stored in a road spring – enough to kill or inflict serious injury – so be very careful when using spring compressors. Make sure the hooks fit the coils well, wind them up evenly, and never point the spring directly back at yourself or at anyone else.*

The most common problem with the dampers is that the rubber gaiters split and fall apart **01**, which is not an MoT failure, but the grit a failed one lets in will eventually wear the damper rod and seal and cause leaks, which is an MoT failure.

New gaiters are inexpensive and on Mk1s incorporate the rubber bump stop **02**, but to change them the spring and top mount have to come off, and that means the spring/damper unit has to be removed. The dismantling involved is the same procedure used to fit new dampers **03**, or uprated or adjustable units to sharpen the handling, a popular mod among MX-5 club members. Removing the springs and dampers is also the first step to taking off the wishbones in order to change their bushes for new or upgraded ones (usually known as polybushes because of their polyurethane construction).

First, clean up all the mounting bolts and nuts with a wire brush, and spray well with penetrating oil or WD-40 to make sure all the fixings come apart easily. If you can do this some time before you start – even the day before – so much the better: you'll have an easier time of it.

Undo the bolts that hold the ends of the anti-roll bar to their drop links **04/05**, one each side – this is so that you're not fighting against the anti-roll bar as you lower the wishbones to release the spring/damper units.

Then unbolt the large through bolt at the outer end of the wishbone **06**, and the through bolt that holds the

01

02

03

04

05

06

07

08

09

10

11

12

13

bottom of the damper (both 17mm) **07**. Tap the damper bolt through with a hammer and brass drift **08/09**. Lever the lower wishbone down until the damper's lower bush is resting just behind the top of its bracket **10/11**. This makes room to go in and undo the second balljoint mounting bolt, which sits vertically inside the wishbone **12**. With that out, you can knock out the balljoint's through bolt with the brass drift **13**.

Then swing the upright away from the lower wishbone **14**. In the engine bay, unbolt the top damper mounting nuts **15/16** – two per side – and let the damper drop through the inner wing **17**. Lever the lower wishbone down with a long bar or length of timber to make clearance and lift the damper out though the top wishbone **18**.

The new dampers don't come with top mounts, so whether you're changing them or just removing the springs to fit new gaiters, the springs need to be compressed so the top mount and spring can be removed. Though garages sometimes make up their own compressing tools involving ingenuity, lengths of steel scrap and semi-retired bottle jacks, at home you'll need spring compressors.

With the spring compressed, you can undo the damper rod nut and lift off the top mount, the spring and the gaiter. Store the compressed spring out of harm's way where it won't get kicked.

Transfer the parts you need, and reassemble the spring/damper unit. The end of the spring at the bottom engages

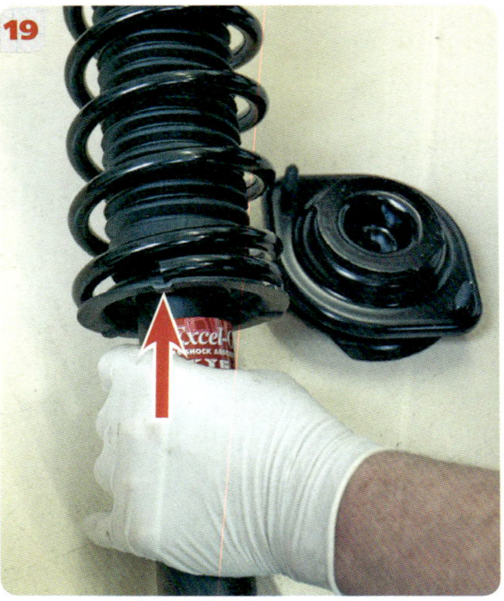

with a notch in the lower spring pan **19**. Very early cars have flat top mounts, but the later dished ones locate the spring much better, so get some if you can. When tightening the top damper nut, ensure that the top mounts bolts line up with the axis of the lower damper bush **20**.

Lift the new or rebuilt spring/damper units back into the car **21/22**, and reassemble in the reverse order of dismantling, starting with the top nuts that hold the dampers to the inner wing.

When you come to bolt the lower balljoints back to the wishbone, fit the through-bolt first, then use a screwdriver to lever the holes for the vertical bolt into alignment **23**. Fit and tighten the vertical bolt before you tighten the through bolt or you'll never get it in.

TIP

Use new plastic gaskets between the top mounts and the body – this will prevent squeaks.

Use a screwdriver passed through from the front of the car to lever the lower damper mounting to line up the holes so you can pass its bolt through.

Finally, tighten the main suspension bolts with the wishbones resting on axle stands to replicate the weight of the car on its wheels **24**. Carefully tighten all fixings to the specified torque.

Rear dampers

Rear damper/spring units require a similar procedure except that, if the lower upright through bolts are too difficult to undo **25/26**, you can undo the top ones instead **27** to release the upright and make room for the damper to come out.

Rather than being held by a bolt and nut, the lower end of the damper is held by a through-bolt that screws into a captive nut. Sometimes, with severe corrosion, this breaks away from the wishbone, but don't panic – there's just enough room to hold it with an open-ended spanner through a slot in the underside of the lower wishbone **28**. The damper's top mounting nuts are inside the boot. On the left-hand side you'll first have to remove the plate protecting the fuel filler neck and the jack handle clipped to the front of it.

25

26

27

28

FRONT SUSPENSION/STEERING BALLJOINT RENEWAL

There are two types of balljoint that commonly fail on an MX-5 – the lower one holding the outer end of the front wishbones to the front suspension uprights, and the track rod ends, connecting the track rods, which control the steering, to the suspension uprights.

You can check them by levering between the wishbone and upright to see of there is any movement **01**, and on the track rod end by grabbing the track rod and shaking, feeling for any play **02**.

Front suspension lower balljoint renewal

Changing a lower balljoint is a similar procedure to separating the joint from the wishbone by undoing the three bolts that secure it, but you'll also need to release it from the upright.

First straighten out and remove the splitpin holding the castellated nut in place, then undo and remove the nut **03**.

To separate the balljoint's tapered pin from the upright you'll need to use a balljoint separator tool, which forces the tapered pin out of its hole in the upright when you tighten the bolt on the tool.

Fit the new taper to its hole in the bottom of the upright first, then push the balljoint body into place on the lower wishbone, line up the holes, fit the bolts and tighten them. Fit the locknut to the balljoint taper. If the nut turns the taper, seat it until it grips by jacking under the lower wishbone, and tighten the locknut to the specified torque. Finally, push in and fold over a new splitpin.

01

02

03

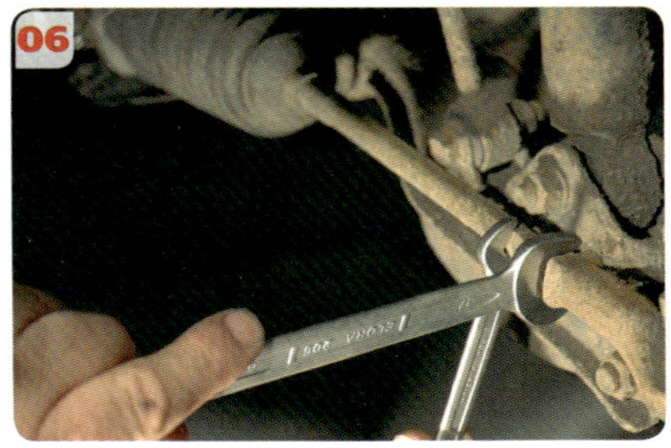

Track-rod end renewal

To change a track-rod end, first clean up the adjusting threads on the track-rod with a wire brush, then mark the position of the locknut using paint or correction fluid.

If a castellated nut is used to secure the balljoint to the steering arm, straighten and remove the splitpin holding the balljoint castellated nut in place **04**, then undo and remove the nut. If a self-locking nut is used, unscrew the nut.

Separate the taper from the steering arm with the balljoint separator **05**.

Holding the track-rod by its flats with an open-ended or adjustable spanner, loosen the locknut slightly **06**, then, still holding the flats on the track-rod, you can unscrew the balljoint.

Screw on the new joint until it meets the locknut that you left on the track-rod and tighten the locknut against the balljoint so it ends up lined up with the paint marks where it started. Then push the taper through its hole in the steering arm. If a self-locking nut was used to secure the balljoint, fit a new locknut and tighten it to the specified torque. If a castellated nut was used, tighten it to the specified torque, then secure it using a new splitpin.

TIP

New locknuts incorporate an undisturbed plastic ring in their top which grips the thread and guards against vibration shaking the nut loose. This might make the taper pin rotate as you try to tighten it so a sharp tap under the balljoint head will seat the taper, making it grip strongly enough for you to tighten the locknut.

FRONT SUSPENSION WISHBONE BUSH RENEWAL

Wishbone bushes very rarely wear – specialist Sam Goodwin has never changed one – but some owners like to change them for polyurethane bushes which deflect less, and many owners feel they sharpen the steering and handling. However, these also give a slightly harder ride, and are usually for racing and track days only. Remember that all the lower wishbone bushes are held to the chassis via eccentrically mounted bolts, and will need a proper four-wheel alignment carried out every time they are disturbed **01**.

The bushes need to be changed with the wishbone off the car, so you'll have to follow the procedure given for damper removal to release the wishbone from the spring/damper unit and the lower balljoint.

Clean up the area around the inner wishbone pivot bolt head, nut and the eccentric washers underneath. Make alignment marks between each eccentric washer and the body with paint or correction fluid, then loosen the nuts, punch out the wishbone bolts and transfer the wishbone to the bench.

To remove the old bushes and fit new ones you will need a special tool, but you can replicate this with a length of threaded bar, a couple of nuts and some deep sockets or tubes, one with a diameter that is slightly smaller than the bush, and one larger than the wishbone eye.

Fit the threaded bar through the bush, then add the smaller socket or tube on one end and the larger to the other, fitting a washer and nut to each end of the bar. Now tighten up the nuts, and the force will draw the bush into the large socket.

Clean up the inside of the wishbone eye, making sure there are no flakes of rust or bits of old bush, then, using the same technique used for removal, pull the new bush into the wishbone eye by winding it on with the nuts.

Refit the wishbone to the car, making sure the marks on the eccentrics and the body line up **02**. This is only a guide, however, because new bushes have been fitted, so when you have finished it's still essential to take the car for a four-wheel alignment check.

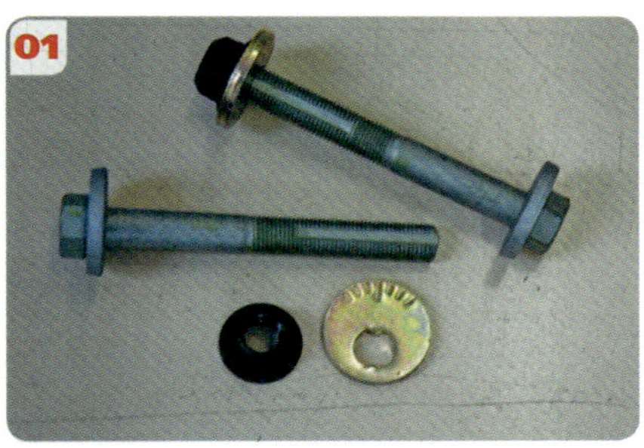

FRONT BRAKE PAD RENEWAL

Chock the rear wheels securely, loosen the front wheel nuts, jack up the car and support it on axle stands. Remove the wheel. Check the brake master cylinder and, if it is quite full, remove some brake fluid with a syringe to prevent overspill when you push back the pistons to make room for the new pads. At the least, arrange a cloth around the reservoir neck to catch any expelled fluid.

The pads are held in by the sliding caliper and the bracket it fits on. Remove the lower lockbolt **01/02**, swing the caliper upward **03**, pull out the upper bolt and support the caliper securely to avoid straining the flexible brake hose – the easiest way is to stand it on the widest (inner) part of the lower wishbone **04**. Remove the springs and pads **05/06**. If the clips come out with the pads, transfer them back to the caliper **07**.

The lower inner brake pad clip has a small tag longer than the others. It's designed to rub on the disc when the pads get near their wear limit, producing a nasty squeal to remind the owner to change the pads.

Check the small rubber gaiters on the lockbolts/slide pins **08**. If they are split, change them because if they are letting in water and grit the caliper will very soon seize and cease to slide.

Save the anti-rattle shims from the back of the pads, if fitted, and transfer them to the new ones **09**. Also fit the clips to the lower ends of the inner brake pads **10**. Slot in the new pads and fit the helper springs to the holes in the pads **11** – if these were missing they can now be bought separately. Now push the piston back into the caliper if you have not already done so, using a G-clamp or a large pair of pipe grips **12** – be very careful not do damage the rubber sealing boot if you do it this way – then check in the engine bay to make sure the brake fluid reservoir has not overflowed.

Clean the lockbolt/slide pins and apply brake grease **13**, then slip the top pin back into the caliper, slip the caliper over the pads **14/15** and replace the lower lockbolt, tightening it and its partner to the specified torque **16/17**. Finally, refer to the 'Warning' box on page 109, and pump the brake pedal a few times.

TIP

Ensure the channels in the caliper bracket that hold the pad end clips are clear of dirt and rust. Scale tends to build up here, with the result that you won't be able to get the new pads in.

12
RECORD

13

14

15

16

17

REAR BRAKE PAD RENEWAL

Changing rear pads is roughly the same procedure as the fronts, but this time the pistons need to be retracted using the manual adjustment screw, which is housed in the back of the caliper near the small levers pulled by the handbrake cables. The screw is protected by a short 12mm setscrew. Remove the setscrew **01** and inside you will find an Allen (socket) headed grub screw. Rotating this adjuster screw anticlockwise as far as it will go with an Allen key **02** will pull the caliper piston inwards. Remove the lower lockbolt (it's got a round rubber boot protecting it with a pip on the end **03**), pivot the caliper upwards and remove the pads, shims and guide plates **04**.

Install the new pads, swing down and bolt up the caliper, then screw the adjuster in until the pads touch the disc, and back it off by $^{1}/_{3}$ of a turn until the disc turns freely – it's easiest to refit the wheel for this, which gives you a better 'feel' of the brake, especially on cars that confuse the issue with a limited-slip differential. Once you're happy with the brake adjustment, refit the setscrew.

If you need to change a rear caliper, follow the brake pad renewal procedure, but also disconnect the handbrake cable by springing it out of its mounting brackets and disconnecting the hydraulic pipes – you will have to bleed the system afterwards.

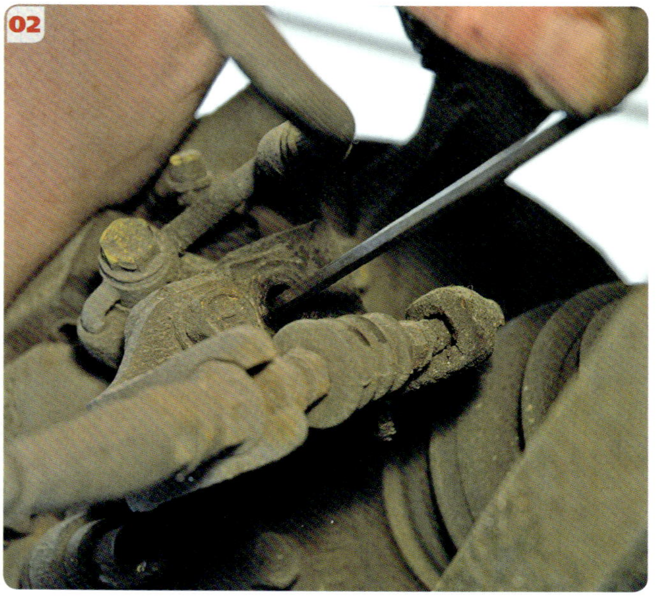

FRONT BRAKE DISC RENEWAL

Changing the discs means going a little further once you have the calipers off. Also unbolt the caliper bracket from the upright (the two bolts will be tight, so you'll need a breaker or extension bar) **01/02** then you can pull the disc off the wheel studs. (Note that the car in the picture has wheel spacers, whose nuts have to be undone first, but normally the disc will just lift off). The disc may be rusted on, in which case you can gently tap it with a soft mallet to free it. Before fitting the new disc, make sure the hub face is absolutely clean and true, otherwise the disc will 'run out', giving a juddery or pulsating pedal. If the hub is rusty, clean it up with a wire brush and emery paper.

Then fit the disc over the wheel studs, bolt the caliper bracket back on, and tighten the bolts to the specified torque, and refit the pads and caliper as above **03/04**. Always change pads and discs in axle sets.

01

02

03

04

WARNING

Once you have finished working on the brakes, pump the brake pedal a few times to bring the pads back to the discs (if you don't you'll have a very exciting time the next time you try to stop), then top up the master cylinder reservoir to the correct level.

REAR BRAKE DISC RENEWAL

Changing the rear discs means removing the caliper, in the same way as for changing pads – save the lower pivot pin somewhere safe and support the caliper, either by resting it on the lower wishbone or hanging it from a length of wire such as an old coathanger – the idea is to avoid straining the flexible pipe.

Unbolt the caliper bracket and remove it so you can slip the old disc off and the new one on – it's vital that the mating face of the hub is clean and free from scale and rust, so clean it up with a wire brush and emery paper if necessary.

Refit the caliper bracket and tighten the securing bolts, then refit the pads and caliper and adjust it, as described previously. Once you have done the other side, pump up the brake pedal and check the fluid level in the master cylinder reservoir, topping up from a new bottle of brake fluid if necessary.

TIP

A poor handbrake (parking brake) is very likely to be caused by the rear brake manual adjustment being incorrect – many owners do not know about the manual adjustment screw, and try to compensate by adjusting the handbrake cable. If the brakes are generally good and the handbrake feels normal but handbrake operation is poor, check this first. If this is not the cause, the next most likely problem is seized calipers.

BRAKE HYDRAULIC SYSTEM BLEEDING

Warning: *Whichever method you use, you will need at least a litre of new brake fluid in a sealed container. Don't use old fluid, because it may have absorbed moisture from the atmosphere. Moisture in the brake fluid heats up and expands, giving at best a spongy feel to the brake pedal, and at worst no brakes at all as the moisture turns to steam and the pedal goes to the floor.*

Hydraulic brakes work on the principle that a liquid doesn't compress, so the fluid can transfer movement – pressing the brake pedal forces fluid out of the master cylinder and down the brake pipes to make the brake caliper squeeze the pads against the discs to slow the car. But air does compress, giving a spongy pedal or no brakes at all, so if any has entered the system it must be eradicated by pumping out the old fluid that contains it until only new fluid with no bubbles remains in the system.

If you have only disconnected one brake – say to change a pipe – then it should only be necessary to bleed that corner of the system. But, since changing brake fluid every couple of years is a good idea, we have detailed working around each of the brakes in turn. If you only need to bleed one corner, simply deal with it and leave the rest – but if you get a spongy pedal, you'll have to do them all.

There are two ways of bleeding the system: the first, with a rubber bleed tube – which usually has a one-way valve in the end – and a helper to push the brake pedal, the second with an Eezibleed. Professional garages use a vacuum device to draw out old fluid from the bleed nipple.

Whichever method you use, start by loosening the wheel nuts, then chock the wheels and jack up the car, supporting it at all four corners, and remove the wheels. You could, if you prefer, work at one end of the car at a time. Start with the brake furthest from the master cylinder.

Bleed tube method

First, clean up the bleed nipple and the area around it, after pulling off its rubber sheath **01/02**. A light wire-brushing is OK. Then check that the nipple can be slackened, using a ring spanner. Once it's released from its seat, push the rubber tube over the nipple, and place the other end into a jar containing enough brake fluid to immerse the end of the one-way valve **03**.

Make sure the master cylinder reservoir is fully topped up, using only new brake fluid from a sealed container.

Open the bleed nipple ¼ turn and get your helper to pump the brake pedal to the floor, returning it slowly, until new fluid containing no bubbles comes down the pipe. You need to keep a close eye on the level of fluid in the master cylinder reservoir every few pumps, because if the

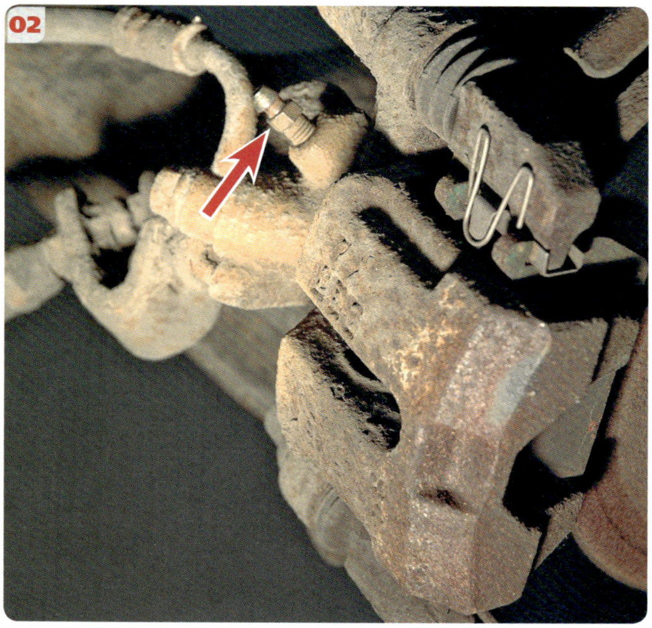

level gets too low and the system sucks air you'll have to start again.

Keep pumping until new, clean fluid free of air bubbles comes out. When clean fluid comes through, get your helper to push the pedal back to the floor and hold it while you tighten the bleed nipple before the pedal is released. Check the fluid level again and move on to the next brake.

Using a non-return valve like this, it's possible to bleed the brakes yourself, though you'll be in and out of the driver's seat because you need to check both what's coming out plus the level in the reservoir. It's still easier with a helper.

Using an Eezibleed

This kit, available from motor accessory stores, uses pressure from a tyre to force old fluid out of the system, and connects via the master cylinder reservoir **04–06**. Its real advantage is that it makes brake bleeding a true one-man job.

Once you have pressurised the system by connecting up the kit according to the maker's instructions, and cleaned up around the bleed nipples, simply go around the car, fitting a pipe to and opening each nipple in turn so that old fluid discharges through the pipe into a suitable catch tank or container. When clear fluid comes out, move on to the next brake. When all the brakes are bled, and you have a nice firm pedal, disconnect and remove the Eezibleed and top up the master cylinder reservoir.

BRAKE HOSE RENEWAL

Mostly, this will be needed because the flexible hose between the chassis and the brakes has cracked or perished on the outside and become an MoT failure point.

Start by removing the master cylinder reservoir cap, stretch a piece of plastic bag over the reservoir and screw the cap back on – this will minimise fluid loss.

Clean up the banjo fitting on the caliper and the area around it, to prevent dirt from falling into the caliper. Undo the banjo fitting's bolt and save it and the washers.

At the chassis end, the hose is held on with a U-clip, and it is secured to the rigid brake pipe by a union nut. Undo this with a brake pipe spanner to avoid rounding off the union. Using pliers, pull off the U-clip that secures the hose to its bracket, then pass the hose through the bracket.

Fit the new hose through the bracket, start the union by hand and then push on the U-clip, then tighten the union with a spanner.

At the caliper end, fit the banjo end to the caliper with the banjo bolt and new copper washers, making sure everything is clean. Make sure the banjo bolt bracket locates with its hole in the caliper.

Bleed the caliper, refit the wheel and lower the car to the ground.

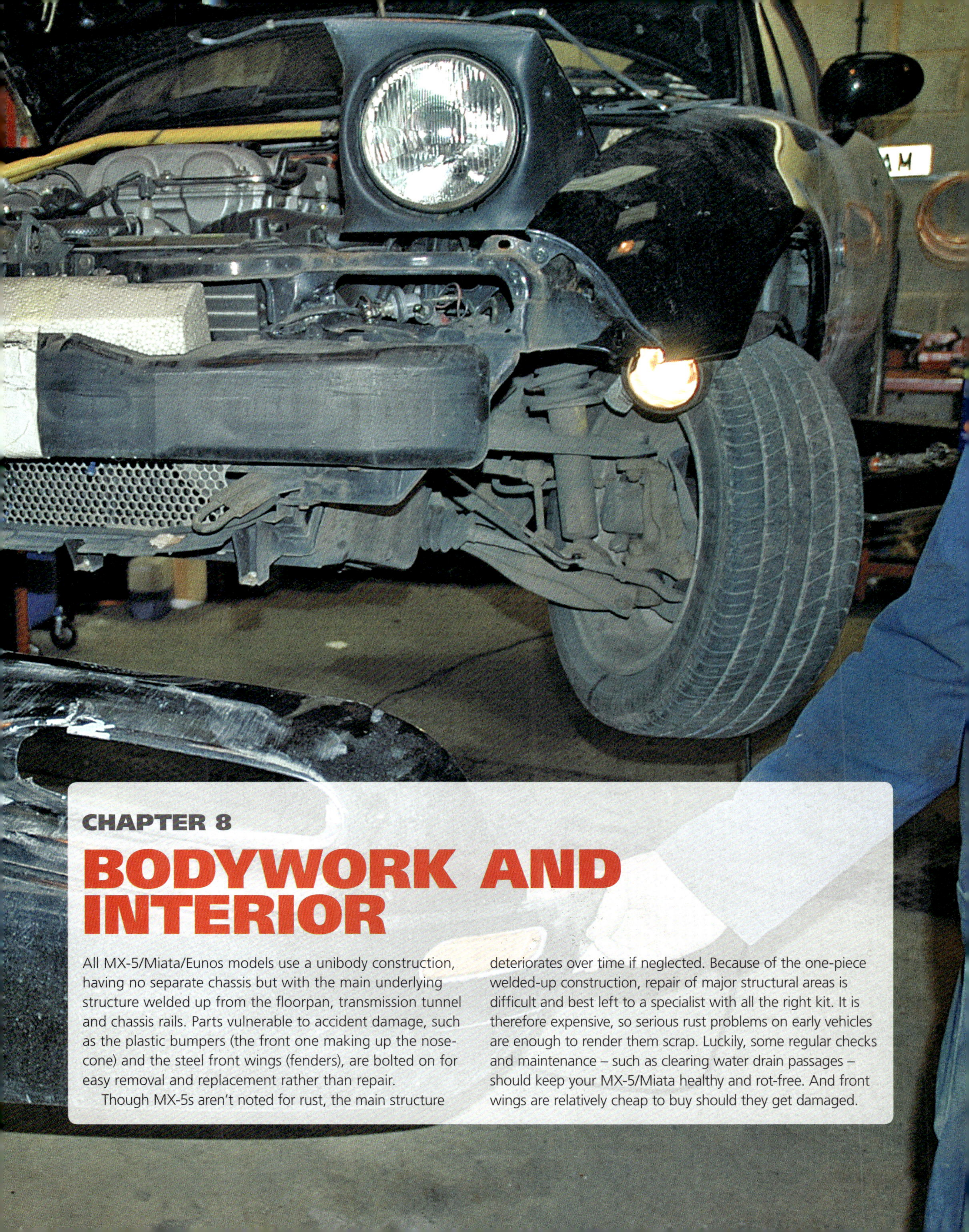

CHAPTER 8

BODYWORK AND INTERIOR

All MX-5/Miata/Eunos models use a unibody construction, having no separate chassis but with the main underlying structure welded up from the floorpan, transmission tunnel and chassis rails. Parts vulnerable to accident damage, such as the plastic bumpers (the front one making up the nose-cone) and the steel front wings (fenders), are bolted on for easy removal and replacement rather than repair.

Though MX-5s aren't noted for rust, the main structure deteriorates over time if neglected. Because of the one-piece welded-up construction, repair of major structural areas is difficult and best left to a specialist with all the right kit. It is therefore expensive, so serious rust problems on early vehicles are enough to render them scrap. Luckily, some regular checks and maintenance – such as clearing water drain passages – should keep your MX-5/Miata healthy and rot-free. And front wings are relatively cheap to buy should they get damaged.

Though there is a perception that European and export cars are better protected against rust than Japanese home-market ones, the evidence seen by UK specialists is that none of the early cars is better protected than others, regardless of original market, and that later cars are less well protected than early ones. UK experts say that Japanese-import Eunos typically display less rot than European cars, possibly because of less salt being used on Japanese roads, and possibly because Japan's tougher vehicle safety laws means that cars leave that market relatively early in their life to come to a more lenient environment.

The MX-5's main body corrosion problems stem from drain holes blocking up. The two main ones are at the rear of the cockpit, where rainwater from the hood drains into channels or 'hoppers', and then out on to the road via two rubber hoses – you can see these from underneath if you get the car up on a ramp. These include rubber flaps a couple of inches up from their outlets, to stop water spray getting up into the car from underneath, and the simplest way to make sure they are clear is simply to probe them from time to time – they will probably drip water for a few minutes afterwards, and you may well even bring out a satisfying amount of grot and gunge when you twist and pull out the probe. Don't use a screwdriver for this job, as it may puncture the hoses – use a tool such as an old car aerial with a ball end.

If these drains are left blocked for any length of time, water builds up and the sills corrode through at the rear. It begins underneath and spreads up to the quarter panels, and sometimes takes the inner sill with it. This can spell the end on purely economical terms for a cheap car.

There are sill drains near the jacking points, and you can unblock them by poking through them with a small screwdriver or length of stiff wire such as an old bicycle spoke.

Sometimes you'll see rust bubbling out from under the sill trims ('kick plates'), where fitted. This is not usually serious or related to internal sill corrosion, though it does need dealing with by unscrewing and removing the kick plates, treating the rust and refinishing the paint.

Other rust spots include the bottom edges of the front of the front wings just above where the nose-cone mates up, the underside edges of all four wheelarch lips, and the back of the boot floor, best checked from underneath. The chassis rails are vulnerable to scuffing, and from damage by careless jacking, but they are thicker at their ends and will tolerate jacking, as long as you use wooden packing to protect the metal and paint.

If the rear of the sills and rear quarter panels behind the doors have 'gone' then taking the car to a specialist is the only realistic choice – they can let in new panels up to the swage lines, and replace sections of sills, though the ideal solution is to buy a car not affected in this area.

One part of the MX-5 that does not last well is the hood, made of vinyl, which suffers with age, use and vandalism. Much better alternatives, such as mohair, are available, which both enhances the look of the car and its value, and are easier to fit.

TIP

Keys

This tip comes from specialist importer Dandycars.com. Any locksmith should be able to cut a spare key for you, though some will protest that they have no Eunos or Mazda key blanks. No problem, the Mazda keys are very similar to Ford keys that will work just as well!

ENGINE UNDERTRAY REMOVAL AND REFITTING

A plastic engine undertray is fitted to protect the engine against road debris and dirt **01**, and most jobs can be done without removing the undertray.

The undertray is secured by a series of bolts, and removal and refitting are self-explanatory **02/03** – though note that one bolt each side holds the wing stays.

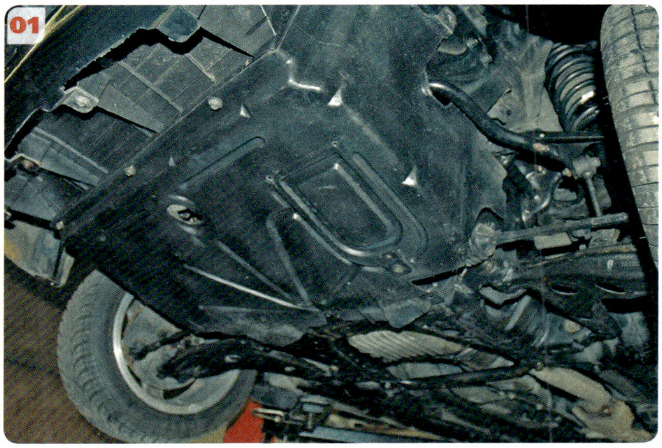

01

02

03

HOOD (SOFT-TOP) RENEWAL

The MX-5's hood is neat, functional and easy to use – but that clean, simple elegance comes from it being fully fitted, meaning that replacement isn't for the faint-hearted. But, as long as you tackle the job logically and in order – and don't panic – there's no reason why you can't swap a hood yourself at home, saving about £150 on fitting costs.

Hoods suffer in a number of ways; wear and tear, accidental damage or vandalism – city street-parked cars get 'knifed' from time to time, and there's not much you can do about that. The other reason for a hood change is to upgrade to a better quality covering, or to the Mk2 type with a glass rear window, though early Mk1s have no wiring loom to power the heating element.

Wear and tear occurs in two main areas. The seams along the tops of the front window top rails tend to crack where the hood flexes when it is folded. By the time the owner tries to fix this with silicon sealer or Gaffer tape, it's the end.

Other problems include deterioration of the gutter, rusting mounting rails, cracking of the hood edges over the windows, splits in the lower side of the hood from surface tension (this lets water into the sills just as surely as blocked drains), and yellowing or cracking of the back window.

The hood's design, fitting inside the car rather than over the rear deck, means water needs to be drained away before it can do any harm. On the MX-5/Eunos/Miata, this is carried out by an ingenious folded rubber/plastic gutter sandwiching the bottom of the hood, which discharges into two small hoppers, one on each side of the car just behind the door pillars. These feed into drain tubes that block up with little provocation, so regular clearing out with a suitable tool such as an old ball-ended car aerial, is a must.

Hood and gutter problems need to be addressed because, left uresolved, water eventually fills the sills which then rot out – and that can 'write off' a cheaper car because the repairs cost more than its market value.

The pros make it look easy, taking about three hours to replace the covering, but warn that the cheaper the hood, the more difficult the job and the harder it is to achieve a good fit. At the top of the tree are genuine Mazda hoods that 'practically fit themselves'. At the bottom are the cheap vinyl hoods that are hard to shut in cold weather.

If you're tackling hood replacement, allow a whole weekend. And, whatever type of hood you choose, it's much easier to fit indoors or on a warm day.

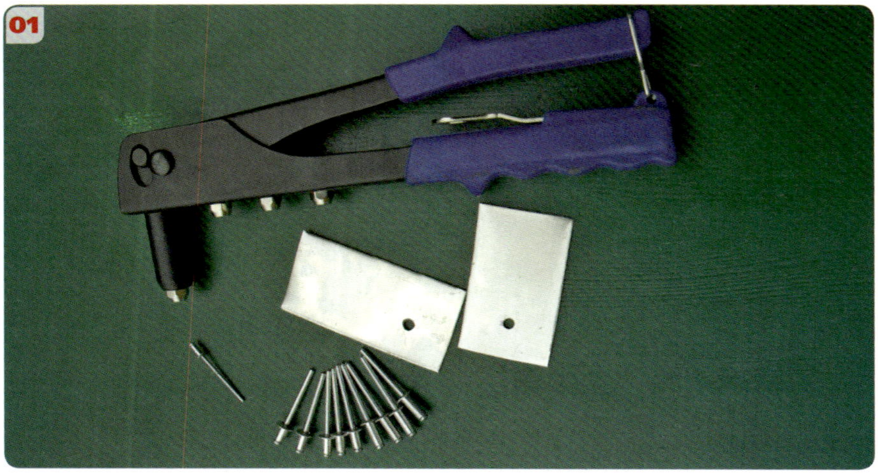

01

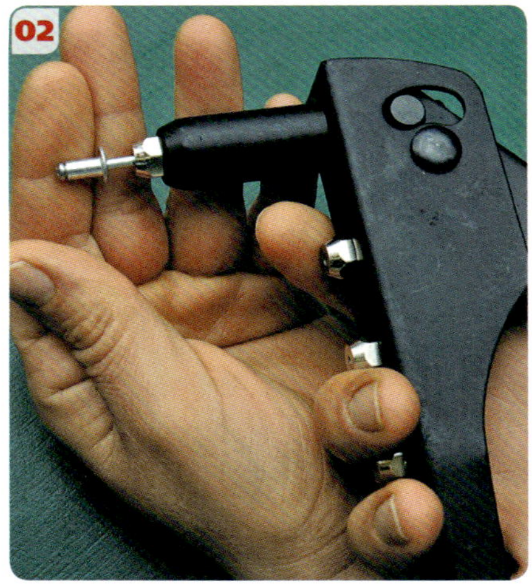

02

Before you start

Make sure you're handy with a rivet gun! The hood is held to its frame with pop-rivets, which you'll need to drill out and replace as the job goes on. If you're riveting for the first time, practise by drilling some holes in pieces of scrap metal **01**. Use a 4mm drill bit, and always wear safety goggles.

Then, using the correct-sized nipple to suit the rivet, insert the steel shank of the rivet into the rivet gun **02**, push the rivet head into its hole **03**, hold it tightly home and squeeze the handles of the rivet gun until the steel shank pulls through and breaks off – you'll need a few 'pumps' **04**. The rivet should end up with its head flush against the work **05/06** but if it goes wrong you can drill it out and start again.

Protect the boot lid and rear deck with an old blanket, and make sure you have a container ready to keep all the screws and nuts in – a multi-compartment Tupperware container is ideal.

03

04

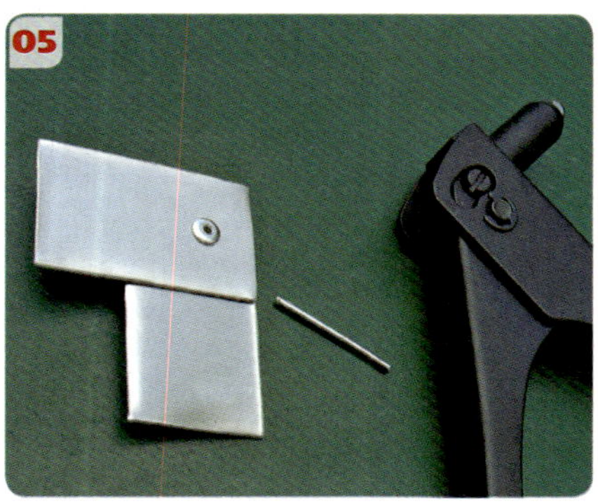

05

06

Removing the old hood (soft-top)

Start by unpopping the carpet from the load deck behind the seats and pull it back so you can undo the row of 13 10mm flat-faced nuts from the back of the car. These secure the three steel rails, one in the middle and one on each side. The endmost nuts are inaccessible, but you should be able to reach them with a small ring spanner – be careful not to drop them down the water drains **01–03**.

When you get the securing rails off, you'll almost certainly find that at least their back faces will be rusty **04**, so this is a good time to give them a good wire-brushing, then rust-treat and paint them. If you use Hammerite Smooth, the rails should be dry by the time you come to fit the new roof.

Pull the hood away from its fixing studs. If this is the first time the hood has been off the car, you'll need to drill out the rivets holding it to the rain gutter **05**. These were used by Mazda to simplify and speed up hood fitting during assembly and don't need to be replaced, so they'll be missing if the hood has already been changed. Tape over any extraneous holes in the gutter or, if it's split, replace it.

Undo the rubber seal retaining screws, then pull out the rubber seals from around the window frames **06**, and undo the cross-head screws holding the stainless steel channels behind them **07/08**. Under these, you'll find rivets holding the hood to the frame, so drill them out **09**.

Unscrew the cross-heads holding the securing channel and the front edge of the hood **10** – these have washers underneath, so be careful not to lose them. Prise the roof covering from the front of the frame and pull it back **11/12**.

Next drill out the rivets holding the tensioning wires to the front of the frame **13**, and pull the wires out of the hood – if it's an old, brittle cover, you'll find you can just rip them through the fabric **14–16**.

Open out the steel channel **17** on the front rail that holds the flap on the underside of the hood, known as a listing, and pull out the listing.

Unbolt the corner caps at the top of the door pillars, and then unbolt the two Torx bolts on each side that hold the hardtop mounts **18/19**.

Unclip the plastic trim from around the seat belt apertures, pull the rubber seal from the door pillar, and then pull the plastic side trim away from the body so you can undo the three bolts each side that hold the hood frame to the car **20**. Lift the frame out of the body - – it's heavier than you think – and sit the frame upside down.

Remove the last rubber seals – held at their top corners by push-fittings **21**. Under each seal is a plate held by a small cross-head screw. The screw will be rusty, so you'll get a better purchase on it by tapping the screwdriver into its cross with a small hammer before you try to twist it **22**. On Mk1s, there is also a rivet 'round the corner' so drill this out **23**, and the last two rivets nearby holding the hood to the frame **24**.

Detach the rear listing, pinched into the rear frame rail. The quickest way to deal with this is to cut through it with a Stanley knife **25**, and discard the remains later, but watch you don't damage the carpet on the parcel shelf. Then you can lift the frame right out of the car, and discard the old roof fabric **26**.

01

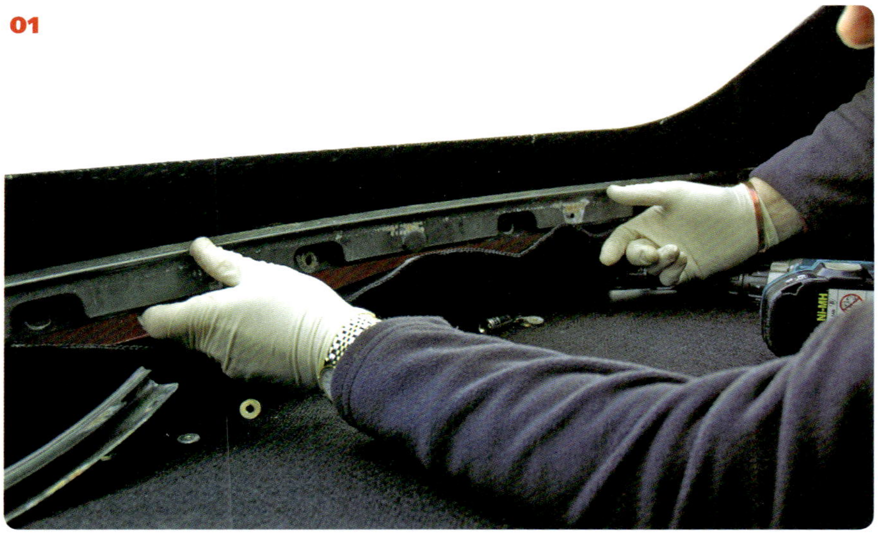

02

03

04

05

06

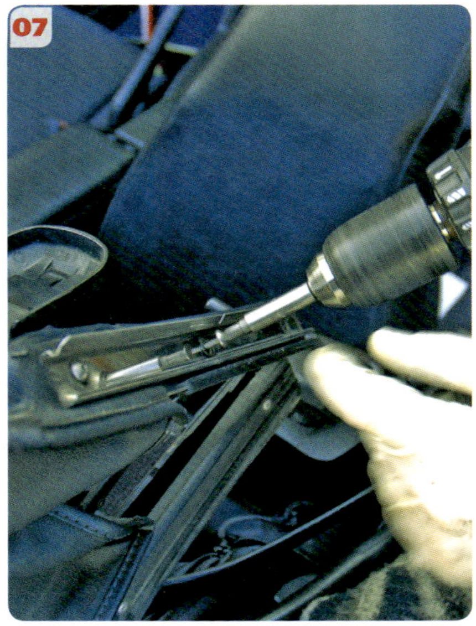
07

08

09

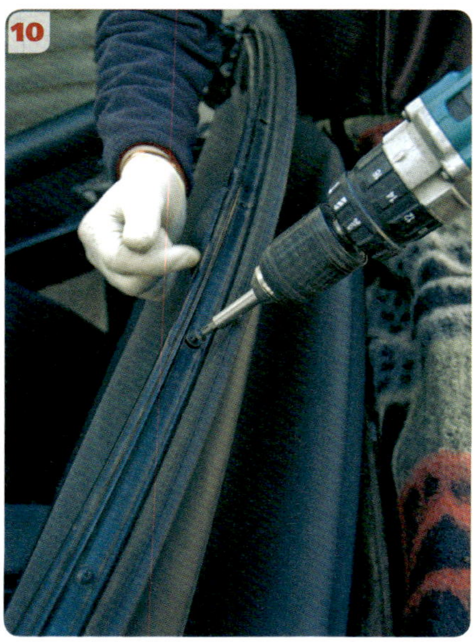
10

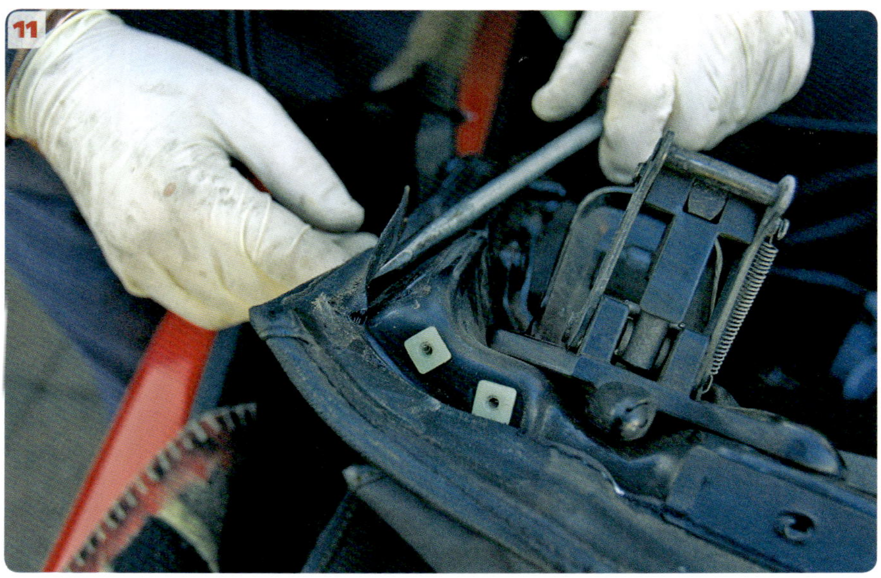
11

12

13

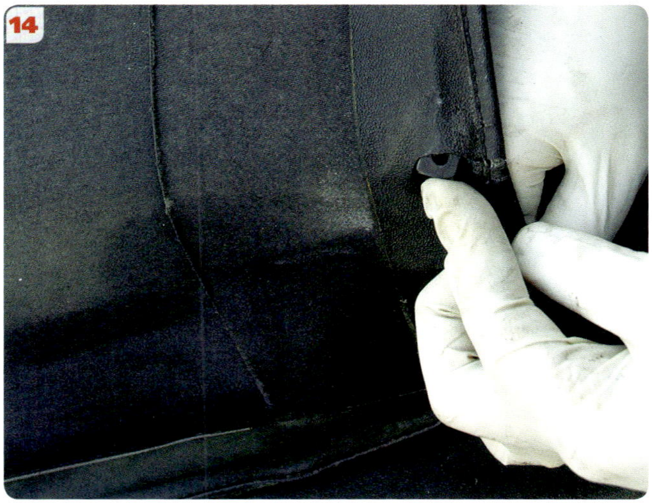
14

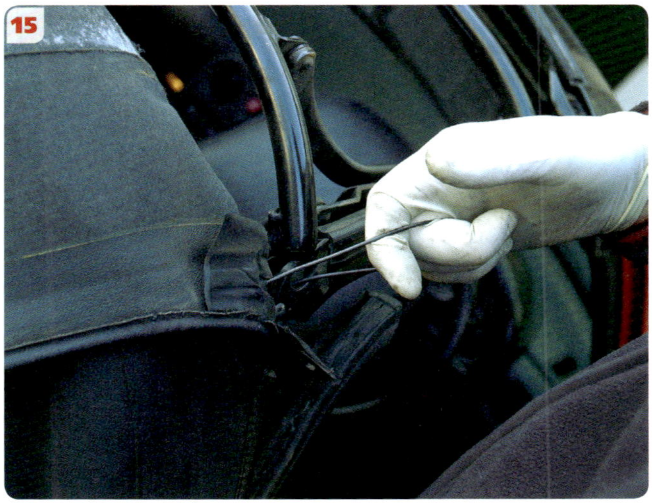
15

16

17

18

19

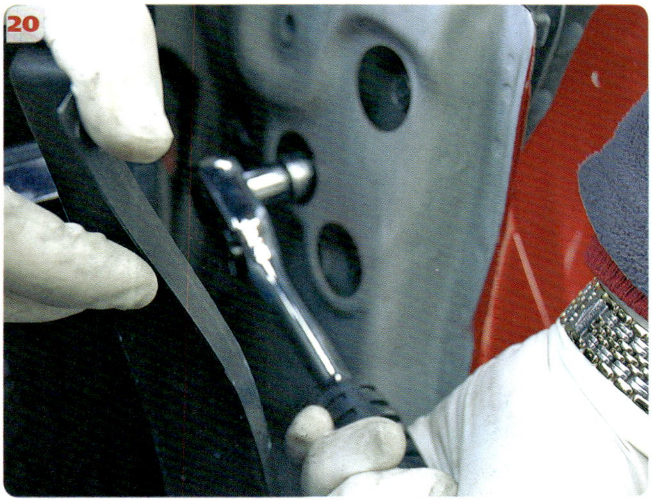
20

21

22

23

24

25

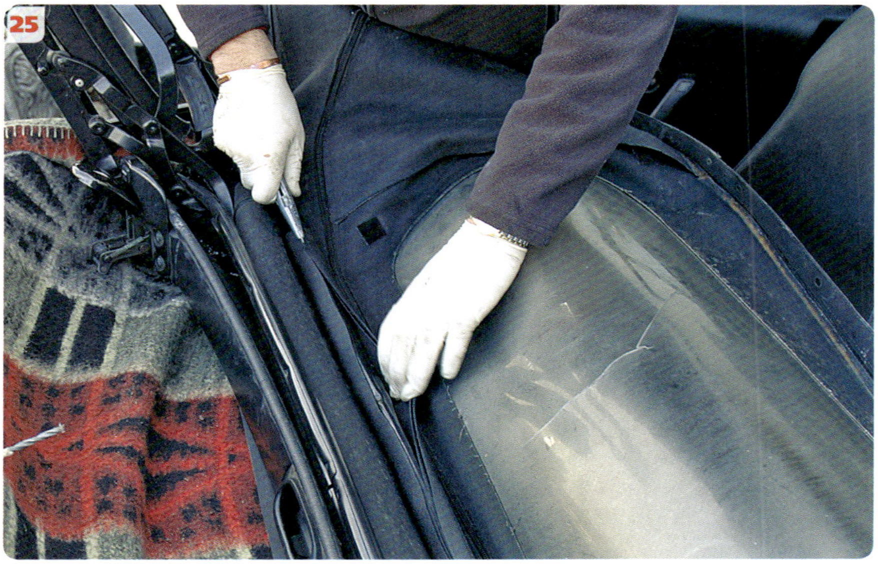

26

Fitting the new hood (soft-top)

If you are fitting a Mk2 hood to a Mk1, drill holes near the corners of the rear frame rail and rivet on the two webbing straps, one each side **01**. This gives the rear corners of the hood a better shape when closed

Unpack the new hood and lay it flat on the car, leaving the packing underneath to protect it. Lift the frame back over the hood.

Pull the tensioner wires through the hood's side channels – pass a straightened-out coathanger with a small loop on its end through the channel, hook on the wire and pull it back through **02** – this is very tight and in extreme cases you may break some of the stitching and have to sew it back up again by hand once the wires are in place. It's easiest if you keep the loop in the end of the coathanger facing the middle of the car **03/04**.

Rivet the sides of the new hood to the window frames – this area is reinforced with vinyl and there are pre-formed holes **05**. If you are fitting a Mk2 hood to a Mk1, only rivet the top holes, or the roof will pull out of shape when closed.

Refit the stainless-steel seal channels and push their rubber seals back into place **06**.

Screw and rivet into position the small steel plates that hold the lower ends of the hood to the frame – it's tricky to keep this neat but try to wrap the fabric tightly as you fix the plates. A tip is to hold each plate in place while you secure it by pushing a long thin screwdriver through the holes for the front seal push-fixings **07**. Once the plates are fixed, refit the front seal, pushing its plastic bolts back in.

Lift the frame and carefully drop the end brackets into place within the sides of the car, replacing the three bolts each side that secure them. Take care here – it is very easy to trap the hood fabric between the frame and the body, so make sure it is clear. Refit the trim and rubber **08**.

Fit the listings into their steels channels on the frame, and pinch the channel tight with pliers **09**.

Rivet the tensioner wires back to their holes under the front plate of the frame **10**.

Mazda-made hoods have a sewn pocket at the front that fits over the front of the frame. On non-Mazda-made hoods, you need to glue the front of the covering to the frame using impact adhesive **11**, turning the fabric over the front edge of the frame and securing it with its steel channel and screws **12/13**. Refit any remaining rubber seals and retaining channels **14**.

If you've not already done so, check the flexible rain gutter and tape up any extraneous holes. If it's split, replace it.

Now you're ready to bolt the back edge of the hood into the car. It'll be tight, so first try to get the centre nut in place to hold the hood back **15** while you fit it over the rest of the studs. The bottom edge of the fabric fits into the gutter and the whole lot is pinched to the car by the three steel channels. The back part of the gutter must go behind the lip on the underside of the plastic body edge moulding. Temporarily remove the centre nut to get the rear channel on and refit it afterwards, then fit the side rails, but don't tighten the nuts yet.

The webbing straps you riveted on to the frame rear rail earlier fit at their other ends on the rearmost stud of

each side channel, pinched between the channel and the gutter.

Now clip the front of the hood to the windscreen frame – you'll need someone pushing down from the outside to help while you squeeze the catches towards their hooks on the inside. Or, to make this step easier, first lengthen the front catches by pulling down their plastic retainers and twirling the adjuster nuts **16**. You can tighten them up again later after the new hood covering has lost some of its initial tension.

Tighten up the 10mm nuts holding the back of the hood **17**, clip in the carpet and then retension the front of the hood using the adjusters on the clamping brackets.

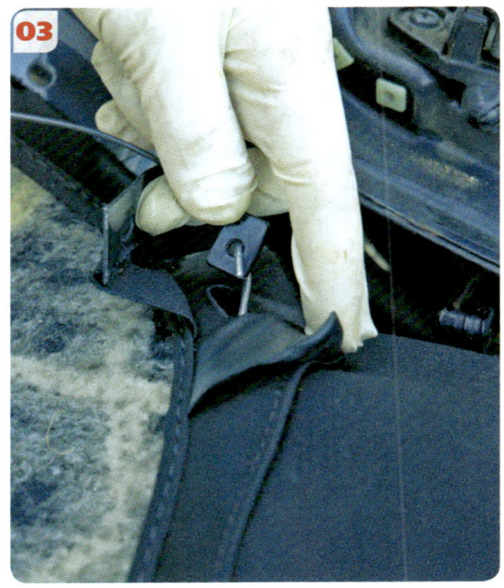

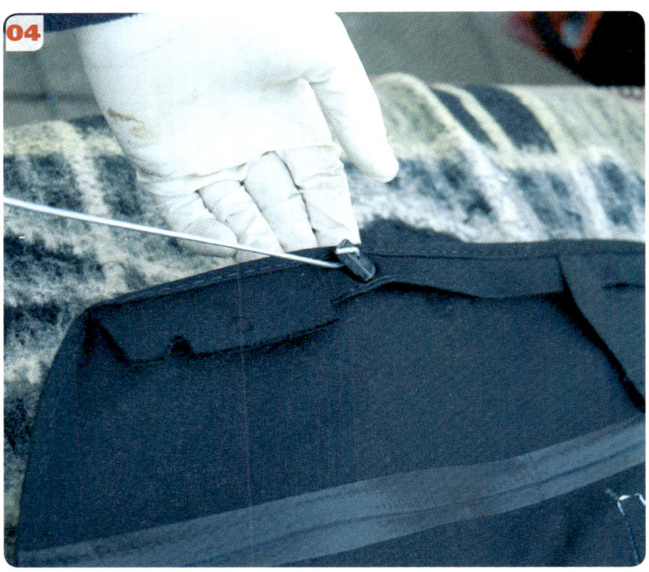

06

07

08

09

10

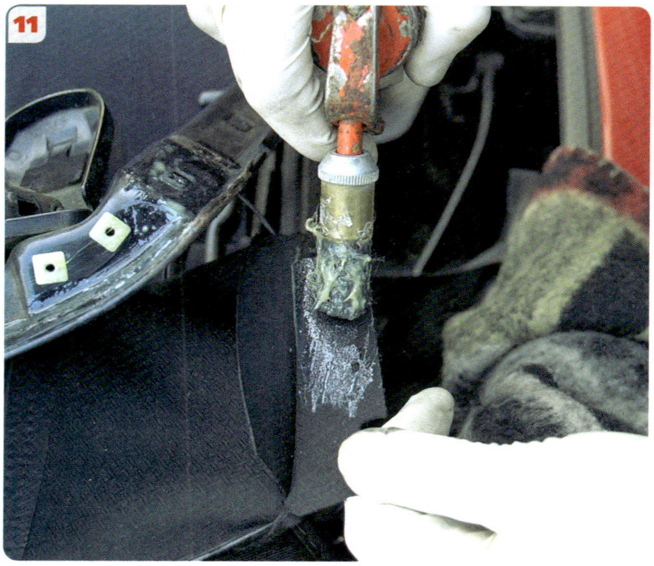

11

13

12

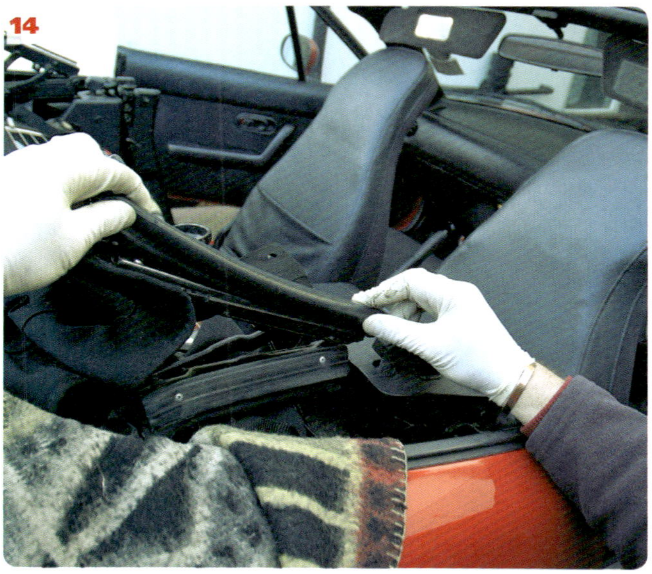

14

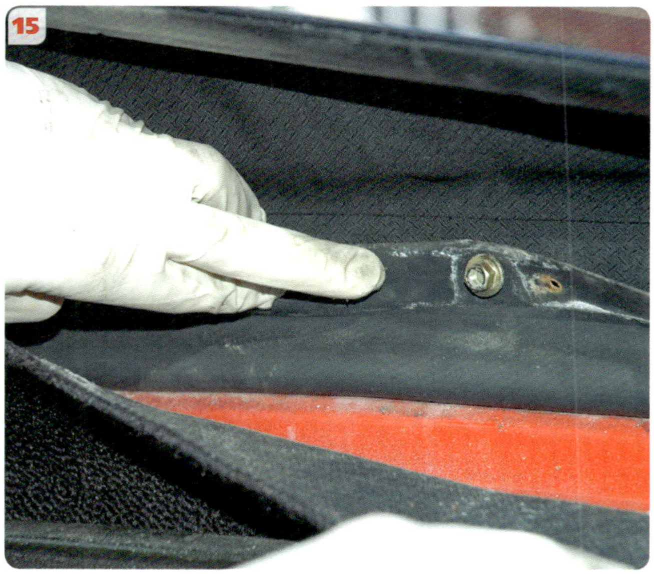

15

16

17

18

REAR SCREEN RENEWAL

With the hood up and window closed, remove the plastic carpet clips around the rear load deck. Pull back the carpet, then undo the 13 10mm nuts holding the rails that secure the back of the hood, and remove the rails. The two corner nuts are inaccessible, but you should be able to reach them with a ring spanner – be careful not to drop them down the water drains.

If there are still rivets holding the hood to the gutter, drill them all out. There are two that you can't reach until you slide the rear section of hood off all the studs and firmly pull up both corner sections of the hood.

Drill out the two remaining flat brass rivets holding the two parts of the hood together.

Remove the metal clips at each end of the zip and unzip the rear panel, making sure you don't lose the slider.

Lay the new screen panel roughly in place. Reattach the zip slider, making sure the two halves of the zip are in line, and then close the zip. Reattach the two small metal clips to each end of the zip.

Release the clamps at the front of the hood to give some slack to work with, and refit the back half of the plastic rain guttering to the studs. Re-rivet where you took out the two brass rivets.

Relocate the rear section of the hood to the studs, making sure you tuck the rear section of hood between the two halves of the plastic rain channel.

Refit the hood-securing channels and refit the 10mm nuts. Clip the front of the hood back to the windscreen frame, and then tighten the row of 10mm nuts at the back of the load area.

Fold back the carpet to its original position and refit the plastic clips and, finally, clean the Perspex screen with spray window cleaner, using a soft cloth.

HARDTOP REMOVAL AND REFITTING

These are glassfibre and are light enough to be lifted by one person – but their awkward size and shape means it's much better to have a helper when putting on and taking off. They are held at the front by the same type of clips that the soft-top uses, plus one more behind each seat. The brackets outside the rear of the roof clip over the small posts that stick up from the rear deck. These can be adjusted by undoing two bolts, but it's not necessary to unscrew and swing back the covers every time you remove and refit the roof **01/02**.

To remove the roof, first disconnect the plug to the heated rear window, if one is fitted, then release the four spring-clips inside. Push the roof back to disengage the rear brackets – you might have to give the backs of the window frames a gentle thump with the heel of your hand. Once the rear brackets are clear, lift the roof clear of the car **03**.

To refit the roof, first drop the rear brackets over the cross-head screws, then push the roof forward until it meets the header rail – the rear brackets might try to ride up over their locating posts, so make sure the roof is correctly seated, then do up the spring clips, the fronts first.

01

02

03

NOSE-CONE (FRONT BUMPER) REMOVAL AND REFITTING

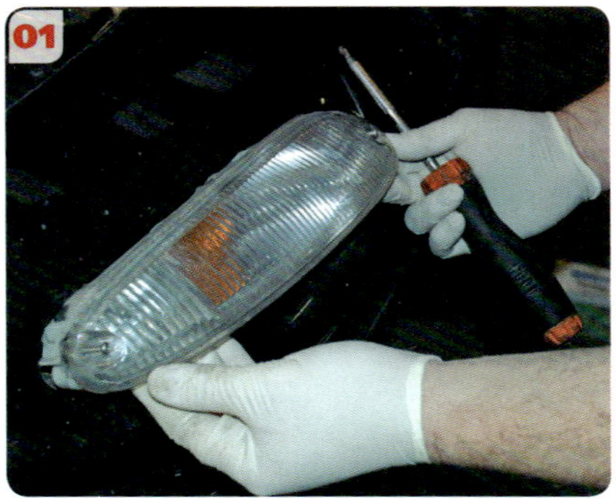

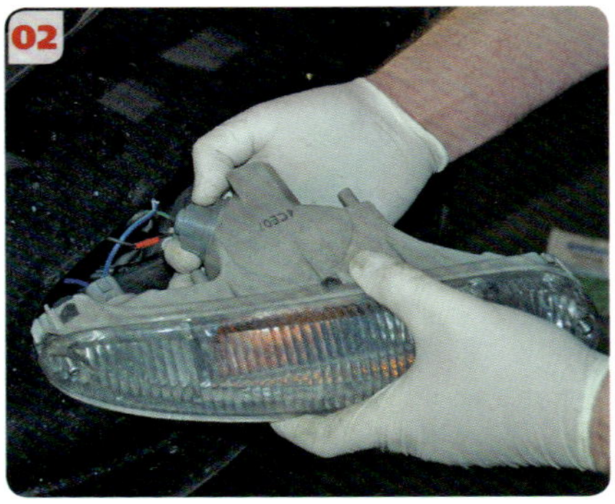

This is a large section to remove. It's not heavy, so it's a job you can tackle yourself – but having a helper when you lift it away from the car will make life much easier.

You'll need to raise the front of the car to be able to reach some of the fixings, so support the front crossmember on axle stands, apply the handbrake and chock the rear wheels. Before you start, wire brush all the steel fixings clean, or at least spray on some penetrating oil.

The main fixings are: three plastic screws inside the top of the 'mouth' of the radiator opening, six bolts and two studs along the front of the bonnet shut plate (called a set plate in some manuals), plus two or four bolts holding the nose-cone to the bottom air duct under the car. On each side, tucked up in the front wheelwells, there are two more nuts on rearward-facing studs that pinch the wings to the nose-cone. These can only be reached with the wheelarch liners out (unless you have a double-jointed eight-year-old who can work backwards by feel). Finally, there are two bumper stays on each side.

Start by opening the bonnet and raising the headlights using the control button on the centre of the dash. Unscrew and remove the combination lights from the front of the bumper – the screws will only back out so far, then you can use them to pull the light units out **01**. Pull the bulb holders from the light body **02** and tuck the bulbs and wiring out of the way **03**.

Then remove the rubber radiator shroud, just inside the bonnet opening, held by four cross-head screws **04/05** – early 1.6s didn't have them, so don't panic if you only find fresh air.

Unbolt the six 10mm bolts that hold the top plate to the nose-cone **06**. At each front corner, just in front of the

06

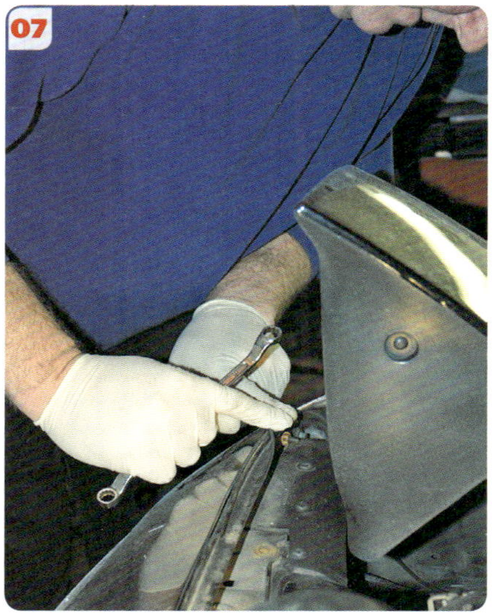
07

headlight, there is a 10mm nut on a rearward-facing stud – pull back the rubber seal to expose it, and you'll reach the nut with a small ring spanner **07**.

Unbolt the bumper stays, just in front of the wheelarch **08–11**. The lower, wire, ones are attached at their inner ends to the forward undertray mounting studs, but these can be left undisturbed. Next to the top stay mounts at the nose-cone end you'll also find a cross-head screw that holds the wheelarch liner to the wing and bumper, so remove them.

Though you can just about manage to reach the front mounting studs by releasing the front few screws on the wheelarch liners and pulling them out of

08

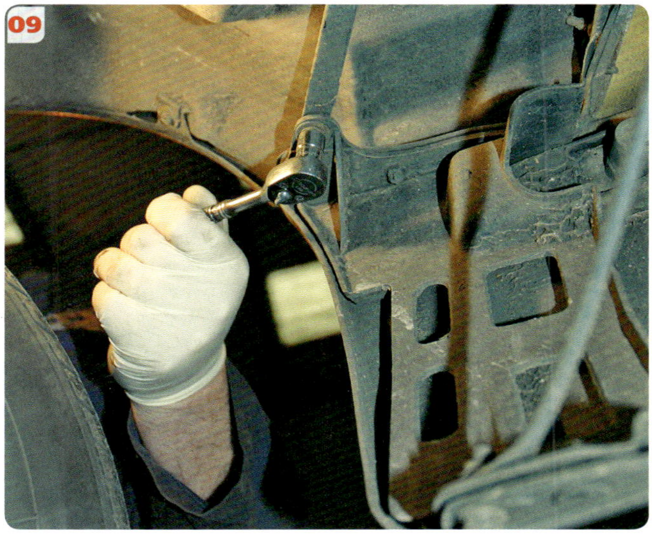
09

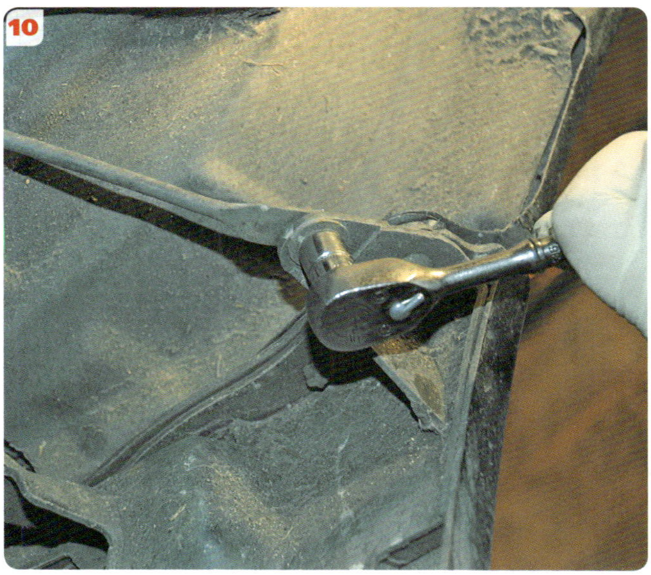
10

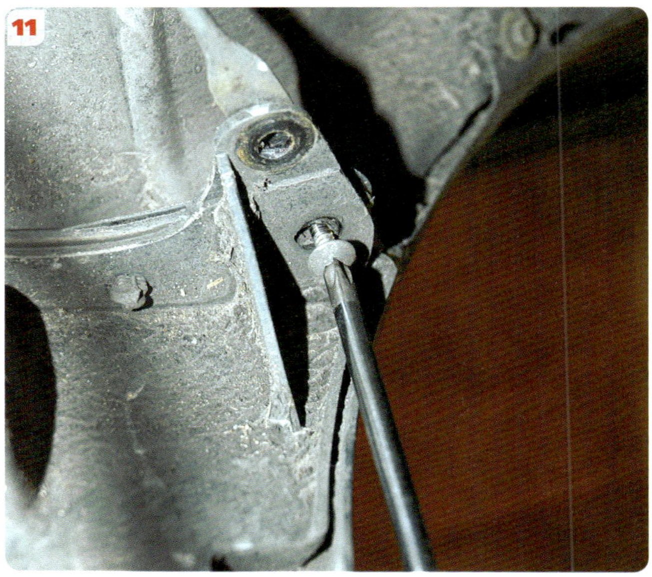
11

the way, it's easier to remove the liners completely – and essential if you are planning to remove the wing later. Each liner is held around its circumference by a series of cross-head screws (the one with a flat plastic block underneath is for the mudflap and will come out with an 8mm socket if it's tight), plus there are two more well inside the wheelwell, one on the lower underside of the wing and one more at the front corner of the liner.

With the liner out of the way, you'll be able to see (or feel) the two angled studs, with 10mm nuts on. Remove these (you'll need a very short ratchet spanner, or a ring spanner and lots of patience **12/13**).

Under the front of the car, remove the two or four 12mm bolts holding the nose-cone integral brackets to the bottom air duct **14**. Now unscrew the three plastic cross-head screws from the air intake, pull out the plastic 'spreaders' that secure them to the car **15**, and the whole nose will now pull forward off the car revealing the metal bumper beam behind **16/17**. If you find this is badly bent, the metalwork behind it is twisted or the inner wings are creased, it's time for specialist help.

Refitting of the nose-cone is quite straightforward – just reverse the removal procedure.

FRONT WING RENEWAL

The front wings (fenders) are bolted on and can be changed quite easily once the nose-cone is off (see previous section). New wings are available direct from Mazda, so, if yours are accident-damaged or suffering from rust, consider changing them. You'll need to get them painted, best done before they are fitted to ensure full paint coverage – though you have to be very careful to avoid scratching them when fitting. One solution is to cover the main areas with bubble-wrap and secure it with masking tape which won't pull off your new paint.

Removing the old wing

Before you start, remove the indicator side repeater lamp, by inserting a small screwdriver into the slot at its rear, 'springing' the plastic retaining tab and withdrawing the lamp from the wing **01**. Disconnect the bulb holder and push it back though the lamp mounting hole, letting it fall back through the wing.

If you have not yet removed the wing-liner, undo the remaining cross-head screws that hold it in place, and remove it.

On each wing there are three 12mm bolts along the top inner edge, one 10mm bolt at the front, accessible after the nose-cone has been removed **02**, and one at the rear bottom edge of the wing under the car. There's one more holding the top rear corner of each wing, accessible with the door open **03**, plus one buried in the wing about half-way up the door pillar, accessible from the wheelarch with a long extension **04** – you don't need to take the wheel off. Remove the front and rear bolts first, then the top three, and work the wing loose. If it won't come off easily, check that you haven't accidentally left a bolt done up.

Fitting the new wing

Don't fit the new wing until you have first painted and undersealed at least the inside faces to protect from corrosion damage, and let it thoroughly dry. Then run a bead of silicon sealer down the top and rear mating faces on the car where the new wing will meet the rest of the body. Make sure you will be able to reach the wiring for the indicator side-repeater light (if you're not sure, tie a length of string to it and bring this through the light's mounting hole from rear to front so you can pull it into place once the wing is on).

Fit the wing into position, and fit the mounting bolts loosely, allowing you to move the wing about until it lines up with the door, bonnet and headlight cover. When you're happy with the fit, tighten the fixing bolts and try the nose-cone into place, having a helper support it while you get the first bolts in – but leave them loose until you have refitted the wing-liner and checked the nose-cone for fit. The important thing is that the wing lines up with the bonnet and door, that the nose-cone lines up with the wings, and then that the headlight covers line up with both.

Finally, reconnect the wiring to the side repeater lamp and push it back into place, and refit the nose-cone, lights and numberplate.

01

02

03

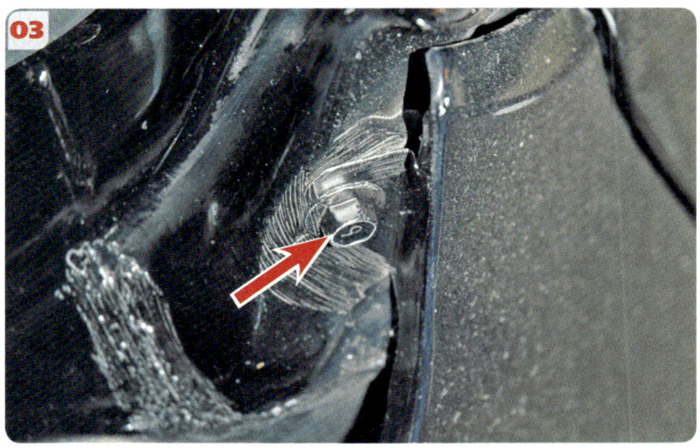

04

SEAT REMOVAL AND REFITTING

Removal

MX-5 seats are held down by four 14mm bolts and are very easy to remove – but be warned; unusually the bolt heads are slightly tapered, so ideally use a close-fitting hexagon socket rather than a 12-pointer.

Pull off the plastic caps that hide the bolts and the ends of the runners **01** then, with the seat slid fully back, remove the front pair of bolts **02**. Then slide the seat fully to the front of its runners, tilt it forward and remove the rear bolts **03**.

If you have a Eunos, which has speakers built into each headrest, you'll see a wire trailing out of the back of the seat and disappearing underneath. Lifting the seat slightly gives enough room to reach underneath and disconnect the plug **04**. Then you can lift the seat out of the car **05**.

Reaching the speakers is easy. Unzip the seat covering from around the head restraint and pull it and the foam behind it to expose the speakers **06–08**.

Refitting

Refitting the seats is easy too, because there are tapered locating plugs at the front of the seat runners that drop into holes in the floor. Once the pegs are located, the seat runners' bolt holes will line up with the captive nuts in the floorpan.

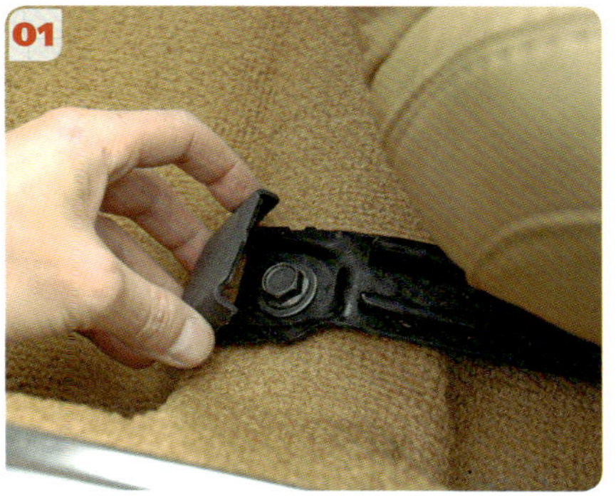
01

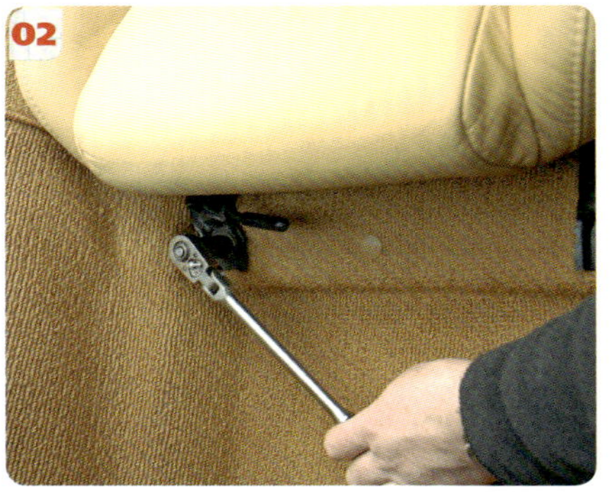
02

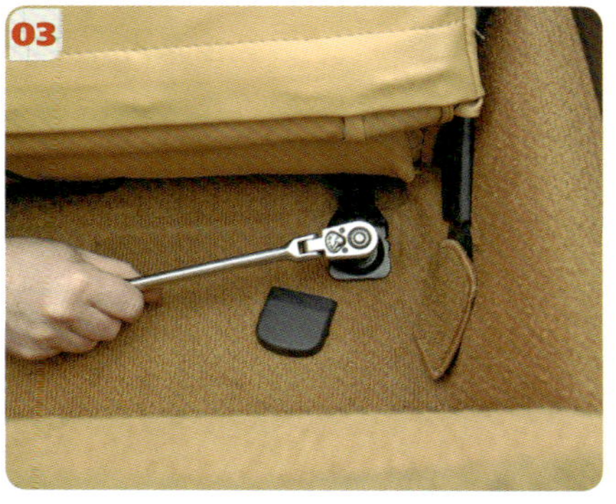
03

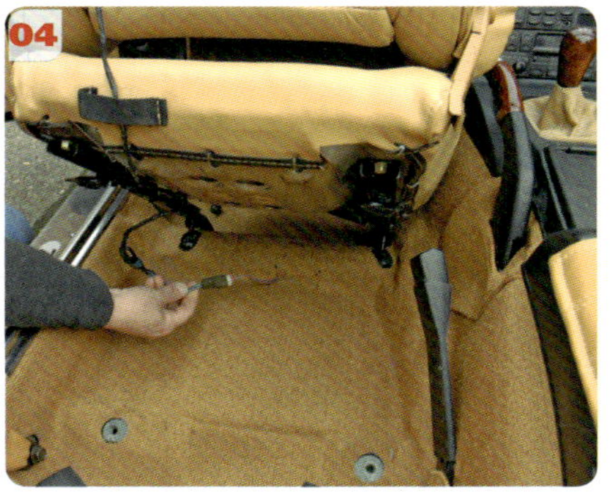
04

05

06

07

08

INSTRUMENT POD REMOVAL AND REFITTING

This needs to be removed if you want to change the dial faces for a different style or colour, to convert an imported car to read mph rather than kph, or if any of the instrument bulbs have blown and need changing **01**.

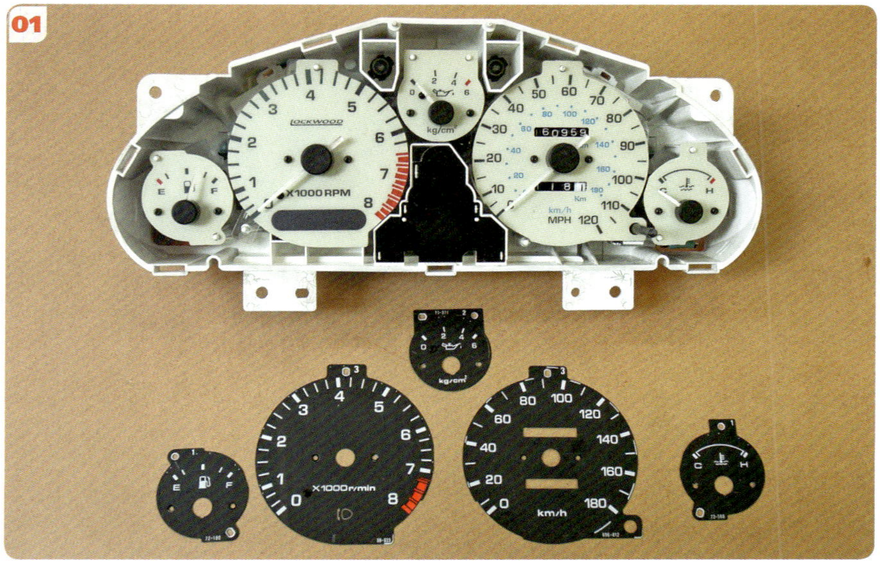

01

Removal

You can do this most comfortably sitting in the driver's seat, with the seat fully back.

Remove the ignition keys, then undo the four screws holding the two halves of the steering column shroud together **02**. Three are self-tappers located high up in tunnels – you'll have to work by feel to find them with the screwdriver. The fourth (a visible one) is a machine screw that is threaded into the bottom of the steering lock casting – don't mix them up when you come to refit them.

Separate the top and bottom halves of the column shroud – they're clipped together – and put them somewhere safe **03**.

Undo the two screws holding the bottom of the instrument shroud, one near each lower corner **04/05**. Then, grabbing the front lip of the shroud, pull it back to remove it from the car **06**. One of two things will most likely happen. If you're lucky, one or more of the three plastic/metal clips that hold the back of the shroud to slots in the top of the dashboard will break off **07**.

02

03

04

05

06

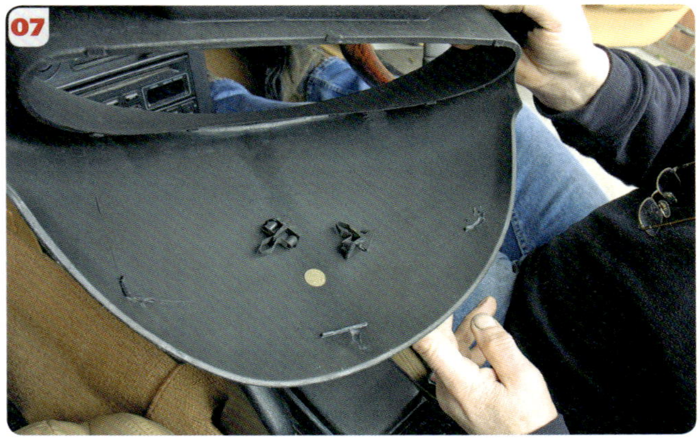

07

This doesn't matter, and MX-5s survive quite happily without them. If you're unlucky, the rear portion of the instrument shroud will break off. This is more likely on cars that have spent years out in the sun, making the plastic brittle. If you're really lucky, the shroud and its tags will survive intact. But then you might also win the lottery.

Now undo the four screws that hold the instrument pod to the dashboard **08**. With the pod pulled slightly away from the dashboard, you can reach in and unplug the electrical connectors, one each side **09/10**, then pull the binnacle a little further out to disconnect the speedo cable. Inevitably the plastic clip that secures it will be on the underside of the connector, and this job may take three minutes or forty-five **11**. Twisting the connector at the cable end usually frees it but, if you're having no luck, try asking somebody with smaller hands and wrists to give it a go. Don't be frightened of reconnecting the cable – it's much easier because the connector just pops into place.

If you're simply replacing blown bulbs, they are a bayonet fit into the back of the instrument pod, and a twist and a pull

08

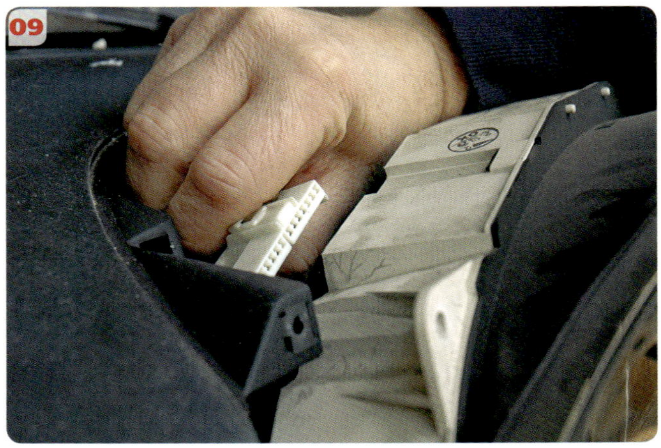

09

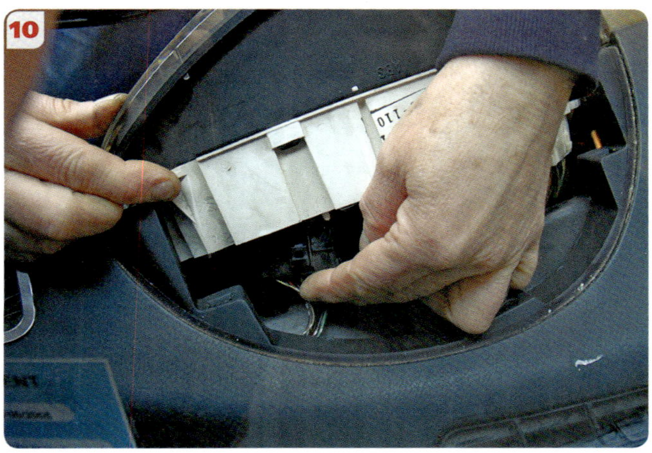

10

11

will remove them – be careful not to damage the delicate printed circuit on the back of the pod.

If you're changing the dial faces, transfer the instrument pod to the bench or the kitchen table and separate the front screen from the white plastic body by releasing all the black plastic tangs with a small screwdriver **12**, working your way around and gently levering the two halves apart **13**.

If you want to remove the dial faces, mark the positions of the gauge needles on the faces, so you have a reference to get them back in the same place. Then prise off each needle with two small screwdrivers **14** – they will simply pull off by hand, but this method is kinder to the spindles.

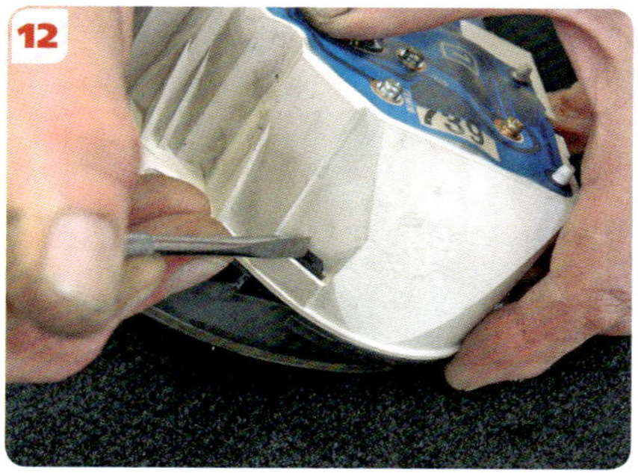
12

13

The faces are held on to each instrument by two small cross-head screws, so, using a small jeweller's screwdriver or similar, unscrew them and lift off the faces **15**.

14

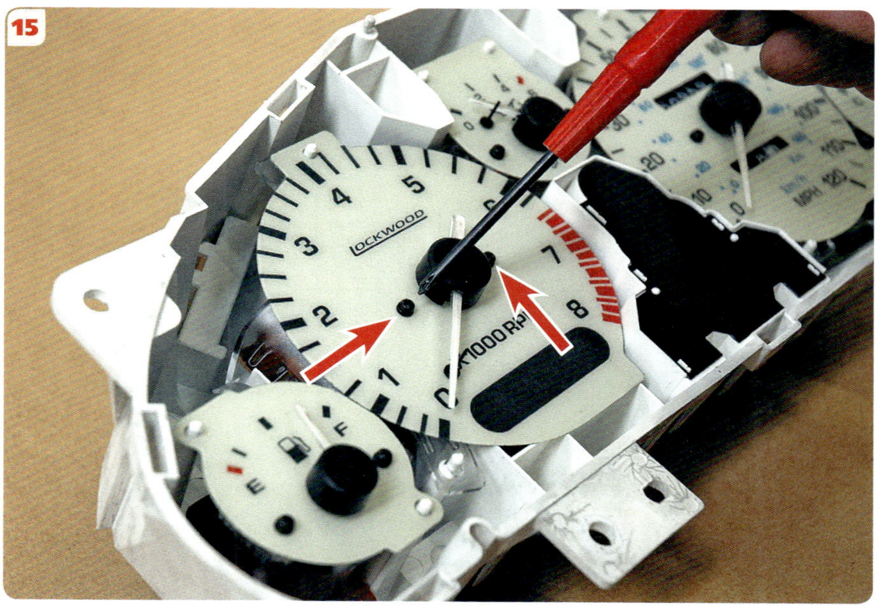
15

Refitting

Position the new faces, then refit and tighten the securing screws. Using the marks you made on the old faces for reference, gently push back the needles in exactly the same places. If you don't, the gauges will lie to you.

Once you are satisfied everything is on in the right place, clip the front screen and its frame back to the instrument pod and refit to the car – reconnect the electrical plugs first, then pushing the pod back to align the locating pegs and holes will 'pop' the rear of the speedo drive into its housing on the end of the cable. Refit the four screws that hold the pod, then refit the instrument shroud – if the securing clips broke off when you removed it, a little Blu-Tack under the back edge will hold it in place and stop it rattling.

Refit the steering column shrouds, making sure you don't mix up the screws. The machine screw is the one that goes in at lower mid-left, and is the only one whose head is visible when the shrouds are refitted **16**.

Road test the car to make sure all the instruments work.

16

ELECTRIC WINDOW PROBLEMS

Though the MX-5 is mechanically robust, some cars suffer from problems with the electric windows. You can help these out by keeping their sliding channels clean, plus giving them a periodic spray with WD-40 (using the fine red pipe that comes with the can to concentrate the spray area). But the mechanisms aren't easily fixable, and if they fail, wholesale replacement is the surest solution.

First, though, check that it's the motor, or more likely the mechanism, that's at fault. If both windows failed simultaneously, suspect the power window fuse in the main fusebox mounted in the footwell by the driver's knee.

If a lifting cable is broken or detached, chances are that it'll be poking up past the window seal outside the door, or you'll see it hanging down once you get the door trim off.

If one window has failed and there are no obvious mechanical problems, you can check if its switch is faulty by checking for continuity through it in various positions with a multi-meter. The only way to the switch and its six-terminal electrical connector is to lift the centre console. This is held down by screws, one under the ashtray, one in the storage compartment and one each side at the front.

An easier check, once you get the door trim panel off, is to disconnect the lift motor's electrical connector, and check with a test lamp to see if power is arriving at the connector with the ignition on and the window switch operated. If not, the switch or its wiring is faulty. A final check, using a 12V battery and small jump leads, is to apply power to the motor side of the connector and see if the motor tries to turn.

If the motor or mechanism has failed, a cheaper alternative to the original type is a worm-drive lifter, but the procedure for changing either type is roughly the same – the main difference is that the worm-drive type has fewer mounting bolts, but either will take about half a day to change.

RENEWING A WINDOW LIFT MECHANISM

Removing the old mechanism

Sitting on the sill or the edge of the seat with the door fully open gives the most comfortable working position. First remove the armrest, held on by three cross-head screws. The top front one is covered by a small plastic cap that you need to prise out first **01–03**. Then remove the screw from the inner door handle cover and lift out the cover **04/05**.

Carefully prise off the plastic loudspeaker cover from the bottom front corner of the door **06**, then pull the trim from the frame **07/08** – it's held by plastic poppers – and lift it off the top of the door. Unscrew the securing screws, then lift the loudspeaker from the bottom of the door **09**. Disconnect the wiring plug.

What's left on the door will be a one-piece clear plastic watershield membrane held on by sticky black 'gloop' around its edge. If you're careful, you'll be able to peel the watershield away from the door, saving it for re-use. Alternatively, you can carefully slice through the membrane **10** and tape it up later when you replace it.

Remove the three screws that hold the inner door handle to the door frame **11**, and peel the watershield over it **12**. Then undo the three 10mm cross-head

01

02

03

04

setscrews that secure the glass to the slider **13**. Undo the two 10mm bolts that hold the window stops, and catch the curved brackets **14/15**.

Then slide the glass up out of the door and store it somewhere safe **16** – not on the ground where it'll get stepped on. Then you can move on to removing the old window-lift mechanism. Unbolt the two 14mm bolts under the bottom edge of the door **17** and the two at the top of the door that hold the regulator **18/19**.

Remove the three 10mm bolts towards the front of the door that hold the electric motor in place **20/21**. Separate the electrical connector **22**, then feed the whole mechanism out through the speaker hole **23/24** – there are also a couple of plastic clips supporting the lifting cables whose heads will need squeezing and pushing back from the door before you can release the mechanism. Cut the wiring off the old motor **25**, because you'll need the connector again.

05

06

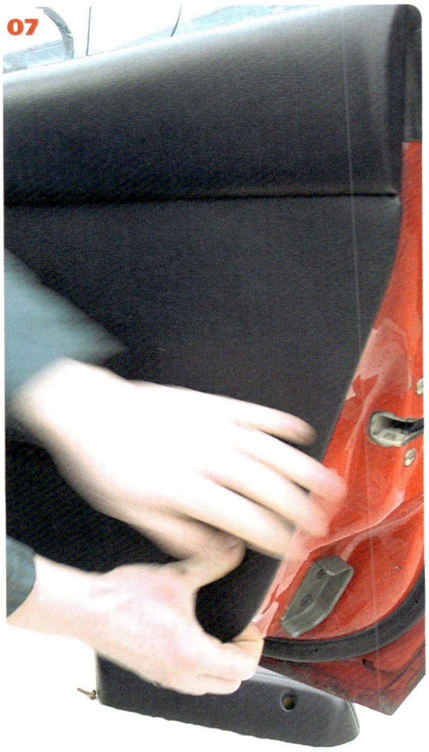

07

08

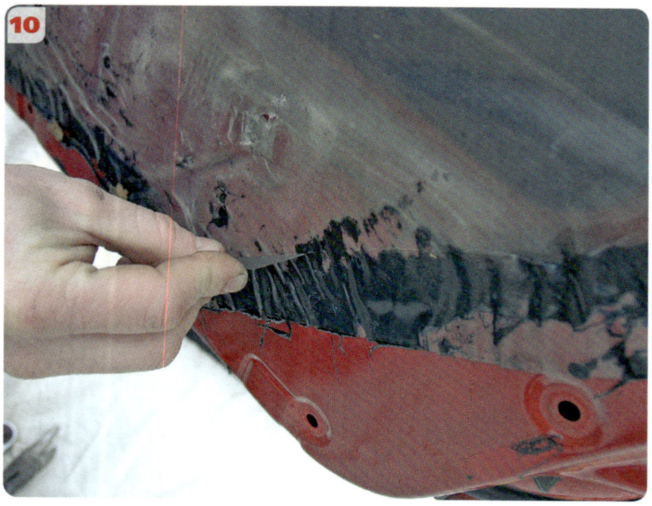
10

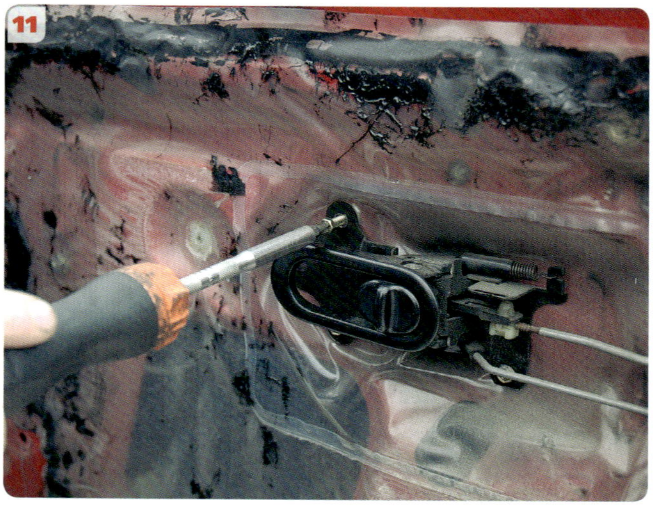
11

12

13

14

15

16

17

18

19

20
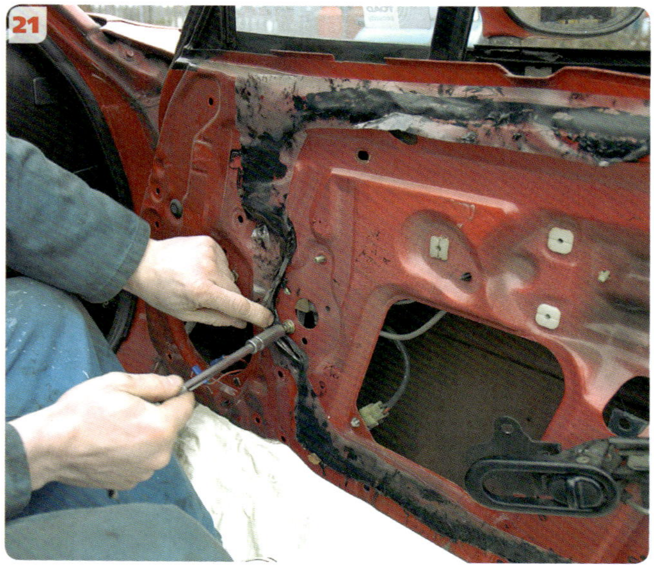
21
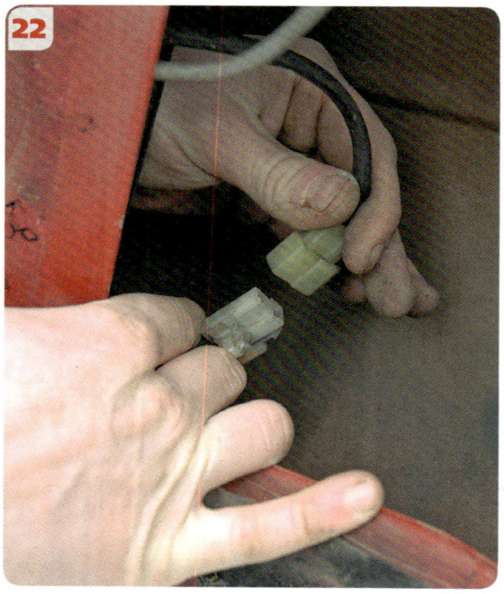
22
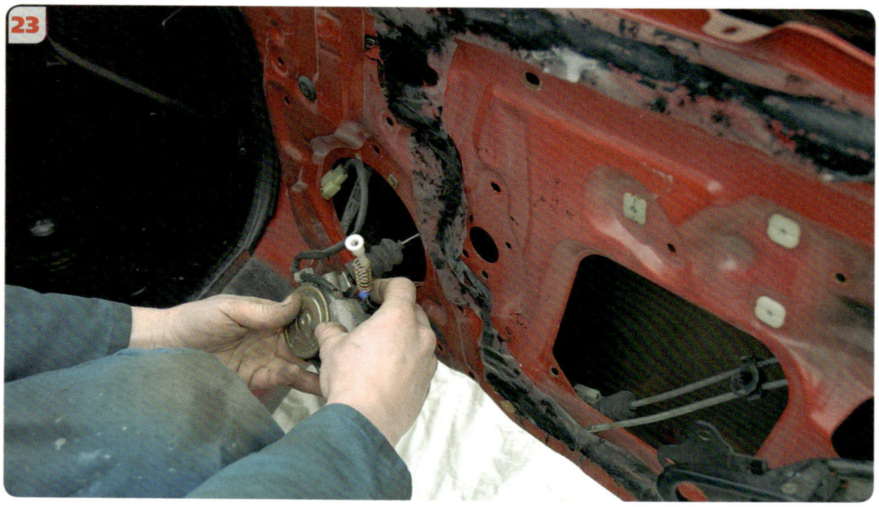
23

24
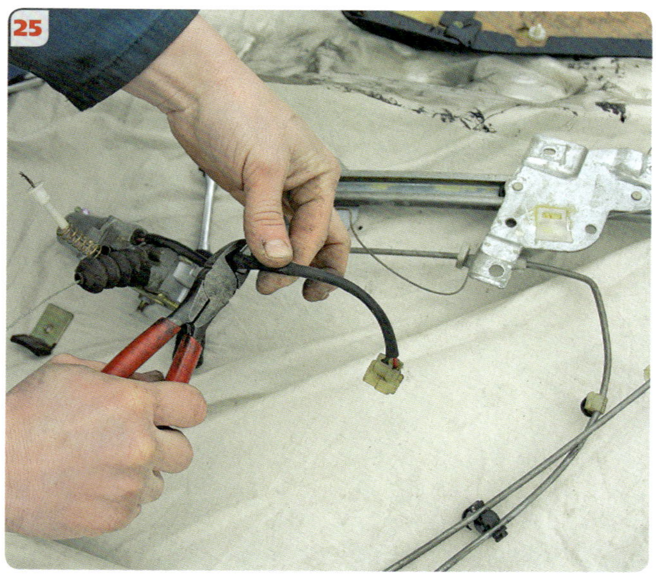
25

Fitting the new mechanism

Pass the new lifter through the middle hole in the door **01/02**, and locate the top of the lifter rail at the top of the door **03**; fit its 14mm bolt so it is snug but not tight **04** (note that the new mechanism is secured by a single bolt at the top). The motor is supported by two cranked s teel straps that bolt to two of the original mounting holes – nuts aren't needed because the holes in the straps are internally threaded **05/06**.

Strip an inch of insulation from the end of the wires you cut off the motor earlier, and from the wires attached to the new motor. Temporarily connect the wires by wrapping them together, then connect the electrical plugs **07**. This is to check that the wires are connected the right way round. With the wires held apart so they cannot touch, turn on the ignition and operate the window switch to test which way the lifter goes. If up gives down, turn off the ignition, undo the wires and reverse the connections.

Now refit the glass **08** – you'll need to help the plastic clips past the window seal with a small screwdriver **09** – then make sure the plastic guides attached to the glass engage with the slider channels. Fit and tighten the three 10mm cross-head setscrews that secure the glass to the lifter – there are nylon mounting pads, but don't overtighten. Two are accessible through the largest hole in the door, and there's a slot in the door inner so that you can reach the

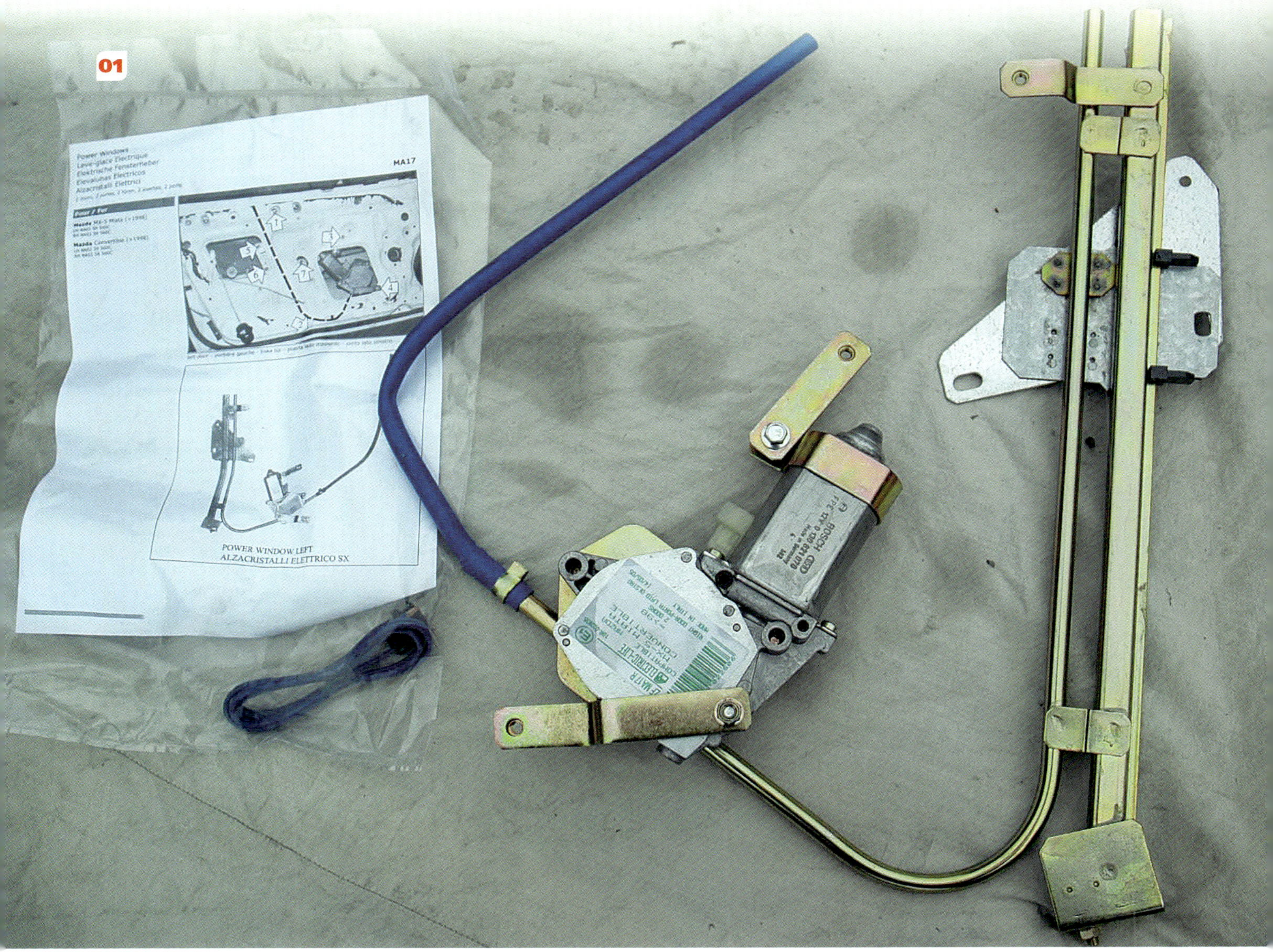

forward one **10/11**. Turn on the ignition and lift the window so that its top edge is flush with the top of the door frame, then refit the window stops so that they fit snugly against the plastic bobbins bolted to the glass **12**.

Outside the car, give the vertical window guide channel a spray with WD-40 **13**, test the window's operation once again and then you can permanently connect the wires, preferably by soldering **14**, and insulating with shrink-to-fit tubing (remember to pass it over the wires before connecting them!) or with block connectors. Tuck the wiring neatly inside the door and refit the watershield membrane, taping it back into place if you cut through it.

Refit the inner door handle and its three screws **15**, and push the foam gasket on the operating rods back so it's against the watershield **16**. Reconnect the speaker wires and refit the speaker. Hook the door trim back over the top of the door and clip it back into place **17**, then reattach the loudspeaker cover **18**, the inner door handle cover, which is attached by a single screw **19**, and the armrest **20**. Finally, give the glass a clean.

02

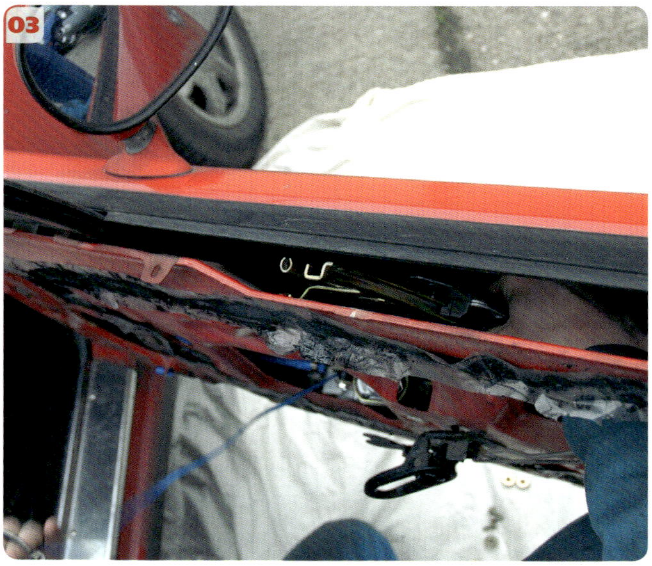
03

04

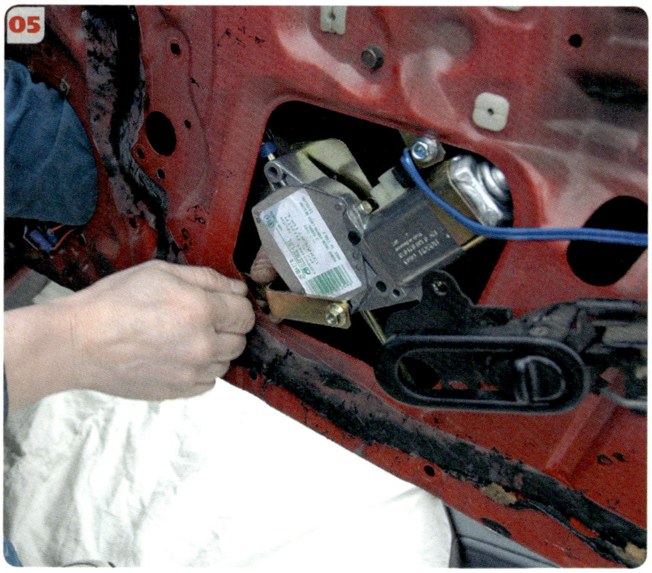
05

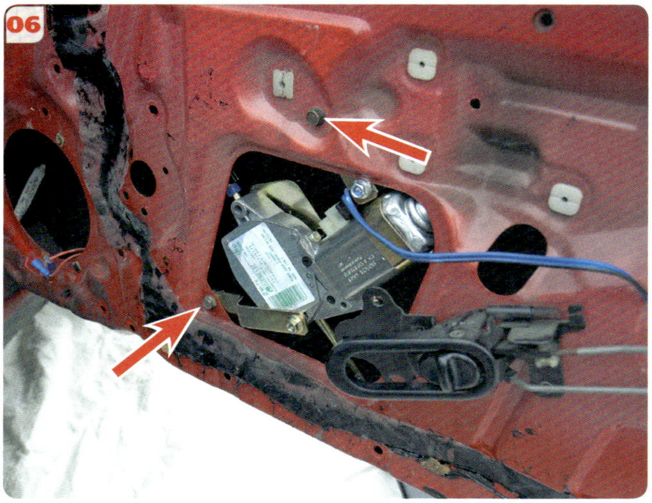
06

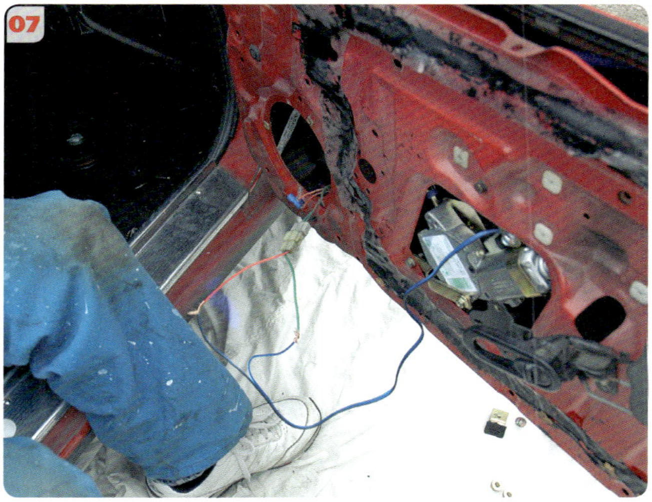
07

08

09

10

11

12

13

14

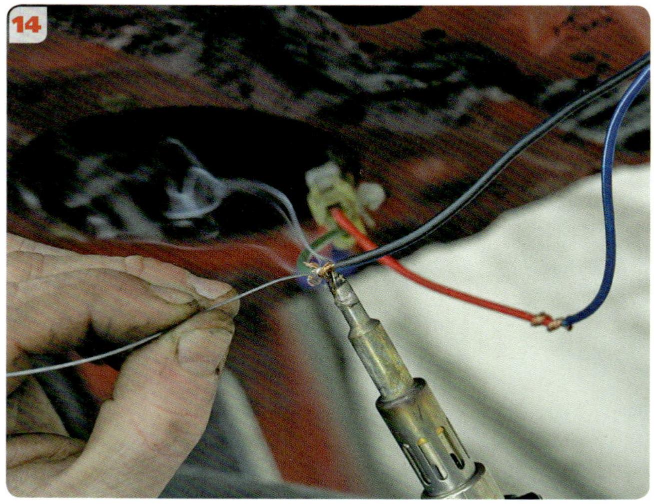

15

16

17

18

19

20

CHAPTER 9

ELECTRICAL SYSTEMS

The MX-5/Miata/Eunos has a conventional negative-earth electrical system charged by an alternator that's belt-driven from the engine. The only peculiarity is that the battery is rather small and, for reasons of space and weight distribution, is mounted in the boot. On Mk1s (NA) it's on the right-hand side of the boot, behind a piece of moulded carpet, and on Mk2s (NB) it's beneath the boot floor.

The fittings and connectors are of high quality and, most of the time, attention to the electrics will be simply a matter of changing blown bulbs and fuses, or cleaning up dirty earth (ground) points – the MX-5 has plenty of them, so before condemning an electrical component as faulty, check all the connections and earths are good.

The electric windows are always pretty slow, but you can ease their passage by keeping their sliding channels clear, and lubricating sparingly once in a while with WD-40. If they pack up completely, check or change them as described in Chapter 8.

There are two fuse boxes in an MX-5/Miata/Eunos. One is under the bonnet, on the right front inner wing. This contains the main fuses and relays. The other, containing the auxiliary (but still important) fuses, is mounted in the footwell by the driver's knee – on the left on a Miata, on the right in an MX-5 or Eunos. Clipped inside this fuse box cover is a pair of tweezers to help you remove the fuses – a visual inspection will tell you if any have blown. Some cars also have more relays under the lip at the rear of the left-hand front wing.

Warning: *Most later Miatas and MX-5s are equipped with airbags, which can go off at any time when the battery is connected. If your car has them, it'll have an 'Airbag' warning light that comes on when you turn on the ignition, then goes off. If it stays on, you've got problems, and need to take the car to a dealer or specialist to have the problem investigated. Therefore, when carrying out any major work on the electrical system, or near the airbag, turn the ignition switch off and disconnect the negative battery terminal. Wait at least two minutes before starting work (the system has a back-up capacitor that needs to discharge before the system is 'safe').*

If any of the instrument bulbs have blown, or if the instrument panel illumination at night is patchy or not what you think it ought to be, you'll need to remove the instrument pod or cluster as described in Chapter 8. It's a lot of hassle just to change a couple of tiny bulbs, but once you reach them they need only a simple twist to pull out, then the faulty bulb can be pulled from its holder and replaced. You then have an hour or so of reassembly work before you can drive the car.

Try not to worry about the main 'brain' or PCM (Powertrain Control Module), which lives either in the left-hand footwell under the carpet and a steel cover, or behind the passenger seat behind the carpet trim, depending on market. It is designed to last the life of the car and very rarely goes wrong. If yours has stopped working and/or is displaying fault codes (see Chapter 5), first try disconnecting and reconnecting the connectors a few times, to see if a build-up of dirt or a poor connection has been preventing signals from getting through. The power going through these connections is minute and it doesn't take much to stop it. You need to unclip the connectors before you can release them – and pull on the plastic connector blocks, not the wires. Working the connectors a few times can sometimes clean up the metal enough to make a good connection again.

TIP

If the car has gone completely dead, most likely after a jump-start, check the main fuse. This is the black square one in the middle of the fusebox mounted on the right inner wing. Also check the 'BTN' fuse, plus the 'ROOM' fuse in the fuse box by the driver's knee.

BATTERY

01

02

Warning: *Make sure you have the code for the radio/stereo before you disconnect the battery or pull a main fuse, otherwise it won't work afterwards.*

This is mounted in the boot – easily visible above the floor on Mk1s **01** and below it on Mk2s. One of the crucial things to check is that the battery overflow/vent pipes are still in place, discharging under the car. These sometimes get missed when a battery is changed, with the result that the battery overflows inside the car, resulting in rapid corrosion in the battery area. The original battery is gel-filled and sealed, so no topping-up is possible, but if your car has a replacement battery which has removable covers in the top, the electrolyte can be topped up, if low, with de-ionised water.

It is recommended that you disconnect the battery before starting any work on the electrical systems (other than changing bulbs and auxiliary fuses). Always disconnect the earth (ground) cable, from the negative terminal first. Unless you're removing the battery, there's no need to disconnect the positive cable.

Pull back the battery's cover and release the terminal from the negative post of the battery **02** – this is the inaccessible one nearer the outer skin of the car. Be very careful not to short the spanner or wrench against the positive terminal – if you do you'll get a very exciting flash and possibly a burn. The positive terminal should be protected by a plastic or rubber cover in any case. If you're going to remove the battery, first remove the spare wheel next to it by undoing the plastic wingnut that secures it to the boot floor. Disconnect the battery positive terminal next, then undo the two nuts securing the battery's clamp bar, and remove the bar and its hooks, taking care not to short it across the bare battery terminals. Disconnect the drain pipes and lift out the battery – careful, it might be small but it's heavy. Check the plastic tray under the battery to make sure it's intact, and that there's no corrosion under or around it.

When you fit the new battery, clean up the terminals and clamps with a wire brush, then smear the clamps and bolt threads with petroleum jelly (Vaseline) to ward off future corrosion. Reattach the drain pipes, then the cables, positive terminal first.

ALTERNATOR

Alternators don't usually deteriorate over a period of time like dynamos – they generally either work fine, or they fail suddenly (in which case the red dashboard warning electrical light will remain on even when the engine is running, and soon the motor will refuse to start or even turn over as the battery's electrical power runs down). Changing a faulty one for a good, maybe second-hand, replacement is the easiest and most cost-effective solution.

Alternator check

Make sure the alternator really is at fault rather than it being a simple problem such as a loose or slipping drive belt, blown main fuse or a partially failed battery, producing less than 12 volts.

If you have a multimeter, which will contain a voltmeter function, you can check the alternator's output. Set the meter to the most suitable DC voltage range – probably 20 volts – and connect it across the battery terminal. It should read 12 volts or just above, with the ignition off or on. Now start the engine and check it again. At idle the voltage should have risen to between 13.5 and 15 volts. If it's still 12 volts, the alternator isn't charging. If it's more than 15.1 volts, the regulator, built in to the alternator, is faulty and needs changing. As a further check, measure the voltages at the large connector post on the back of the alternator, after removing its cover – be careful not to let anything get caught in the drive belts when the engine is running. The readings should be the same as at the battery.

Removing the alternator

The alternator is buried under the inlet manifold on the front right-hand side of the engine. It's most awkward to remove from early 1.6s, and slightly easier on 1.8s. Disconnect the negative earth lead from the battery. Unplug the power steering pressure switch connector, if fitted, the coolant thermoswitch connector (built into the thermostat housing) and the idle air control valve connector (on the throttle body housing, part of the inlet

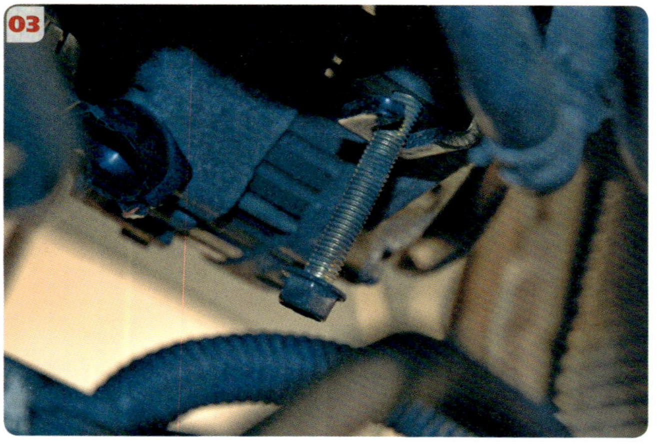

manifold). Then undo the nuts that hold the two leads to studs on the back of the alternator and pull the leads away **01**.

Loosen the alternator's tension adjuster (the sideways-facing bolt) **02/03**, then the clamp bolt (behind the alternator on a 1.6, and facing forwards on a 1.8) and the lower pivot bolt, push the alternator towards the engine and detach the drivebelt. Remove the upper clamp bolt and adjuster bolt and block **04**, and the lower pivot bolt **05**, and remove the alternator **06**.

Refitting the alternator

You will have to transfer the adjustment bracket to the replacement alternator and maybe the pulley too. If you don't have the puller you'll need for this, ask if the store you are buying the alternator from will swap the pulley over for you.

To refit, with the adjustment clamp loosely in place, place the alternator in position and fit the pivot bolt, followed by the adjustment bracket-to-engine bolt, but don't tighten them yet. Fit the drive belt – use a new one if there are any signs of cracks or wear on the old one – and tension it using the adjuster bolt until the maximum play on the top run is about 10mm, then tighten all the other bolts and reconnect the plugs and cables.

Make sure the ignition light goes out once the engine starts, and/or retest the system with a voltmeter to make sure it is now charging correctly.

WIPER MOTOR

The MX-5/Miata wiper mechanism is fairly simple, and accessible by modern standards, which is lucky because specialists say failures aren't unknown. The motor lives in the rear left corner of the engine bay on right-hand drive cars **01** and in the right-hand corner on left-hand drive cars, at the base of the windscreen, and the cranking mechanism is mostly visible between the two bulkheads (firewalls). If your motor isn't working, or there's excessive slop in the bellcrank joints on which the wipers move through their arcs, consider changing the parts for second-hand ones from a vehicle dismantler instead of going to the expense of replacing with new.

Note: *When checking the motor, to avoid scratching the windscreen (windshield) by repeatedly dragging dry wiper blades across it, lift the wipers clear of the screen, so long as they'll clear the open bonnet. If they won't, wet the screen first to lubricate the wiper rubbers.*

Wiper motor check

If the wipers are not working, first check the 20amp fuse in the interior fusebox – it's the top right one, which you can see without removing the fusebox cover, but to do so you'll have to get your head right down in the footwell by the clutch pedal. To reach it, you'll probably have to climb upside-down head-first into the footwell with your legs over the backrest. If you're not up to such contortions, get a thin adolescent to help. He or she will find they need to remove the cover anyway, as clipped to the back of it are the tweezers you need to pull out the fuse. If the fuse has blown, replace it. If it blows again, there's a short-circuit, most likely in the motor. You can also check whether the wiper motor or the wiring to it is at fault by using a length of wire long enough to reach from the motor feed terminal to the power terminal at the left front of the engine bay.

First, disconnect the main plug supplying power to the wiper motor. Then connect the jump wire to the power terminal (it's under a blue cover that simply pulls off) and touch the wire to the outer of the two top terminals in the connector block on the motor. The motor should run at low speed. Then touch the wire to the other top terminal. The motor should run at high speed. If the motor runs, you have a problem in the wiring or switch, which will need further investigation.

Removing the wiper motor

If the motor doesn't run, you'll need to replace it. First, remove the black plastic cover over the cranking mechanism. This is held by cross-head screws at the lower edge of the windscreen, one more screw to the inner wing and a couple of clips. Underneath, you'll find the cranks. Disconnect the crank arm from the wiper mechanism – it's a press fit into a plastic bush **02**, and needs levering with a screwdriver until it pops out.

Disconnect the motor wiring plug **03**, then unbolt the three bolts that hold the motor to the forward bulkhead **04** – one holds an earth lead – and remove the motor **05**, feeding its cranking arm through the hole in the bulkhead.

On left-hand-drive cars to make room to get the wiper motor out, you'll first need to move the fusebox out of the way, after undoing the two 10mm nuts that hold it to its mounting studs.

When you refit the motor, don't

forget the earth lead that goes under the lower inner bolt. The three wiper motor securing bolts need to be just nipped up hand tight with a short spanner. Squeeze the motor's cranking arm back into the wiper mechanism, then refit the black plastic cover and reconnect the wiring block. Make sure the motor works.

If the spindles or gearboxes that support the wiper blades have worn and need replacement, you first have to remove the wiper arms. These are held by 13mm flanged nuts under black plastic covers at the bottom of the blades that simply prise off. After removing the nuts, you'll need to twist and pull the wiper arms to get them off the spindles. The spindle gearboxes are each held by two 13mm bolts – which are hidden by another black plastic trim. This is held by cross-head screws – but these are hidden under black plastic caps that are very hard to remove – they won't prise out from above and the only way to release them is from behind the plastic panel by bending an old thin screwdriver or strip of steel so you can reach the tangs that hold them. Disconnect the cranking mechanisms by snapping the joints apart with a screwdriver.

Refitting the wiper motor

This is the reverse of removal: refit the spindles, cranks, cover, motor if you're changing it, electrical connector. When you reassemble the mechanism, leave the wiper arms off but reconnect the wiper motor plug, then switch the wipers on and off to make sure the spindles are at the 'park' position before you refit the wiper arms. Positioning them should be obvious from the dirt on the screen.

HEADLIGHT MOTOR

Raising a headlight manually

Headlight motors, like the rest of the MX-5, are pretty reliable. If one headlight won't raise or lower, first check that nothing has got stuck in the mechanism – if it's stuck down, first wind it up manually after removing the retractor fuse (see below) and check.

If there's nothing jamming the light, suspect the motor, but first disconnect the connector and use a test light to see if power is arriving at the motor. If only one light is affected, suspect a wiring fault.

If both lights fail to raise and lower, it's likely that the fuse or relay has failed. The 30A retractor fuse is in the main fusebox on the right-hand inner wing (on rhd cars), and it's usually green – there's a diagram on the lid to help. The relay lives under the steering column next to the flasher relay, and you need to remove the column shroud to get at it.

If the headlight motor has failed or its power supply has been interrupted, you can raise or lower the light using the winding knob near the back of the light – it lives under a pull-off rubber cover **01**. But if the motor is working, it will fight you and first you need to disconnect the motor's wiring connector, or pull the 30 amp retractor fuse from the main fuse box (as described previously).

Removing and refitting a headlight motor

Warning: *The headlight motors are strong and geared down to give them a considerable mechanical advantage – so be very careful to keep your fingers clear of the light shut when you reconnect the power, otherwise your MX-5 can give you a nasty bite. This has happened to Steve Chapman at Sam Goodwin MX-5 Specialists, and he says it's not pleasant trying to beat the headlamp off while simultaneously scrabbling around to try to part the connector again so it lets go.*

To change a motor, first remove the 30 amp retractor fuse from the main fusebox on the right-hand inner wing (on rhd cars) and manually raise the light if it is closed. Unplug the electrical connector next to the headlight – the female part stays attached to the car. Using a flat screwdriver, prise off the bellcrank that raises the light unit, then undo the three 10mm bolts than run through the lower part of the motor body. You might need to move hoses or wires so you can withdraw the motor. On the left side, on cars with power steering, you might need to unbolt and move the power steering fluid reservoir.

Don't bother trying to withdraw the motor's mounting bolts – there's no room and they are meant to come away with it. If your replacement motor has none, you'll need to prise off the plastic washers stopping the bolts from falling out, and transfer the bolts to the new motor.

Bolt in the new motor, snap the lifting bellcrank back on and reconnect the electrical connector.

If you need to adjust the closed position of the headlight, the adjuster stop is underneath **02**. Prise off the lifting bellcrank, then adjust the stop a little at a time, checking that the closed headlight lines up with the closed bonnet.

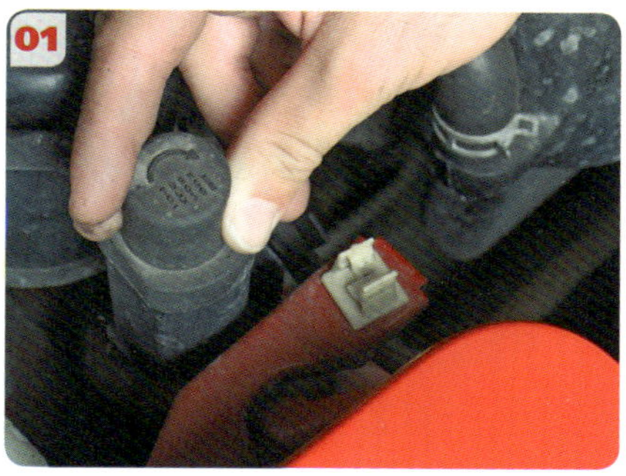

BULB RENEWAL

Headlights

Caution: *Don't try removing headlight bulbs if the lights have been in use in the last five minutes – the bulbs get very hot. And, don't hold the bulb by the glass if there's any chance you'll be re-using it – to get you home when you don't have a replacement, for example. Even the moisture from your fingers will crystallize and shatter the glass envelope once the bulb is up to operating temperature.*

Though many have been uprated to the H4 halogen type, the Mk1 has sealed-beam units as standard – the same as used on older British cars such as Minis – so you can't change the bulbs. If a filament blows, then you have to change the lamp unit.

Start by opening the bonnet, then raising the headlights, using the button on the dash **01**. Undo the crosshead screws that hold the matt-black cover around the light unit, and withdraw it **02/03**.

The headlight is held in by a matt-black trim ring that has three fixing screws. You don't need to remove these completely, because the ring has three slots leading to larger holes that will clear the screw heads. Simply loosen the screws **04**, twist the rim and withdraw it **05**, and the headlight practically falls out in your hand. Catch it in one palm, then pull off the connector on the back.

To fit the new lamp, push on the connector, fit the headlight into its housing, fit the trim ring and twist, then tighten its screws. Refit the matt-black cover and its screws.

On the Mk2 (NB) the lights changed to fixed, moulded units to save the weight of the raising motors. These lights use conventional H4 bulbs, protected from the elements by rubber covers at the back of the light unit. To change or check a bulb, open the bonnet and pull off the rubber cover at the back of the light **06**, then pull the connector off the back of the bulb. Unclip the spring-wire retainer that holds the bulb in and remove it **07** – you should easily be able to see which filament has blown by holding it up to the light.

When you fit the new bulb, make sure the three tangs on its body engage properly with three slots in the lamp unit – it will only fit one way. As a guide, this is when the three spade

01

02

03

04

05

06

07

terminals on the back of the bulb form an inverted U. Clip the spring-wire retainer back under its locating hooks and check the bulb is secure, push the connector back on and then refit the rubber cover.

Sidelights and indicators (combination lights)

These are forward of the headlights, held in by two cross-head screws. Unscrew these until they'll come no further **08** – when the threads begin to bite into their plastic housings you can use them as grab handles to withdraw the light unit **09**. The indicator bulb is in the larger of the two grey bulbholders in the back of the light unit – it's a bayonet fitting, so twist and pull to remove the bulbholder **10**, then push and twist to remove the bulb. The sidelight, the smaller of the two, nearer the outer edge of the car, is a push-fitting. Pull the bulbholder from the grey plastic light unit housing **11**, then you'll find the bulb pulls straight out. The new one just pushes into place.

08

09

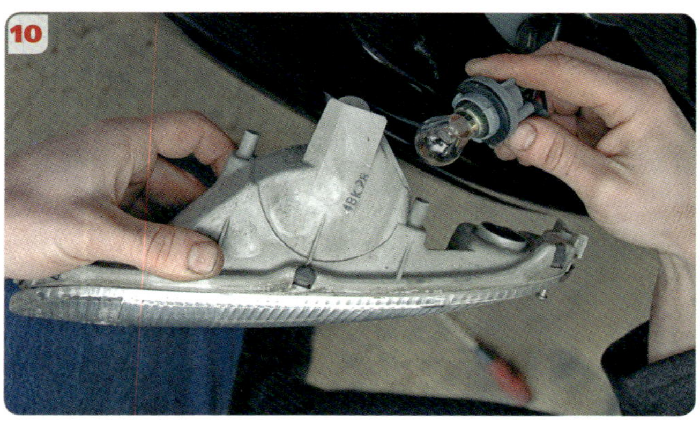

10

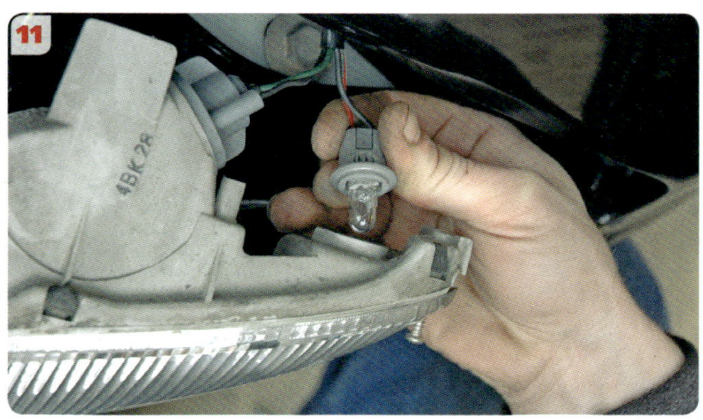

11

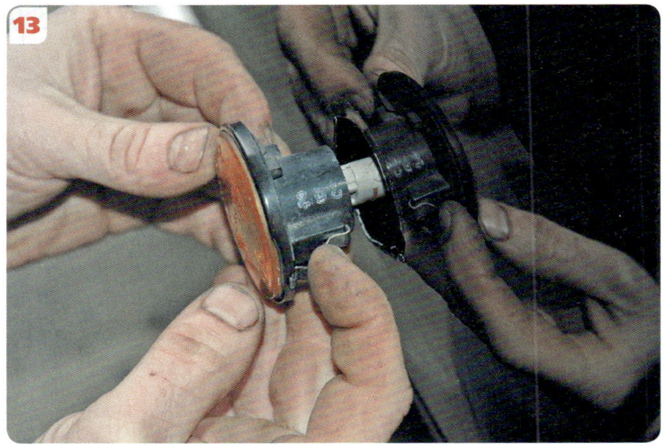

Side repeater indicators

These are push-fitted into the front wings, and retained by a steel spring clip. The slot to release this is at the rear of the repeater, so push in a small screwdriver to retract the spring clip **12**, being careful not to damage the surrounding paintwork, and prise the light unit out of the bodywork **13**. The bulb holder is a bayonet fit, and then the bulb pulls straight out **14**. When you've fitted a new bulb, and the holder back in place in the light, the light unit push-fits back into the wing until its spring clip snaps into place behind the body panel.

Tail lights

The tail/stop light and reverse light bulbs are held into the back of the tail-lights in a removable white plastic bulb housing. Open the boot (trunk) lid, reach behind the lights and pinch the 'ears' of the white bulb holder together so you can withdraw it **15**. Push and twist each bulb to remove and check it. When you've fitted the new bulb, clip the bulb holder back into its housing. Don't get these mixed up – one is for the stop/tail light, and the other (inner) is for the reverse light.

The indicator (turn) signals are in separate holders at the outer ends of the tail light. Once again, from inside the boot, twist and pull the bulbholder to remove it, then push and twist the bulb to get it out.

To completely remove the tail light, follow the above steps to remove the bulbs, then remove the four 10mm nuts that hold it to the car **16**. The entire light unit will come out backwards – give it a gentle push from inside the boot if it's stuck.

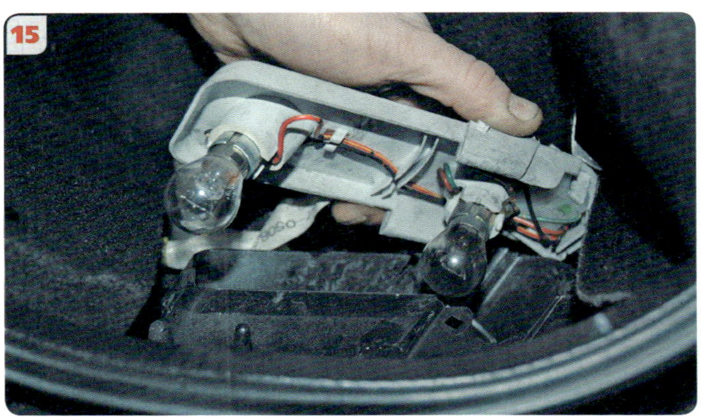

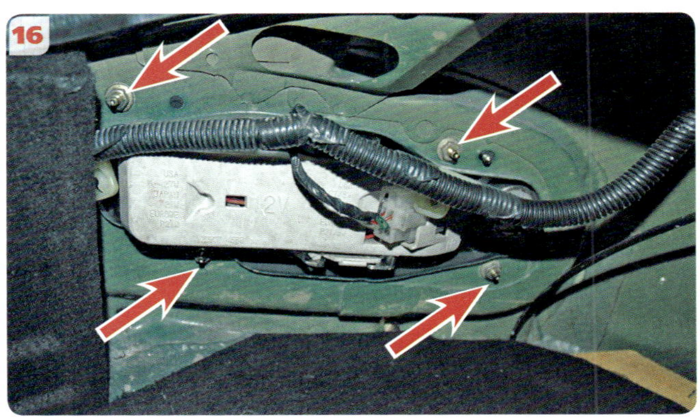

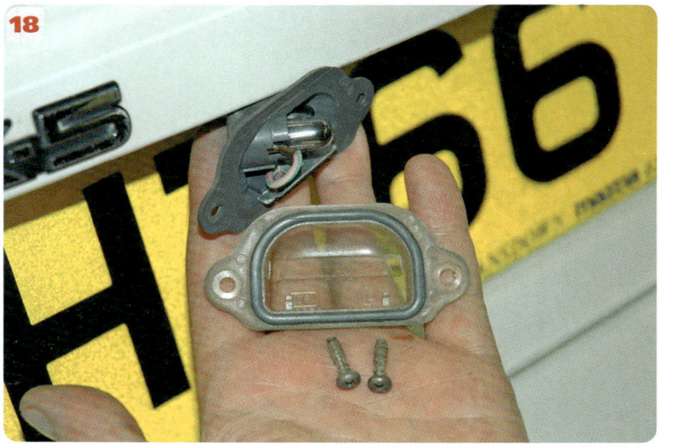

Number plate light

On certain models, the number plate (license plate) light is accessible from inside the boot too – its holder is a bayonet fitting. Twist and pull to get it out, then push and twist the bulb to remove it.

On models where the number plate light is not accessible from the boot, unscrew the two screws above the numberplate securing the light unit in place **17**, then pull off the lens and the light for access to the bulb **18**.

Rear fog light

On imports, the fog light will almost certainly be a square add-on dangling from the back bumper. Undo the two cross-head screws to remove its red lens, then the bulb inside has a simple bayonet fitting – push and twist to remove the bulb.

Side marker lights (where fitted)

Remove the two housing securing screws, pull the light unit from the car, then twist and pull the bulb holder from the back of the light. Pull out the bulb to remove it.

Boot-lid-mounted brake light

On cars with a third brake light in the centre of the boot lid, the bulbholder is a bayonet fitting into the back of its housing, so reach up behind the number plate, grab the bulbholder, twist and remove it. The bulb is held in by a standard bayonet fitting – push and twist to remove it.

Boot light

The boot light bulb sits in the underside of the boot lid – pull to remove, and the new bulb just pushes in to place.

Interior courtesy light

Mounted on the header rail. Prise off the plastic cover, then pull out the festoon bulb inside. You might find it easier to use a small screwdriver to help work it out of its sprung terminals. Push the new bulb into place, making sure it works, then snap its cover back on.

Map reading light

Some models have a map reading light mounted on the passenger's side of the facia, next to the glovebox. To change the bulb, simply prise out the lens and lever out the festoon bulb **19**.

FUSES

Fuse boxes

There are two fuse boxes on an early MX-5 – later cars have an auxiliary fuse box in the boot for the heated rear window and electric aerial, that doesn't apply to the NA. We'll deal with the main ones.

Under the bonnet, towards the rear of the right-hand inner wing (on rhd cars) is what Mazda calls the 'main fuse block'. In it you'll find the fuse box containing the main 80 amp fuse, plus the 'BTN' fuse that powers the engine brain, and the 30 amp headlight retractor motor fuse, which you'll need to temporarily remove if you want to raise the headlights manually. There are also a couple of relays for the cooling fan and fuel injection. This fusebox should have a clip-on black plastic cover that identifies its contents, because there will be minor variations depending on the car's original market.

Inside the car is another fusebox that's very difficult to reach (and even harder to photograph) that Mazda calls 'fuse block No 1'. It's mounted on the outer side of the footwell near the driver's knee and you should be able to see it by kneeling down next to the car with the door open, and peering up under the steering column **01**. However, to reach it, it can be easier lying backwards in the seat with your head in the footwell and your feet over the head restraint. Remove the access cover first – it's held by two cross-head screws and is clipped to the dashboard. This fusebox also has a clip-on black plastic cover identifying the contents, and on the inside a small pair of plastic tweezers should be clipped in place to help remove fuses. There is also provision for a spare fuse. This is where you'll find the fuses for interior lights and instruments, plus the 'room' fuse (located at bottom right of the fuse box). On pre-1996 cars, there should also be, in the centre of the fusebox, a resettable circuit breaker for the heater blower motor.

Also... on some cars you may find extra relays on the inner wing on the opposite side from the underbonnet fuse box.

Fuse renewal

Most fuses on an MX-5/Miata/Eunos are the miniature push-in type, and there's a small pair of plastic tweezers clipped to the inside of the fuse box lid in the passenger compartment to help you remove them without damage. If any circuit has failed, identify its fuse from the diagram on the fuse box cover, pull it out then hold it up to the light or against a light background to inspect it – a blown fuse is obvious because the thin wire between the two spade terminals will be burnt through or missing. Replace the fuse with a new one of the right value – they are colour coded, and the fuse's value is moulded into its plastic housing. If it blows again almost immediately, you've got a problem in the wiring or associated componentry – probably a short circuit, which needs investigating. Don't just fit a bigger fuse or an electrical fire could result and destroy the car.

If the fuse has not blown, but the circuit still does not work, then the bulb or other component at the far end of that circuit is most likely faulty – this may just be a blown bulb. If not, then you may have a wiring problem. The simplest way to check is to identify the terminal at each end – fuse box and component – and temporarily bypass the wire to see if the problem is now solved.

One fuse is very different: that's the main power fuse **02**, an 80amp unit in a square black plastic body, mounted in the middle of the fuse box under the bonnet. This is held each side by a 10mm bolt, each of which also secures a cable. If the car has suddenly gone completely dead and the battery is OK, this is the most likely cause. To remove it, undo the bolts, withdraw the fuse and if it's blown replace it with a new one, making sure you reconnect the wires.

CHAPTER 10

MODIFICATIONS, EXTRAS AND IMPROVEMENTS

There's so much kit on the market with which to improve or modify your MX-5/Miata that it's rare to find two cars exactly the same. Totally standard cars are few and far between, although owners of some of the earliest 1.6s have realised their cars' historical value and are trying to keep them standard.

Because the MX-5 is fundamentally easy to work on, it's easy to swap cosmetic parts and, because it is so well engineered, the chassis can handle extra power easily. Slightly stiffening and lowering suspension is always popular, because it sharpens the handling still further, and makes the car look lower and meaner – but regard a 50mm drop as the absolute maximum, and 25mm more sensible.

In the case of early cars, parts from the later models can often be fitted to confer a performance advantage. Here, the Internet is invaluable, where owners discuss what's possible and whether it works. Whatever you can think of, it's almost certain to have been done before and you can read about it – even a 5-litre Ford Mustang V8 engine swap. And UK company mx5parts.co.uk publishes a league table showing the ten most popular aftermarket parts that it has sold.

HOOD

One of the most popular upgrades is to fit a Mk2 (NB) hood to an NA, because the glass rear window was never offered on early cars. Fitting is just the same, because the cockpit dimensions, including the windscreen frame, are the same on both types. The only difference is that if you want to power the heated rear window that comes with these hoods, you'll need to arrange a power supply. Late NAs are fitted with a power socket by the left-hand rear seatbelt upper mount, and specialists sell the extra piece of connecting loom. If desired, you can simply swap the zip-out rear window panel, but you still need to unbolt the rear of the hood to change it over – refer to Chapter 8 for details.

CABIN

The inside of an MX-5/Miata doesn't quite live up to the fresh and attractive lines of its body – though neat, ergonomic and well put together, it's most often trimmed in unremitting black vinyl, and can be a gloomy place to be. Many owners like to fit add-ons to brighten up the inside, from aluminium gearknobs and handbrake sleeves to a complete leather retrim in contrasting colours **01–04**.

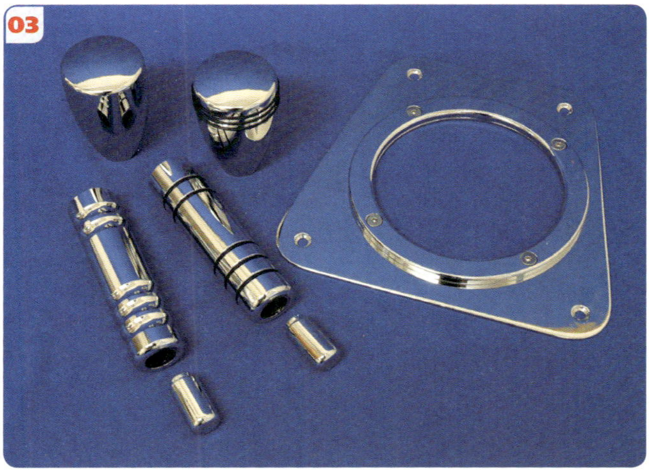
03

04

One of the most popular interior swaps is to fit white coloured dial faces in place of the original matt black. Mazda changed the dial faces to white on the so-called Mk2½, but many other colours are available from aftermarket suppliers **05–07**. They aren't too difficult to fit, though disconnecting the speedo cable can be a matter of trial and error (see Chapter 8). Some of the instrument pod retaining clips will get broken but don't worry – they seem to manage quite happily with a few missing, and new instrument pod tops are available from specialists.

Trim rings for the air outlets in the dash simply glue into place using self-adhesive pads. After cleaning the vent outlet trims with an alcohol wipe, you simply whip off the pads'

05

06

07

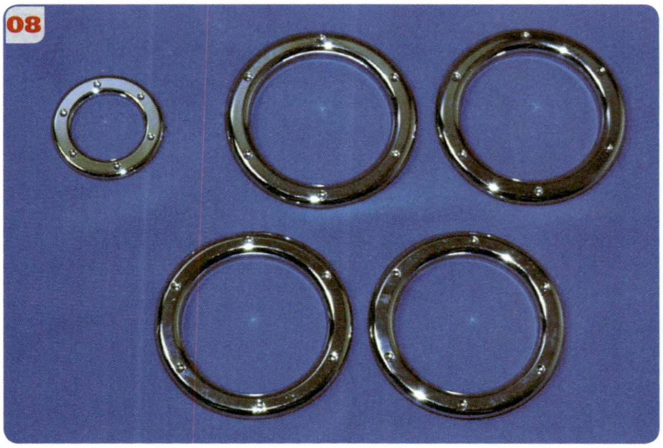
08

09

10

11

12

adhesive backing, and press them into place **08–10**.

Last on the shiny front are roll bars – or, more correctly 'style' bars because they won't do much to protect you in an inversion. These bolt to the upper seat belt mountings **11**. Sometimes, to make them fit neatly, you have to cut a slot in the plastic side trim before the bar mountings will locate properly.

Proper roll cages are available for racing (and advisable even if you're sprinting, hillclimbing or taking part in track days), but the floor will need drilling to mount them, and you may not be able to fit a hardtop afterwards – check carefully with the maker that the soft-top will still fit. Full roll cages also need a rear restraint for the driver's helmet to satisfy RAC Motor Sports Association regulations.

On soft-tops, wind deflectors do a great deal to increase comfort on chilly days. These either bolt to the rear seat belt towers, or sometimes clip to the style bars **12**. And, from specialists, there's a huge range of mats, carpet sets, luggage and branded clothing (see Appendix 2 at the back of this book).

BODY

General

Everything from a hardtop to a bewildering variety of add-on shiny parts can make your MX-5 stand out from the crowd, but make sure it's all for the right reasons.

Glassfibre hardtops are easy to fit and cost about £500 – though you'll have to decide whether or not you want to go to the trouble of removing the soft-top, which is at least half a day's work.

Rear spoilers, as fitted to several special editions, need the bootlid drilling to fit, and will need spraying to match the body. Even alternative nose-cones with alternative sculpting and deeper front spoilers are available for that individual look. Less extreme are extra lips that bolt on under the car's 'chin'. But if you're going to make the body look butch, remember the question of balance – you'll probably need some bigger wheels and tyres to fill the arches better. Slightly lowering the car can have a similar effect.

There are smaller add-ons a-plenty for the MX-5/Miata, from chrome-effect washer jets that push-fit into the bonnet **01** to chrome door handles **02**, and a huge choice of shiny grille inserts **03**, most of which need the tie-down loops, or 'baby teeth', removing first to fit them.

01

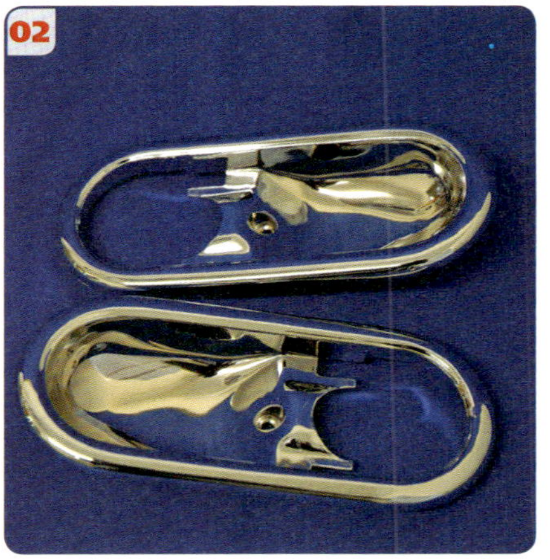

02

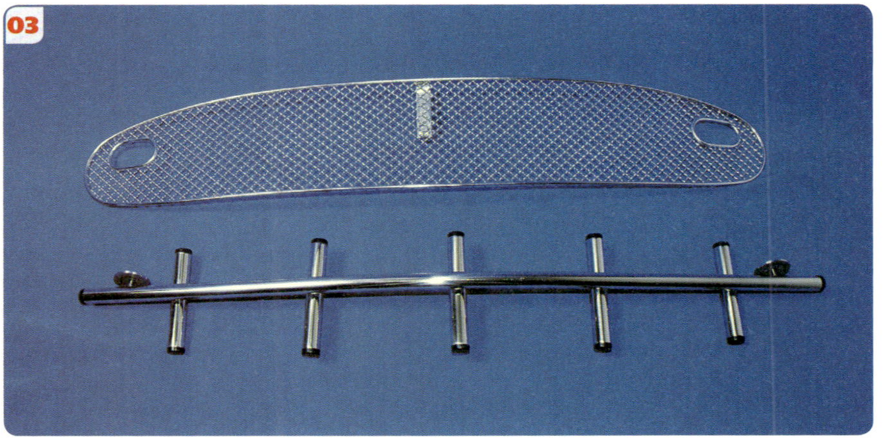

03

Baby teeth

For many owners, especially in the US, removing the 'baby teeth' is considered a rite of passage. These are the tie-down loops fitted in the 'mouth' and are not suitable for towing **04**, so you might as well get rid of them and enjoy cleaner looks and less rust potential. They are attached to the chassis with three 14mm bolts **05**, and you'll need both a socket and an open-ended spanner because access is very tight. The left-hand side can be reached from the front, while the right-hand one is more easily accessible through the right-hand wheel arch.

Colours

Consider colours too – though you might not want or need a full paint job, one way to personalise your car, and sometimes the best way to liven up an insipid all-white one, is with a bold stripe or two running down the middle – think cool American racing colours, not Herbie goes to Monte Carlo. You can add stripes at home using a self-adhesive vinyl kit.

04

05

SECURITY

You can't do much if someone's determined to knife your roof, but a very visible steering wheel lock will act as a deterrent, because the thief won't be taking the car away and may not bother breaking it. There are plenty on the market, from general car accessory stores as well as Mazda specialists.

LIGHTING

Ditching the sealed-beam headlamps from Miatas and Eunos is a good idea. Replacement halogen units cost much the same, they fit straight in place of the old (about 20 minutes per side) and they are the biggest performance upgrade you can make to a standard sealed-beam equipped car. In the UK, Raybrig H4s are popular **01/02**, relatively inexpensive and give a bluish light. In the US, the popular choice is Hella.

For a more radical look, there are low-profile headlights using four projector lamps by Hella **03**. These require more work, because you have to change the headlight stops – the lights open only about half as high as the originals and the stops stop the lamps fluttering at high speed.

Front indicators that incorporate an air scoop are a straight swap **04**, though to make best use of them you'd need to fit flexible trunking from behind them to blow on to the discs – however, MX-5s tend not to run out of brakes.

At the rear, Lexus-type lights are a popular choice **05**, and are very easy to change – the wiring simply unclips, and the lights come rearwards out of the body after removing four 10mm nuts.

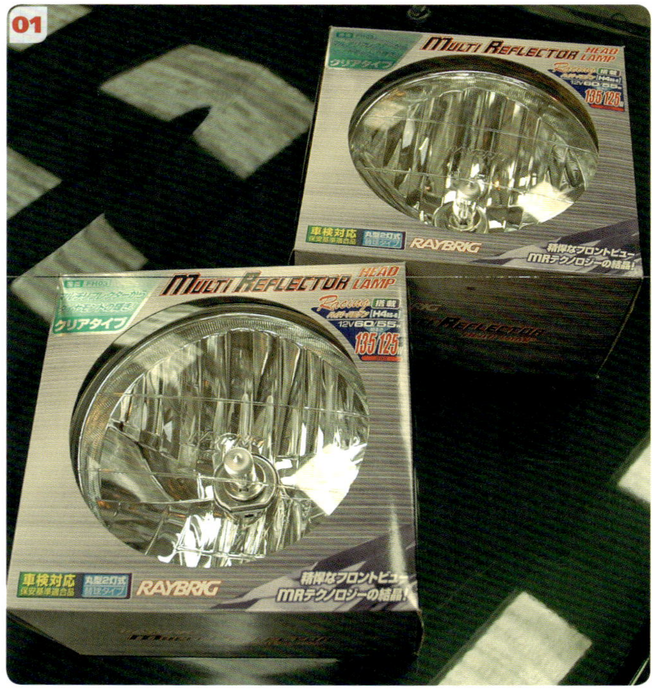

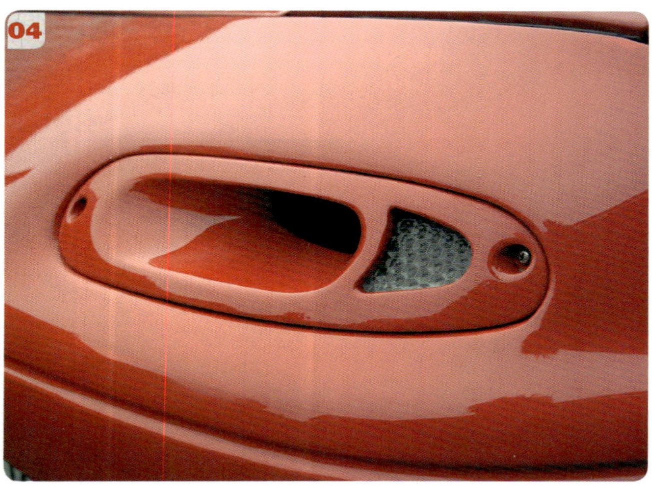

SUSPENSION, WHEELS AND TYRES

Handling

These cars handle brilliantly; or they should. Generally, the suspension is fine as it is, but the cheapest performance mod is a proper four-wheel alignment check and, if needed, adjustment to make sure everything is pointing in the right direction. The factory settings have wide tolerances, so even balancing the car up from side to side should make it feel better. (See the sidebar for factory-recommended settings.)

Let's not forget the difference between grip and handling. Traditional old sports cars had not very much of the former and lots of the latter, which is what made them so much fun – and the MX-5/Miata is entertaining partly because it follows this reasoning. Now, we're not saying that you need to drive sideways everywhere – that would be irresponsible, and besides, it wears out tyres and suspension bushes – just that too much grip can make life a bit boring; witness modern hatchbacks. A car that talks to you, drifts about a little, is a far more entertaining companion than one that just stodgily goes round, its messages masked by too much rubber, both on the wheels and in the suspension joints.

For this reason, many owners like to lower and stiffen the car a little, perhaps adding harder suspension bushes to further sharpen messages, while retaining the standard wheel sizes and investing in a decent set of rubber. MX-5s are not hard on their tyres – unless you're a member of a drift club, in which case you need a second set of wheels and tyres for the rear, to keep costs sane.

When this book was written, adjustable KYB dampers were popular in the UK **01**. They allow owners to easily fine-tune the car to their preferences using an external knob. If you're going to change the dampers, this is the time to change springs and the suspension bushes if needed, because the suspension has got to come apart anyway. This would also be a good time to derust and repaint the wishbones, which become very rusty on older cars, to the extent that they can cause an MoT failure.

Don't lower the car more than 50mm, or it messes up the steering geometry (the steering rack ends up too high relative to the rest of the suspension, causing bump steer). Lowering is best done by changing to shorter springs, or better still, using dampers with adjustable spring platforms. If you decide to cut down your own, remember that shortening a coil spring also stiffens it, because there are fewer coils to deflect – in short, less spring.

Once you've put it all back together (with new, uprated wishbone-to-body bolts – the originals have sometimes been found to twist), you'll need to take it for that four-wheel alignment check. Because suspension height affects wheel alignment, if you normally drive the car alone, ballast it to simulate your weight by placing a sack of spuds on the driver's seat while the suspension is adjusted.

01

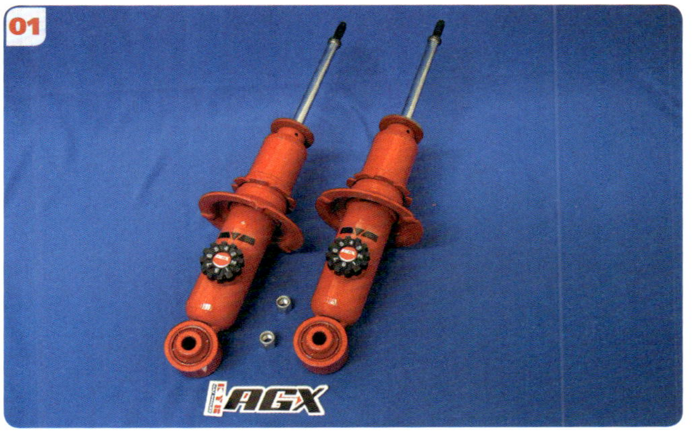

Strut braces

Strictly these should go in the body section, but since a stiff body helps the suspension to work properly, they're here. These are a very popular suspension mod, partly because they're highly visible and easy to fit **02/03**. Basically, they stiffen the chassis/body structure. Mazda progressively added more and more underside bracing tubes as it increased the power output (the later your car, the more you'll have to unbolt to get the exhaust or transmission out), and early cars certainly benefit, especially when stiffer springs or anti-roll bars are used, because they help make the suspension do the work, instead of the body flexing. Flyin' Miata in the US has even developed a whole 'butterfly' brace, covering most of the underside of the floorpan, that is claimed to be the ultimate for rigidity and precision.

02

03

Most conventional strut braces simply bolt between the top damper mounts at each end of the car, their main bars having a threaded adjuster for length to allow for manufacturing tolerances. Get them in aluminium, or a bright colour, and they look good too. If you fit a rear brace to a Mk1 you'll need to relocate the spacesaver spare wheel – though most owners leave it at home and carry a can of tyre gloop instead.

SUSPENSION SETTINGS

Factory-recommended

Front	
Caster	5deg ±1deg
Camber	0–1deg ±1deg
Toe-in	3mm ±4mm
Rear	
Camber	-1–0.5deg ±1deg
Toe-in	3mm ±4mm

Max difference side to side 1.5deg

As recommend by Flyin' Miata for best handling

(FM's Keith Tanner says these won't wear the tyres oddly, even when used on the road.)

Front	*road*	*track*
Caster	-5deg	-4.5deg
Camber	-0.7deg	-1deg
Toe-in	1⁄16in	0
Rear	*road*	*track*
Camber	-1.2deg	-1.5deg
Toe-in	1⁄16in	1⁄16in

Remember that adjusting any suspension parameter will throw the other settings off, so start with rear toe-in and work from there. This is the most critical setting, and not enough of it will make the car very oversteery. Tolerances sometimes stack up, so if you can't quite achieve the ideal settings, at least get both sides the same. Setting the front wheels parallel – i.e. with no toe-in – will liven up the steering feel, but make the car 'darty' on the road.

Wheels and tyres

The easiest way to ruin an MX-5/Miata's delicate, finely balanced handling is to put big wheels and tyres on it. Lightness was key on the original, and for this reason the Mk1 wheels had only seven spokes instead of the traditional Minilite lookalike eight, plus specially-designed Dunlop tyres.

It was all done for lightness and the standard size for a Mk1 1.6 is 6 x 14 with a 185/60 tyre. 1.8s used a 195/50 x 15 tyre and wheel, which fits earlier cars too. The rolling diameter of a standard wheel/tyre combination is about 22.7in. If you increase the overall diameter to anything more than 23.2in, you'll mess up the gearing and the speedo may read inaccurately.

The widest recommended tyre is 195mm, as used on 1.8s. To wear 17in diameter wheels, a Mk1 or Mk2 would have to use 35-profile tyres to retain the standard gearing – and even if they were widely available, they would make the ride harsh.

A couple of other dimensions to remember; the hub flange diameter is 54mm, so whatever wheels you use must match that. The offset used is 45mm and any aftermarket wheel with less probably won't clear the brake calipers, especially if you are running later brakes.

Alloy wheels, when bent, can't usually be straightened, but if they're dull or scruffy they can usually be refinished to as-new or better by specialist companies such as Diamond Styling.

What actual rubber you use is a matter of choice and budget – Dunlop D60 and Yokohama A509 are club favourites in the US. Pressures, like tyres, are a matter of choice – but website consensus is that 28–29psi works well.

BRAKES

You can never have enough brakes and, although the MX-5/Miata's are fine, they were improved (basically, enlarged) as the car developed. So to get more stopping power you can either use brakes from the next model up or, more simply, use grippier pads and discs.

Drilled and grooved discs, along with a choice of different pad compounds, are the usual option **01**. These are certainly worth considering if you're planning some track days, which can wear out the pads of any standard car very quickly. Again, check the Internet to see what people are using. One popular option is the EBC Green pad, which warms up fast enough for road use, coupled with a grooved disc – they won't fade on the track, and look good through the wheels too. In the author's experience, they're not as dust-free as claimed but they certainly work, and give good pedal feel. For changing discs and pads, see Chapter 7.

01

Swapping to later brakes

WARNING: *Though standard 14in wheels fit over all these brakes, aftermarket ones might not. Ask first.*

Brakes from the later model fit: there was a jump in size from 9.25in front/9.1in rear discs of 1990–1993 cars to 10in front/ 9.9in rear for 1994–2002 cars, and then again to 11in front/10.9in rear on 2001–2002 Sport cars and on all others from 2003. All will fit within the standard 14in wheels, and you can use your existing calipers (unless the rears have seized!) except when fitting Sport (11in) brakes to the front when you'll need the mounting brackets too because they are different – the larger the disc, the further they mount the caliper from the spindle centre.

For the ultimate in braking, companies in the US such as Flyin' Miata sell conversion kits involving even bigger discs and racing Wilwood or AP calipers – just make sure your wheels will clear them.

ENGINE

General

Though the early cars had only 114bhp, remember, too, that they were the lightest and weren't significantly slower than later models, whose extra torque mostly compensated for the car's middle-aged spread. Experts say the early 1.6s seem to go amazingly well.

But they're not fantastic at dishing out low-down punch – which shouldn't matter in a sports car. Remember the engine revs to 7,000rpm, and much of the power lies in the upper reaches of the rev range. If you simply want to go faster, you are using all 7,000, aren't you? If you want a little more prod, you can help the car to breathe a little better, on both the induction and exhaust sides.

On the induction side, a performance air filter kit is very popular and seen on many cars. This replaces the air box with a conical gauze air filter, blanking off the original air intake with a plain sheet of aluminium. But remember, you need to clean the filter gauze from time to time, a more arduous business then simply changing a replacement paper filter element.

One side-effect of an aftermarket filter kit is that it might make your car a bit louder because of extra induction roar. English-spec MX-5s were always more subdued than the Eunos and Miata, so a different exhaust is always worth considering if yours is due for replacement. In the UK, club members have written positive things about Larini stainless steel systems, which are available in a variety of styles and configurations to fit all models. The front pipes tend to last better than the rear sections and are a pain to remove, so replace an exhaust from the rear forwards (see Chapter 5).

01

02

Regular oil changes will help keep the engine healthy, as will changing the spark plugs every 15,000 miles, and their leads (wires) every 30,000 – if your MX-5/Miata is misfiring, check these first. The men who work on them all the time say that advancing the ignition timing to 14° BTDC (at tickover) makes the cars more lively. See Chapter 5 for how to adjust this, but be very attentive to pinking (pinging) – a light metallic rattling, especially with the engine under load, and worse when accelerating from low speeds in high gears. If there's any hint of it, and you're not comfortable driving around the problem with lower gears and more revs, return the timing back to standard settings. If ignored, serious engine damage can eventually result, such as a holed piston.

Engine swaps

For people who want more work, there's always an engine swap – fitting a 1.8-litre engine into a 1.6 car. The engines swap straight over, using the 1.8's engine mounts, and the transmissions are the same, apart from the clutch size, but the ECUs, manifolding and exhausts aren't, so unless you know what you're doing, leave alone. Same goes for using an NB cylinder head, which has better breathing, on an NA engine. If using the NB inlet manifold you'll need to devise some way for the engine brain to trigger the VICS butterflies, which open around 6,000rpm. The NA inlet manifold won't fit, unless you weld (aluminium – gulp!) and remachine the mounting flange. Post 2001 heads aren't suitable because they need an oil feed to control the variable valve timing.

Supercharging and turbocharging

Supercharging and turbocharging are popular **01/02**: BBR used to market a turbo option in the UK, with Mazda's blessing and warranty – testimony to how tough the engine is. Turbo kits are still available from a number of sources – but remember, adding a turbo or tuning gear is no solution for a tired engine, and will just wear it out quicker. If you plan any tuning, aside from an engine swap (and there have been Ford V8 conversions in the US), make sure the car is mechanically up to scratch first. And, if you do change any hardware, tell your insurance company or you might end up not being covered.

RUSTPROOFING

You've found a lovely rust-free Eunos import in the UK. It won't stay that way through many English winters unless you are fastidious about hosing off the underside every spring to blast off accumulated salt.

But you can help the car out a great deal by rustproofing it yourself at home. Get a large (5-litre) can of rustproofing compound with pump kit from Waxoyl or similar and use it to spray the underside of the car and inside cavities. By removing trim panels, you can get to most internal parts of an MX-5. If your car wears kick plate trims, you can remove them and drill small holes in the tops of the sills to access these box sections, then plug them with grommets which will be hidden by the kick plates. Make sure you don't get any of the rustproofer on the exhaust, or it'll smoke and smell horrible when you start the car up; and keep the slippery stuff well away from the brake discs. Only apply the proofer in a well-ventilated area, because the solvent will evaporate off. Some may even drip out of the car, leaving only a waxy coating. Repeat every year after pressure-washing off the underside and leaving to dry.

APPENDIX 1 – SPECIFICATIONS

MX-5 Mk1 1.6i
From 1990

Body
Steel unitary construction with bolted-in front and rear steel subframes and pressed-alloy PPF tying engine/gearbox to rear axle. Folding convertible soft-top, hard-top optional.

Engine
Iron block, alloy head, in-line four-cylinder with dual overhead camshafts driven by belt from crankshaft nose. Hydraulic bucket tappets, lobe-type oil pump, multi-port fuel injection, watercooled.
Capacity 1,597cc
Bore and stroke 78 x 83.6mm
Max power 114bhp @ 6,500rpm
Max torque 100lb ft @ 5,500rpm

Transmission
Five-speed all-synchromesh manual gearbox driving rear wheels. Four-speed automatic optional in Japan and US, and in UK from 1995. Limited-slip differential optional.
Final drive ratio 4.3:1

Suspension
Unequal-length wishbones all round, with coil-over dampers and anti-roll bars front and rear. Anti-drive geometry incorporated at front.

Brakes
Discs all round, ventilated at front, with assistance from vacuum servo. Dual hydraulic circuits, ABS optional.

Steering
Rack and pinion, power assistance optional.

Wheels and tyres
Seven-spoke cast alloy.
Size:
Wheels 5.5 x 14in to Mazda design.
Tyres 185/60 x 14 Dunlop.

Dimensions and weights
Length 3,948mm
Width 1,675mm
Height 1,230mm
Wheelbase 2,265mm
Track front 1,410mm
Track rear 1,428mm
Weight 995kg

Performance (Mazda figures)
Top speed 121mph
0–62mph 8.75 secs

Note: *Eunos roadster has generally higher spec: air conditioning is standard, leather interior, extra speakers in head restraints.*

MX-5 Mk1 1.8i From July 1993

Engine
Capacity 1,839cc
Bore and stroke 83 x 85mm
Max power 128bhp (133bhp from 1995, along with shorter 4.3:1 final drive)
Max torque 110lb ft
Compression ratio 9:1

Transmission
Final drive ratio 4.1:1 until 1995

Wheels and tyres
Size:
Wheels 6 x 14 from 1994;
6 x 15 optional from 1995
Tyres 195/55HR15 optional from 1995

Dimensions and weights
Weight 1,025kg
Weight distribution 50/50 unladen

MX-5 Mk2 1.6i From 1998

Engine
Capacity 1,597cc
Bore and stroke 78 x 83.6mm
Max power 108bhp @ 6,500rpm
Max torque 99lb ft @ 5,000rpm

Wheels and tyres
Wheels 6 x 14
Tyres 185/60RHR14

Dimensions and weights
Length 3,975mm
Width 1,680mm
Height 1,225mm
Weight 1,025kg

Performance
Top speed 119mph
0–62mph 9.7secs

MX-5 Mk2 1.8i and 1.8iS From 1998

Engine
Capacity 1,839cc
Bore and stroke 83 x 85mm
Max power 140bhp @ 6,500rpm
Max torque 119lb ft @ 5,000rpm

Wheels and tyres
Wheels 6 x 15
Tyres 195/50VR15

Performance
Top speed 126mph
0–62mph 7.8secs

MX-5 Mk2 1.8i 10th Anniversary

Engine
Max power 140bhp@ 6,500rpm
Max torque 119lb ft @ 4,500rpm

Transmission
Six-speed manual

Performance
Top speed 126mph
0–62mph 8.4secs

MX-5 'Mk2.5' (2001 facelift)

1.6i
Engine
Type dohc iron-block, alloy-head inline four with sequential valve timing
Max power 110bhp @6,500rpm
Max torque 99lb ft @ 5,000rpm

Performance
Top speed 119mph
0–62mph 9.7secs

1.8i (1839cc)
Engine
Max power 146bhp @ 7,000rpm
Max torque 124lb ft

Performance
Top speed 127mph
0–62mph 8.5secs

1.8i automatic
Engine
Max power 139bhp @ 6,500rpm
Max torque 125lb ft

Performance
Top speed 118mph
0–62mph 11secs

1.8i Sport (six-speed)
Engine
Max power 145bhp @ 7,000rpm
Max torque 124lb ft

Dimensions and weights
Weight 1,100kg

Performance
Top speed 129mph
0–62mph 8.4secs

APPENDIX 2 – USEFUL CONTACTS

Useful websites

www.miatanet.com
The website for MX-5/Miata owners. Find everybody else here.

www.miataclubs.com

www.miataforum
If it's been done, it's here. FAQs, pitfalls, active discussion forum.

www.miataprojects.com
Flyin' Miata's expert Keith Tanner's own site. Hands-on projects for the more ambitious.

www.v8miata.com
Where 'too much horsepower isn't enough': Owner Martin Wilson has converted more than 100 Miatas to Mustang power.

Specialists (parts and services)

Bourne Road Garage Ltd
Bourne Road
Crayford
Kent DA1 4BU
01322 521595
www.mazda-accessories.com

Brain Storm
12569 W Washington Boulevard
Los Angeles
CA 90066, USA
001 310 313 0088
Tuning parts and accessories.

ChromDesign
Biberweg 31
D-53842 Troisdorf/Spich
Germany
+49 (0)2241 945920
Fax +49 (0)2241 9459229
www.chromdesign.de

Cox & Buckles
Avebury Foundry
Elm Grove Industrial Estate
Elm Grove, off Worple Road
Wimbledon
London SW19 4HE
020 8944 7100
www.cox-and-buckles-workshop.co.uk

Dandycars
330–332 Eastern Avenue
Ilford
Essex IG4 5AA
0845 450 4589
www.dandycars.com

www.donutz.co.uk
(Web-based parts service only in north of England)
07785 507200

Mike Edginton Cars Ltd
Silverstone Garage
63 Little London
Silverstone
Northants NN12 8UP
01327 858000
www.carsatmec.co.uk

Eric's MX-5 Centre
17 Heathfield Park Drive
Romford
Essex RM6 4FB
(by appointment)
020-8503-8921
www.mx5centre.com

Everything MX5.com
01708 754882
07773 229362
www.everythingmx5.com

Flyin' Miata
331 South 13th St
Grand Junction
Colorado 81501, USA
001-800 359 6957)
www.flyinmiata.com

GoMiata
7525 Ethel Ave, Suite M
North Hollywood
CA 91605,
USA
0001 866 466 4282
www.GoMiata.com

GoodWin Racing, LLC
8380 Vickers Street, Suite D
San Diego
CA 92111,
USA
001 858 775 2810

Griffin Style bars
100 Heathfield Avenue
Ilkeston
Derbyshire DE7 5EH
0115 9163990
www.mx5rollbars.com

Sam Goodwin MX-5 Specialists
Unit 2 Kelsey Close
Attleborough Industrial Estate
Nuneaton
Warwickshire CV11 6RS
02476 353909
www.samgoodwin.com

Hard Dog Fabrication
Bethania Garage, Inc.
5391 Bethania Rd
PO Box 50
Bethania, N.C. 27010
001 800 688 9652
(International and tech;
001 336 922 3018)
www.bethania-garage.com
(See this website for some scary pictures showing their roll bars really work)

HotHoodsMX5.com
07957 273270

IL Motorsport
www.ilmotorsport.de

Jackson Racing
440 Rutherford Street Goleta
CA 93117, USA
888-888-4079 (toll free)
805-681-3410 (local)
www.jacksonracing.com

Jimparts
Japanese Import Motor Parts
8 Myrtle Close, Barwell
Leicestershire LE9 8GU
0845 890 1159
www.jimparts.co.uk
Parts, hoods and fitting.

Larini Systems
0870 777 9060
www.larinisystems.com
Stainless steel exhausts.

Miata Mania.com
Moss Motors Ltd
440 Rutherford Street
Goleta
CA 93117, USA
800-667-7872
(From outside US: 001 805 681 3400)
www.mossmotors.com

Mazmania
Kell Green Hall Farm
Marthall, Knutsford
WA16 7SL
01565 873588
www.mazmania.co.uk

Milcars Mazda – Watford
Otterspool Way, Watford
Herts WD25 8HL
01923 257755

Milcars Mazda – St Albans
229–235 Hatfield Road
St Albans
Herts AL1 4TB
01923 257755
www.milcarsmazda.co.uk

Moss Europe
Main office
Hampton Farm West
Hampton, Middlesex
0800 281182
www.moss-europe.co.uk

MX5parts.co.uk (Scimitar International)
4 Cluster Industrial Estate
Rodney Road
Portsmouth PO4 8ST
0845 345 2384
www.mx5parts.co.uk

MX5 Mad.com
XS-Speed Limited
215A North Street
Romford
Essex RM1 4QA
0845 345 2727
www.mx5mad.com

MX5 City
Sheffield Road
Conisborough
Doncaster DN2 2BY
0845 2300 856
Fax 08452300 857
www.mx5ccity.com

Panache
382 Enterprise St, Suite 108
San Marcos
CA 92069, USA
0001 760 510 9682
www.v8miata.com

Performance5
PO Box 418
Pinner
Middlesex HA5 9AA
0845 230 4505
www.performance5.com

Prestige Car Hoods
Prestige Autotrim Products
Oak Tree Place
Expressway Business Park
Rock Ferry
Birkenhead
CH42 1NS
UK 0151 643 9555
www.prestigecarhoods.com

Priory Fives
Priory Mazda
Cambridge Autopark
315–349 Mill Road
Cambridge CB1 3DF
01223 242222

Racing Beat
4789 E Wesley Drive
Anaheim
CA 92807, USA
001 714 779 8677
www.racingbeat.com

Raven Wing Performance
19079 Grovewood Drive
Corona
CA 92881, USA
Order 001 8877 581 3278
Tech support 001 951 817 5644
www.ravenwingperformance.net

Select Imports
Broadmere Garage
Ipswich Road
Grundisburgh
Woodbridge
Suffolk IP13 6TJ
01473 738958
07720 398914
www.select-imports.org

Serious Auto Accessories Inc
Santa Cruz
001 831 425 5722
www.seriousauto.com

Soft Top Windows (UK) Ltd
66 Hartland Way
Shirley
Croydon CR0 8RF
020 8777 6764
www.softtopwindows.co.uk

SFT MX5 Parts
991 Wolverhampton Road
Oldbury
West Midlands B69 4RJ
0121 544 5555
Fax 0121 544 4340
www.davidmanners.co.uk

Wolf Auto Accessories Ltd
A1 Seedbed Centre
Coldharbour Road, Pinnacles East
Harlow
Essex CM19 5A
01279 411014 Toll-free fax from US 1-888-229-6378
Freephone from England 0800 435439
www.wolfmiata.com

Westco Battery
1645 South Sinclair Street
Anaheim
CA 92806,
USA
800.372.9253 – 714.937.1033
Fax: 714.937.0818
www.westcobattery.com
Gel batteries.

3rd Millennium Strategies
34 Cogswell Road
Essex
MA 01929,
USA
www.3rdstrategy.com
Improved headrest speakers.

Clubs

There are more than 200 Miata/MX-5 Clubs worldwide. We can't list them all, or their full addresses, but here are the websites of the major ones. Find more on www.miatanet.com

UK
www.mx5oc.co.uk

www.clubmazda.co.uk

www.mx5nw.co.uk
MX-5 Clubs, North Western Region

www.southerncoasters.com

USA
www.mscw.com
Mazda Clubs Sportscar of Washington Inc

www.lonestarmiata.net
Texas

www.foothillsmiataclub.com
Foothills Miata Club of Carolinas

www.miata.pace.net
Pennsylvania Central Area Miata Owners Club

Canada
www.trilliummiata.com
Trillium Miata Clubs, Toronto and Ontario

www.mroad.com
Mroad Miata Clubs, Texas

www.sunriders.com
Miata Clubs of Tampa Bay

www.myus.com/tmr
Triangle Miata Clubs

www.socalm.org
Southern California Miata Club

Australia
www.mx5.com.au
Central homepage for all Australian MX-5 clubs

www.mx5club.com.au
Mazda MX-5 Clubs of Western Australia

www.miata.net.au
MX-5 Club of Queensland

www.mx5.com.au/sa
Mazda MX-5 Clubs of South Australia

www.mx5.com.au/nsw
Mazda MX-5 Clubs of New South Wales

www.mx5vic.org.au
Mazda MX-5 Clubs of Victoria

Austria
www.mx5.at
Austrian MX-55 Clubs (Kurt Walter)

www.mx-5.at.gs

Belgium
www.mx5.be
MX-5 Club Belgien

www.mx-5club.be
Flanders MX-5 Club

France
www.mx5passion.com

Germany
www.miataclub.de

www.asian-car-club.de

www.mx-5-freunde.de
MX-5 Freunde Essen (Rüdiger Döll)

www.owners.de

www.mx-5club.com
MX-5 Clubs Franken Power

www.mx-5-club.de
MX-5 Clubs, Köln (Peter Mohr)

www.mazda-crew.de

mazdaclub.come.to

Ireland
www.mx5ireland.com

Italy
www.miataclubsicilia.it

Japan
www.roadster.hotspace.jp

The Netherlands
www.mx5owners.nl

New Zealand
www.mx5club.org.nz

Spain
www.clubmx5.com

www.mx5zone.com

Sweden
www.miata.se

Switzerland
www.mx5.ch

www.mx-5-team.ch

INDEX